H   AB

635

4383 401

£35-00

Asian Gardens

The lotus, *Nelumbo nucifera*, was sacred in West, South and East Asia.

Asian Gardens

History, beliefs and design

Tom Turner

Routledge
Taylor & Francis Group

LONDON AND NEW YORK

First published 2011
by Routledge
2 Park Square, Milton Park, Abingdon, Oxon, OX14 4RN

Simultaneously published in the USA and Canada
by Routledge
270 Madison Avenue, New York, NY10016

Routledge is an imprint of the Taylor & Francis Group, an informa business

© 2011 Tom Turner

Designed and typeset by Sutchinda Rangsi-Thompson
Printed and bound by Grafos, Barcelona

British Library Cataloguing in Publication Data
A catalogue record for this book is available from the British Library

Library of Congress Cataloging- in-Publication Data

Turner, Tom (Thomas Henry Duke), 1946
    Asian gardens : history, beliefs, and design / Tom Turner.
        p. cm.
1. Gardens–Asia–History. 2. Gardens–Asia–Design. I. Title.
SB451.36.A78T87 2010
712.095–dc22
2009036189

ISBN13: 978-0-415-49687-2 (hbk)

Contents

Preface

All the world's ancient gardens are on the fringes of Asia; none are in the Americas, South Asia, North Asia, Oceania or Africa-outside-Egypt. Why should this be? When flying over the steppes, mountains, rivers and forests of Central Asia, I always requested a window seat and while gazing at the scenery an idea about the influence of these landscapes on gardens began to take shape. My hypothesis is that the art of making gardens originated in the zone of interchange between the lifestyles of nomads and settlers.[1] The gods of the nomads, known only from linguistic analysis, were associated with natural phenomena. They included the sky, the dawn, the rivers, the mountains and the earth.

When nomads became settlers, they retained a love of wild landscapes. In Iran, for example, Aryan settlers made a type of space which they called a paradise. It is likely

P.1 Anapurna, the Goddess Mountain. Garden design on the fringes of Asia was influenced by wild places with connections to the spirit world.

P.2 Ranthambore Fort was founded in 944 and is surrounded by a maharajah's hunting park, showing enthusiasms both for settlement and for wild nature.

P.3 When nomads became settlers, some gardens reflected wild nature and other gardens drew on the geometry of civilization.

to have been a walled enclosure used for hunting and stocked with exotic plants and animals. Similar enclosures were made in other parts of Eurasia's 'Garden Fringe'. We call them hunting parks but they also had ceremonial, didactic and religious roles. This is recorded in connection with the great landscape parks of China and survives in the Islamic and Christian use of the word 'paradise'. Ancient parks reminded kings of the wild landscapes in which their ancestors had lived and roamed, as in the story that the 'Hanging Gardens of Babylon' were made for a beautiful concubine who, on the plains of Mesopotamia, yearned for a garden to remind her of 'meadows on mountain tops' in Persia (see p. 38). Settlers' gardens could reflect the nature of the wilds and the nature of civilization. These two natures remain the most astonishing things on earth. Gardens are sometimes described as a Third Nature.[2]

According to the creation myths of Mesopotamia and Egypt, the world began in watery darkness. The gods then made land, light and life – and were honoured in sanctuaries comprising mounds, pools, plants, buildings and terraces. These were the earliest symbolic landscapes and their components, with the sky, remain the compositional elements of garden and landscape design. In the millennia after 3000 BCE, great gardens were made on the fringes of Central Asia. They occupy a belt which, from Sumer, runs west into Europe and east into China (see p. 29). It was a zone of interchange, a landscape in which horsemen encountered farmers and the design of symbolic gardens and landscapes began. I define garden and landscape design as the art of composing landform, vegetation, water, paving and structures in relation to the forces of nature and human needs. The ancient design objectives are *commoditas*, *firmitas* and *venustas*, with the latter often translated into English as 'delight', referring to qualities associated with Venus' oldest-known equivalent deity: Inanna of the Sumerians.

The word 'Asia' comes to us from Herodotus, who used it for the region which remains the meeting point of East and West: Anatolia. He may have got the word from Akkadian, in which it meant 'the land of the sunrise'. The divide between Europe and Asia is now taken to run north, from Anatolia to the Ural Mountains. Agriculture, cities and gardens developed around the southern end of the line and the horse was domesticated in Central Asia. The northerners were not literate, but the ideas and technologies they developed spread with their chariots into China, India, the Fertile Crescent and Europe. 'Nostalgic nomads' appear to have made enclosures to symbolize the primeval landscapes in which their gods lived; 'proud settlers' appear to have made gardens to symbolize the abstract ideas which, as gifts from the gods, made civilization possible. Gardens could, therefore, symbolize wild nature *and* civilized nature – the realms of the Sky God and the Earth Mother. We might summarize thus:

- Nomads, believing the chicken came before the egg, developed natural gardens which were symbolic landscapes.

- Farmers and settlers, believing the egg came before the chicken, developed geometrical ('formal') gardens which were walled and watered orchards.

'Formal' gardens reflect the primary geometrical forms ('the egg') used by Gods to make the world and by mankind to make gardens. They involve straight lines, rectangles, circles, geometric solids and the forces of nature, as when gravity is used to deploy and disperse the miracle of water. Both 'formal' and 'natural' gardens were made in the settlement zone on the fringes of Asia. Some settlers arrived from the south. Others, whom I would associate with symbolic landscapes, were returnees from the north. In the settlement zone, gardens balanced the call of the wild with the call of the hearth. Personally, I feel pulled in both directions. When settled, I yearn to travel; when travelling, I want to return home. In a garden, anywhere, I feel at peace. So I prefer to sleep in garden hotels, to live in a house with a garden and to holiday in cottages with gardens.

P.4 A garden appeals to the desire for scenery and the desire to settle.

The *National Geographic Magazine*'s Genographic Project has let me discover that my paternal ancestors migrated round the East Mediterranean and then turned north-west through Anatolia and the Balkans to reach England; my maternal ancestors swung further east, via the Caucuses and the Baltic, before turning south to the Alps and then north to Germany before settling in England. Curiously, my investigation of garden history followed this route in a backward direction for thirty years and then struck east from Egypt. My interest in the religious, philosophical and artistic aspects of garden and landscape design came in part from my maternal grandfather (Henry Meulen) and in part from Professor G. P. Henderson at the University of St Andrews. The latter introduced me to aesthetics and the philosophy of religion. He also invited Ninian Smart to give a series of lectures.[3] Henderson had a special interest in the didactic character of Byzantine art. My grandfather claimed descent from seven generations of atheists, explaining that his family had suffered in the religious wars of the seventeenth century and concluded that religion 'must be a bad thing'. His arithmetic makes me a ninth generation sceptic but we could both pass muster as 'religious atheists' on account of our interests in the 'what, why and how' questions relating to life on earth. They arise in debates on philosophy, ethics, art, design and natural science. I should add that, being a careful man, my grandfather classified himself as agnostic rather than atheist.

Lord Fisher supported a failed invasion of Asia, at Gallipoli in 1915, and advised that one should 'Never contradict. Never explain. Never apologize.' But he was a Sea Lord and, as a modest writer, I would rather preface my work with an apology: for my ignorance of Asian languages. In mitigation and compensation, I have visited most of the places discussed, taken many photographs and made use of London's excellent library resources. The text contains words from languages with sounds that cannot be represented in English. Philologists use a sophisticated system of diacritical

P.5 This is how I imagined Suzhou, though it is Zhouzhuang.

marks (accents) to indicate the sounds. In the interests of readability, and with an acknowledged loss of accuracy, I have not used these marks. Non-English words are written in italics when explaining their meaning or drawing attention to their origins. The reason for discussing word origins is that many words do not have precise English equivalents and etymologies assist comprehension.

However much one reads, visits are an essential part of the garden historian's work. I have, for example, two images of Suzhou in mind which I still find hard to integrate. One dates from before I visited the city. It is of a sleepy city with low buildings, narrow lanes, steamy canals and a profusion of quiet shady gardens. The second image is of a bustling city with glaring sunlight and broad highways flanked by tall modern blocks. Expecting Suzhou gardens to be dark, peaceful and slightly grotesque, I found them brightly lit, noisy and of high design quality. My misjudgement of the gardens may have been a consequence of their being often photographed in the early morning. Photographers like to work when there are few people about and the lighting is soft.

Overview of the book

The organization of this book is chronological and geographical. Parts 1, 2 and 3 have chronological accounts of West, South and East Asia. Part 4 has comments on North Asia and on the vagaries of modernism in Asia. West Asia includes the countries which are now Iran, Iraq, Saudi Arabia, the Gulf States, Syria, Jordan, Israel and Egypt. South Asia includes the countries which are now Pakistan, India, Nepal, Sri Lanka, Bangladesh, Myanmar, Cambodia and Indonesia. East Asia includes China, Japan and other countries which, though not specifically mentioned in the text, come within the same cultural sphere: Vietnam, North and South Korea. Chapter 8 includes North, West, South and East Asia with Russia, Mongolia and the countries discussed in earlier parts of the book.

The general plan was to use text to carry the argument and illustrations for visual support. The book has few verbal accounts of gardens but all the gardens mentioned can be found on a companion website with additional photographs, aerial images, garden descriptions, source material and links to local garden websites: http://www.gardenvisit.com/history_theory/asian_gardens_companion. The organization is similar to that used in my previous book, on *Garden History: Philosophy and Design 2000 BC to 2000 AD* (Spon Press, 2005) which dealt with gardens found north and west of the Fertile Crescent. This current volume is about garden design in Asia. Geographical regions could have been used in the titles of both books, so that the earlier volume could have been entitled *European Gardens: History, Philosophy and Design 2000 BC to 2000 AD*. I would probably have used this title if I had known I was going to write the present book and plan to use it for a revised edition of the 2005 book, though this may cause problems. First, Europe and Asia are part of a single landmass. Second, the story of American gardens, so far, belongs with that of European gardens. Third, styles of garden design were internationalized in the twentieth century.

Another difference between what could be the first and second volumes of a single book on Eurasian gardens is that I would still want to use 'philosophy' in the title of Volume 1 and 'beliefs' in the title of Volume 2, for two reasons. First, there was more separation between religious and philosophical ideas in the West – and it was philosophy which influenced garden design. Second, there was less separation between sacred and secular affairs in the East. Palace gardens, though not untouched by religion, were dominant in the West. Sacred gardens, though not untouched by residential use, were dominant in the East.

The development of Asian gardens and designed landscapes will be traced through fifty centuries in eight chapters. Owing to the shortage of examples in many periods, the discussion is more about garden types than design styles, and it has not been possible to give more than one or two examples of each type. Worse, it has sometimes been necessary (e.g. for hunting parks in Ancient China) to invent a diagram without any visual information about historic forms. If archaeological or graphic information comes to light, these inventions can be corrected, but, in view of the 'word and image' nature of the book, it seemed best to provide graphic versions of my hypotheses.

The geographical coverage is mainly of West, South and East Asia, with some mention of Central and North Asia in Chapter 8. There are two excursions. The first, in Chapter 2, follows the influence of West Asia into Greece and Italy. The second, in Chapter 3, follows Islamic beliefs to Spain. Since the book covers a wide geographical region and a long historical period, it is sure to contain some errors, which I regret. There is also some guesswork. As Barry Kemp wrote of his work at El-Amarna: 'It has proved impossible to write a history of Akhenaten's reign which does not embrace an element of historical fiction.'[4] When speculating on my own behalf, in text or plan, this is stated.

Architectural historians sometimes use elevational diagrams to show the compositional elements of buildings (walls, doors, windows, floors, roofs and stairs). I use style diagrams to summarize the characteristics of garden plans. The book also has diagrammatic garden and landscape plans, with scales and north points, to show the compositional elements. The art of composing landform, water, vegetation, horizontal structures and vertical structures to make places is my subject. This explains why I have strayed 'beyond the garden wall' into, for example, temple sanctuaries, cities and modern landscape architecture. Generally, new plans and new photographs have been used instead of old plans and old drawings. My drawings often show archaeological details with modern vegetation, because details of the ancient vegetation are

P.6 This is how I remember much of Suzhou.

P.7 a, b My bicycle in Bukhara and in Orchha. It was safe throughout Asia before being stolen near SOAS in Central London.

unknown. Contours are included where they could be found but this was rarely possible. I look forward to more information becoming available as Asia advances.

The travel required for this book left me feeling guilty about the size of my carbon footprint. On arriving in a city, I therefore did as much travel as possible by bicycle. After using a similar method in Europe, I felt nervous when venturing forth. The first trip, to Egypt, went well. On a January dawn in Luxor, the hotel doorman saluted and I set out along a carless street, delighted to see groups of old men burning litter to keep warm. The sun rose on the ferry and the West Bank smelt of diesel and spice as I began to re-explore the Domain of Amun. The next trip was to Iran, where I did not cycle and found crossing streets alarming. In Isfahan, a beautiful girl dressed like a European nun, who said Islam forbade her shaking my hand when we were introduced, suddenly grabbed my arm and yanked me into the traffic with the words 'Come on – we must be brave.' She was right. In China, cycling is normal, for the present, and I was peacefully ignored. In India, my cycling was accompanied by friendly calls along the lines of 'Where from? Very nice bicycle. You have lights! Hello one rupee. Goodbye chocolate. Welcome to India.' But my first day cycling in Delhi was an awesome pre-vision of hell. In Japan, where the people were wonderfully helpful, only one person called out 'Very nice bicycle' and I looked up to see a smiling Indian. Like me, he was trying to ignore the gusts of an approaching typhoon. I thank all those who continue Asia's ancient tradition of befriending travellers. Nearer home, I thank my family for personal support and my students and colleagues at the University of Greenwich for academic support. Richard Hayward runs an enlightened and outward-looking school; Robert Holden, Benz Kotzen and Patrick Goode always encouraged me to press on; Mehrdad Shokoohy gave me wide ranging advice on the art, architecture and history of Asia. At Routledge, I thank Caroline Mallinder for her encouragement through many years.

Part 1
West Asia

CHAPTER 1

Beliefs and gardens

1.1 Farming began in fertile valleys. Tombs, temples and temple gardens symbolized beliefs.

1.2 a Nomads in Kazakhstan.

1.2 b Boundaries turn nomads into settlers.

Defining boundaries, building houses and forming gardens are foundational activities. They assert claims to the ownership of land; they convert nomads into settlers; they allow permanent structures; they enable the growth of civilizations. John Locke, famed for his political thought but also a writer on gardens,[1] saw property as a natural right. He argued that 'mixing' one's labour with a part of nature creates ownership rights and a necessity for the rule of law. He asserted that 'the reason why men enter into society is the preservation of their property'.[2] Structures are the simplest means of protection and people still remark that 'high walls make good neighbours': they reduce the causes of conflict.

In making children and gardens, we interact with nature in the most profound ways, experiencing creation, growth and change. 'Golden lads and lassies must, like all things, come to dust.'[3] But historic gardens outlive generations of 'lads and lassies' to inform us about the characteristics of the peoples, laws, technologies, societies and beliefs which influenced their design. Why do we have children? As an ancestral duty? For immortality? For the pleasure of their conception? Because we must? One cannot know, but the urge to create comes from afar and leads to rights and duties of care, protection and inheritance which can be explained only with the aid of abstract ideas. The influence of beliefs on procreation and garden creation is ancient and profound, particularly in Asia. And it contributes a fascination to gardens: designs derive from local circumstances and general concepts, from particulars and universals, from the ancient and the modern worlds.

*Throughout history and beyond in the dark recesses of men's earliest cultures, religion
has been a vital and pervasive feature of human life. To understand human history and*

human life it is necessary to understand religion, and in the contemporary world one must understand other nations' ideologies and faith in order to grasp the meaning of life as seen from perspectives often very different from our own. But religion is not something that one can see. It is true that there are temples, ceremonies and religious art. These can be seen, but their significance needs to be approached through the inner life of those who use these externals. Consider the ceremony of baptizing a baby. How can we understand it, save by knowing the hopes and feelings of those who participate in the occasion?[4]

No more can we understand historic gardens 'save by knowing the hopes and feelings' of those who participated in their creation. Often, they were the hopes and feelings of peoples who lived in the zone of interchange between the lifestyles of the nomad and the settler. They were peoples who often fought and often co-operated.

Garden origins

Homo sapiens is believed to have a common ancestor who was born in Africa *c*.150,000 years ago. Known as Mitochondrial Eve, she is our matrilineal most recent common ancestor. A group of her descendants, 'Haplogroup L3', migrated out of Africa and into West Asia about 70,000 years ago. By 30,000 BCE their descendants had crossed the Baring Straits to occupy the Americas. By 10,000 BCE nomads were settling in West Asia and developing ideas about the origins of mankind. Similarities between the

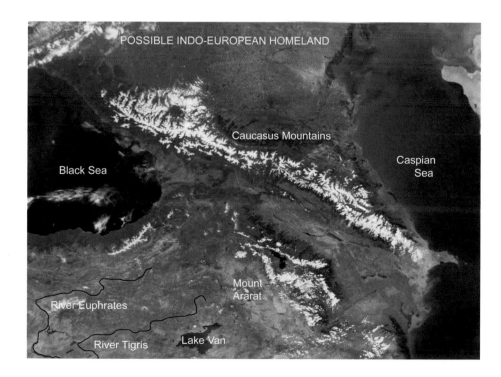

POSSIBLE INDO-EUROPEAN HOMELAND

Caucasus Mountains

Black Sea

Caspian Sea

Mount Ararat

River Euphrates

River Tigris

Lake Van

1.3 Many theories about the Proto-Indo-European (PIE) homeland centre on the Caucasus Mountains, which stand between the Eurasian Steppes and Anatolia. The Euphrates and the Tigris run from this region into Mesopotamia.

creation myths of early societies could mean that humans are predisposed to certain ideas, that a common set of beliefs was carried with the 'daughters of Eve' from the African motherland, or that god exists.[5] Writing was invented c.3,500 BCE and there are references to beliefs, temples, cities, sex and gardens in the oldest literary works, with archaeology and linguistics providing information on the pre-historical period.

The belief that male and female deities created both the Earth and the human race was widespread. Mother goddesses, associated with the earth and fertility, are common in Palaeolithic societies throughout Asia. Sky fathers are particularly associated with Central Asian nomads, including the Proto-Indo-European (PIE) tribes of West Asia, the Turkic/Altaic tribes of East Asia and the Celtic tribes which settled in Europe. Their pantheon had 'a god called Father Sky, whose name is securely reconstructable from the exact equation of Vedic Sanskrit *dyaus pitar* "(o) Father Sky", Greek *Zeu pater* "(o) Father Zeus", and Latin *Iu-pitar* "Jupiter" (literally "father Jove")'.[6] Often, the Earth Mother was 'fertile' and the Sky Father was 'creative', as when water irrigates a desert. E. O. James, who wrote about the Mother Goddess and the Sky God, made this point:

> *Especially in arid regions and in oases on the fringes of deserts where water was the most urgent need, particularly with the rise of agricultural civilizations, it was to the celestial powers who controlled the elements that resort was made in the first instance for the life-giving rain or inundation. It is not surprising, therefore, that in almost every ancient pantheon from the Neolithic onwards the figure of the Sky-god recurred, primarily concerned with the weather and the atmosphere, and with the creative process in general.*[7]

Cultivation may also have begun 'on the fringes of deserts': agriculture with the harvest of wild grains and horticulture with the planting of wild fruits and vegetables.[8] Irrigation allows plants to grow in dry places. Fencing protects crops from animals. Walls provide additional shelter from wind, weeds and rodents. Such advantages underlie the *Encyclopaedia Britannica* definition of a garden as a 'plot of ground where herbs, fruits, flowers, vegetables, or trees are cultivated'.[9] But this book is only peripherally concerned with growing food. Its focus is on what the modern world regards as 'the garden as a work of art' and the ancient world saw as the layout of sacred enclosures for spirits, Gods, Kings and God-Kings.

The word 'sacred' derives from the Latin *sacrum*, meaning 'set apart' and referring to the space in which an altar or temple was set. 'Holy' (from Holly, as in Holly Tree) is an equivalent word derived from the Old German *hulis*.

Central Asian beliefs centered on spirits. In Sumer, kings were part-god and part-human. In North India, the Sky God and the Earth Mother were Indra's parents, so that beautiful landscapes with water, mountains and forests were sacred. In Egypt, kings were living gods. The Egyptians distinguished residences for living gods and afterlife gods. Relationships between gods, kings, gardens and sacred landscapes

1.4 Cultivation is thought to have begun 'on the fringes of deserts' (River Euphrates, in Turkey).

continued until, in the nineteenth and twentieth centuries, thinkers and designers turned away from religion to analyse the nature of the world through science. This produced an abstract style of garden design, a few masterpieces and a great many dull and 'soulless' places (see Chapter 8).

The influence of ideas about nature on the design of cities and gardens is profound, ancient and on-going, leading to such questions as:

- What is the 'nature of Nature'?
- How should the works of man relate to the works of Nature?
- What are the aesthetic and functional aims of garden and landscape design?
- How should we form the conceptual and physical boundaries between gardens, landscapes and cities?

In discussing these questions, there is much to be learned from history. Philosophically and artistically, garden and landscape design constitute a single discipline, but there is an important distinction: gardens are enclosed and tend to be in private ownership; landscapes are unenclosed and are often designed to create public goods.[10] Both garden and landscape design involve composition with six elements: buildings, landform, vegetation, sky, water and paving. I agree with Jellicoe that 'we may be moving into a phase when landscape design is regarded as the most comprehensive of the arts.'[11] Landscapes *can* be designed as discrete elements but *should* be integrated to create places which are greater than the sums of their parts.

Design origins

In what Karl Jaspers called the Axial Age, from 800–200 BCE, key thinkers put forward ideas which gave birth to philosophy and influenced older belief systems.[12] It was an age when urban-agricultural societies were coming under the rule of law. Zoroaster, Buddha, Plato, Confucius, Elijah and other thinkers could move from city to city, able to live in comparative safety and with some independence from the old military, political and priestly castes. This facilitated the development of general ideas and specialized professions. Kings valued the new thinking and, eventually, gave it state support. Neo-Platonism, Neo-Confucianism, Mahayana Buddhism and Islam flourished in this context. Philosophical concepts brought sophistication to belief systems and professionalism to design. In the West, a separation of powers developed, with philosophy, law, natural science and politics becoming specialized academic and professional activities. Monotheism contributed to the trend.

When there are many gods, each can personify a concept or guiding principle. In Ancient Rome, for example, Venus personified beauty and Justita personified justice. But if there is only one god, abstract concepts and professional disciplines gain importance in the specification of ideas. Further, if everything is done in the name of religion (government, worship, art, law, etc.), then all aspects of life will be inter-related. But if each professional activity is carried on solely for its own sake, abstracted from the totality, there will be problems with their integration: law may be separated from justice, agriculture from fertility, and garden design from the fine arts. As will be discussed in Chapter 8, the lack of integration between competing objectives has contributed to the urban and agricultural atrocities of the twentieth century. Religion also suffers from the separation: if priests can speak with authority only about religion, they will be abstracted from everyday concerns and confined to a 'god slot'.[13] One cannot deny the benefits of each subject having its own specialists – but integration remains essential and harmony remains the goal.

The design of aesthetic gardens began as a religious activity and developed into a professional activity. Since the manipulation of outdoor space on a large scale is a daunting challenge, compositional ideas have often developed at the garden scale and then been applied at the urban scale. Palace cities were planned like royal gardens, giving garden design great importance beyond the walls of gardens. Between 1000 and 2000 CE, garden design became a specialized profession in Japan, Europe, China and elsewhere.

Palace gardens, though not untouched by religion, were the dominant garden type in the West. Temple gardens, though not untouched by domesticity, were dominant in the East. Sumerian cities had been sacred in their entirety, founded and protected by city gods and ruled by kings with divine qualities. The emperor of China was a Son of

1.5 a, b The island of Philae was so sacred that birds were said not to fly over it. As in Mesopotamia, temples stood on mounds near water and vegetation.

Heaven and the emperor of Japan was a 'heavenly ruler' (*tenno*). Moving west, we find a gradation. Indian kings depended on Brahmins for their legitimacy. Buddhism began by separating itself from kingship but in South East Asia kings became Bodhisattvas, with god-like attributes and aspirations. Gilgamesh of Uruk was two-thirds god and one-third human. Shia Islam is still led by descendants of the prophet. In Europe, kings claimed no descent from gods or prophets, but did claim a divine right to rule – until such ideas were thrown out by rationalism, revolution and modernism. Many of these cultures eventually turned to specialist designers instead of priests to design their palaces, temples and gardens. Yet many of the religious and philosophical ideas underpinning the design process were retained. One cannot analyse the history of Asian garden design without a focus on belief, or the history of European garden design without a focus on philosophy – and nor can one draw a precise boundary between the two modes of thought. Mircea Eliade, a great historian and philosopher of religion, believed that 'humankind is *homo religiousus*, and therefore every human has a need to find meaning, to discern patterns, though each culture, indeed each individual, may fill in the broad outlines differently'.[14]

The design of gardens which express ideas about the nature of the world was often unique to specific cultures, leaving garden historians 'to discern patterns', which are partly physical, partly conceptual and partly religious.

Sacred places

Sacred places express general ideas at specific locations. If the general ideas are about the nature of the world, they are likely to include symbolic representations of sky, water, stones, earth, plants and buildings. Information about the symbolism

1.6 Sky is rich with mythological significance.

1.7 Water is the supreme magic; nothing is more noble than a majestic rock.

1.8 The moon 'governs all those spheres of nature that fall under the law of recurring cycles: waters, rain, plant life, fertility'.*

Note: *Eliade, M. *Patterns in Comparative Religions*, London: Sheed and Ward, 1976, p, 154.

of these elements can be obtained from archaeology and from the comparative analysis of myth. James Frazer collected myths from around the world and Mircea Eliade, having learned English to read Frazer,[15] wrote a book entitled *Patterns in Comparative Religion* which sets out the context in which the design of symbols evolved. The following notes comprise quotations from Eliade with brief comments on the sacredness of what later became the compositional elements of landscape and garden design.

Sky

The sky, of its very nature, as a starry vault and atmospheric region has a wealth of mythological and religious significance. 'Height', 'being on high', infinite space . . . what is supremely sacred.[16]

The sky remains a primary element in garden and landscape design, always visible and always necessary for plant growth. It is the 'ceiling' over designed gardens and landscapes.

Water

Symbol of creation, harbour of all seeds, water becomes the supreme magic and medicinal substance; it heals, it restores youth, it ensures eternal life.[17]

Water is the source of existence and a prerequisite for life on earth. It precedes and upholds creation. In ritual, contact with water confers re-birth. In gardens, it is the most common focus.

Stones

Nothing was more direct and autonomous in the completeness of its strength, nothing more noble or more awe-inspiring, than a majestic rock, or a boldly-standing block of granite. Above all, stone is. It always remains itself, and exists of itself.[18]

Stone symbolizes the hardness and permanence of matter. It was not the stone itself which was worshipped but the 'something other' it represented: stones manifest power. Stone altars were made in places which had been set apart because they were sacred.

The Earth and the Moon

From all the beliefs we have so far looked at, the earth emerges as a mother, that is, as giving birth to living forms which it draws out of its own substance. The earth is 'living' first of all because it is fertile. Everything that comes from the earth is endowed with life, everything that goes back into the earth is given new life.[19]

The Sky God and the Earth Mother (Gaia) gave birth to a family of gods, to the family of man and to all living things. When living matter returns to earth, it is reborn in another life form. The moon is a symbol of birth, growth, death and rebirth. Ishtar and Hathor were divinities of the moon.

Vegetation

A divinity manifested in a tree is a motif that runs through all Near-Eastern plastic art; it can also be found in the whole Indo-Mesopotamo-Egypto-Agean area. Most often, the scene represents the epiphany of some divinity of fertility. The cosmos reveals itself to us as a manifestation of the creative powers of God.[20]

There is a mass of myths and legends in which a Cosmic Tree symbolizes the universe (with seven branches corresponding to the seven heavens).[21]

The entire cosmos is symbolized by the World Tree. It connects the three cosmic regions: the sky, the earth and the underworld, making wood essential to the practice of shamanism.[22] This led to individual trees being regarded as sacred, to the planting of sacred groves in association with temples, and to the siting of altars in natural groves. Hindu culture retains the sacredness of trees.

Cultivation

Agriculture taught man the fundamental oneness of organic life; and from that revelation spring the simpler analogies between woman and field, between the sexual act and sowing, as well as the most advanced intellectual synthesis: life as rhythmic, death as a return.[23]

Agriculture and horticulture involve human intervention in the natural world and are ritualistic. The actions and labour of the husbandsman are holy. Farm labour is a rite. 'The fertility of women influences the fertility of the fields, but the rich growth of plants in turn assists women towards conceiving.'[24] In ancient China this led to springtime orgies with 'as many couples as possible' encouraged to mate in the fields and reawaken the fertility of the land.[25]

Enclosures

The enclosure, wall, or circle of stones surrounding a sacred place – these are among the most ancient of known forms of man-made sanctuary . . . The same is the case with city walls: long before they were military erections, they were a magic defence, for they marked out from the midst of a 'chaotic' space . . . a place that was organized, made cosmic, in other words, provided with a 'centre'.[26]

Sacred places are discovered, not chosen.[27] They then become places to worship, to build cities, and to make royal gardens. Each sacred place is a 'centre'.

Structures

The sacredness of cities, temples, palaces, groves and gardens derives from three complementary beliefs:

1.9 A Cosmic Tree is a symbol of the universe (in Kathmandu).

1.10 Agriculture led men to see life as rhythmic and to find 'analogies between woman and field, between the sexual act and sowing'.*

1.11 City walls were magic defences 'long before they were military erections'.*

Note: *Eliade, M. *Patterns in Comparative Religions*, London: Sheed and Ward, 1976, p, 154.

1.12 Kailash is a sacred mountain, close to the sources of three great rivers. It is regarded as a symbol of Mount Meru.

1. The 'sacred mountain' where heaven and earth meet, stands at the centre of the world.
2. Every temple or palace, and by extension, every sacred town and royal residence, is assimilated to a 'sacred mountain' and thus becomes a 'centre'.
3. The temple or sacred city, in turn, as the place through which the *Axis Mundi* passes, is held to be a point of junction between heaven, earth and hell.

Mount Meru, in Hindu and Buddhist belief, stands at the centre of the world.[28]

> *There is no other mountain comparable to Kailas(h), because it forms the hub of the two most important ancient civilizations in the world, whose traditions remained intact for thousands of years: India and China. To Hindus and Buddhists alike Kailas(h) is the centre of the universe. It is called Meru or Sumeru, according to the oldest Sanskrit tradition, and is regarded to be not only the physical but the metaphysical centre of the world.*[29]

The mountain home of the gods was conceived to have palaces and gardens, which, in their turn, became models for the design of earthly temples, palaces and gardens throughout South and East Asia. Sacred places inspired secular places.

As garden design, like painting and architecture, became a professional activity, theoretical questions and responses arose:

- *Why* should gardens be made?
- *Where* should gardens be made?
- *What* types of garden should be made?
- *How* should gardens be designed?

These questions are reviewed below.

1.13 Asian palace gardens were often made within fortifications (Bundi). (See also Figure 3.64.)

Design objectives

The oldest Asian texts on design theory have links with religion. In India, the earliest references to design of any kind are in the *Rig Veda* hymns, thought to have been composed *c.*1500 BCE (see p. 113). The *Vedas* gave rise to the *Shastras* with detailed instructions for the rituals which should guide designers and builders. In China, the *Rituals of Zhou* are thought to have been composed between 500 and 200 BCE (see p. 195). They explain how to lay out a city but do not mention the parks or gardens which, it is known from other sources, were located outside the walls of ancient Chinese cities.

The first books specifically about garden design are of more recent origin but retain close links with religion. The first book in any language exclusively about the design of gardens is the *Sakuteiki*, in Japanese.[30] It dates from *c.*1070 CE and makes use of principles drawn from Buddhism, yin–yang theory, feng shui and the appreciation of 'nature' (see p. 253). The oldest Chinese book about garden design is the *Yuan Ye*.[31] It was written *c.*1620 and draws on China's hermit tradition (see p. 198). Both these manuals place garden design in a religious context, implying that the reason for making symbolic gardens (the 'Why?' of garden design) was to create places that evoke the religious and aesthetic sentiments which contribute to a 'sense of awe' – an experience the modern world continues to seek out in National Parks. The garden design objectives implied by the *Sakuteiki* and the *Yuan Ye* are non-utilitarian. They make no mention of gardens as places to grow vegetables, collect plant varieties or enjoy an outdoor meal. Far from it.

Locations

The location of Asian gardens was determined by the planning of Asian cities. It was necessary for kings to live in cities both for religious reasons and for personal safety. Therefore gardens were made in or near walled cities. The Indian palace gardens described in the *Ramayana* (see p. 117) are within fortifications, like the garden in which Sita was imprisoned on Lanka. In a similar period (500–100 BCE), Chinese emperors had courtyards in palace compounds in walled cities and great landscape parks with detached palaces outside the city walls. Since mountains and water were highly valued, one can imagine that parks included areas where these features were present. There are rivers and mountains sufficiently near Chang'an (Xian) and Luoyang for them to have been within their landscape parks. Fortified cities, protecting palaces, were characteristic of West Asia from early times. The building of free-standing castles with independent defensive structures and castle gardens, was less common in Asia than in Europe. In North India and Japan, castle-building was stimulated by the introduction of European firearms after the fifteenth century.

Garden types

Garden types can be associated with building types and music types (see Table 1.1) and it is a useful aid to thinking about garden design. Music speaks to the soul and is studied in a cultural context by ethnomusicologists.[32] There is scope for a new academic discipline, ethnogardenology, which would examine gardens in their cultural context. Only confusion results from a discussion of 'Chinese gardens' without consideration of culture, contexts and typologies.

Table 1.1   Correlation between types of gardens, buildings and music

Gardens and parks	Buildings	Music
Courtyard gardens	Dwellings	Romantic music
Horticultural gardens	Farm buildings	Folk music
Hunting parks	Fortifications	Military music
Palace gardens	Palaces	Ceremonial music
Temple gardens	Temples	Religious music

Courtyard gardens

Courtyard housing is characteristic of Asia. It is only in climatic extremes, like jungles, that open courtyards were not considered the most useful kind of domestic outdoor space. But courtyard usage varied. In palaces, courtyards were used for feasting, entertainment, ceremonies, cooking and craftwork. In monasteries, they were

1.14 a, b Courtyards have many uses, including entertainment and trade (Samarkand).

communal areas for domestic and devotional activities. In farms, they were used to protect animals at night. In West Asian cities, they were often used for markets. In town houses, courtyards were places to cook, eat, wash and work (see p. 127). The safest generalization about planting in courtyards is that it was more often absent than present.

Horticultural gardens

Horticultural gardens, distinct from courtyards both physically and functionally, varied in size and location. When a city wall was first raised, especially in China, much of the enclosed land was unbuilt and available for horticulture. Chinese cities endured many sieges and the more food produced within their walls, the longer besiegers could be held at bay (see p. 176). But compared to the relatively large fields used for

1.15 a, b Some domestic courtyards were used for work; others accommodated ornamental plants and family life.

growing cereals, outside city walls, it is safe to guess that farm and family gardens were smaller and nearer dwellings, because fruit and vegetables require endless care. No unchanged examples survive and horticultural gardens are not the main subject of this book (see p. 37).

Hunting parks

Hunting parks were characteristic of Asia's desert fringe. The idea of fencing land to create a royal hunting preserve seems to have arisen when nomadic horsemen from Central Asia began to settle and cultivate the land. The earliest known hunting parks were in North China, Iran and the Fertile Crescent. Hunting was also popular in Egypt but it took place in deserts and on the Nile, not in fenced parks. The early kings of India set aside land for hunting but it is not likely to have been fenced, because a relatively low proportion of the country was under cultivation. There is still a deer park at Varanasi (see p. 151) but, like other Indian deer parks, it is now a fenced enclosure. Southern and western areas did not have hunting parks because horses do not flourish in hot humid conditions.

1.16 Asia has had small fields for fruit and vegetables since ancient times but they are not the subject of this book.

1.17 Sikandra was built as a tomb garden but now offers the ancient pleasure of watching deer graze beneath trees.

1.18 Bharatpur was once a maharaja's hunting ground and is now an Indian national park.

1.19 a, b Palace gardens were designed to provide their owners with as many of life's pleasures as possible (Udaipur, India).

Palace gardens

Because the rich and powerful have sought to enjoy all the pleasures life can offer, their gardens and parks have generally had many roles: as symbols of power, as sacred symbols, as ceremonial space, as social space and as places to grow fruit and vegetables. Chinese palaces had covered walks, used like European peristyles, but did not have gymnasium-type facilities of the kind found in Macedonian and Roman palace gardens. Greek gymnasia had social and educational roles separate to those of sacred groves (sanctuaries). Roman emperors incorporated both gymnasia and sanctuary roles into their palace gardens, perhaps because they were gods. In West and East Asia, some kings were gods and others expected to join the gods after a life on earth. This blurred the distinction between palace and temple gardens.

Temple gardens

Mesopotamian cities were sacred in their entirely. Egypt had sacred and royal cities as well as non-sacred and non-royal settlements. The palaces and parks of the Sons of Heaven, in China, were 'centres' where heaven and earth met. Retired Japanese emperors, hoping to join Amitabha in his Western Paradise, chose to live as abbots in temple-palace gardens. In pre-Islamic India there was a clear separation between priests and kings. They belonged to different castes: Brahmin and Kshatriya. Hindu temples were homes for gods, but not for kings. They were built in walled enclosures,

1.20 Indian temples have significant positions in the landscape, and, occasionally, garden settings (Ranakpur).

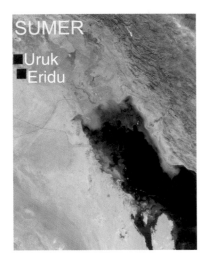

1.21 Sumer, where the oldest literature was found, was on the west shore of the Gulf. Since then, the shore, indicated with a blue overlay, is thought to have been pushed east by sediments from the Tigris and Euphrates.

1.22 The Egyptian goddess Isis, equated with Ishtar, Astarte, Aphrodite and Venus is identified by her solar disc headdress (from the Temple of Isis at Philae).

sometimes with step-wells. There is no evidence for Hindu temples having had gardens before the Islamic conquest but they were located in significant landscapes (e.g. beside water, mountains and trees). Islamic palace gardens were sometimes near mosques but were physically and functionally separate, because of the ban on idolatry. Mughal tomb gardens, however, had both religious and secular aspects. Family members came to pay their respects and to pray for distinguished relatives, assumed to be in paradise. The Taj Mahal garden contains a mosque and an almost identical building thought to have been used as a guest house for family visitors.

Garden aesthetics

The branch of philosophy called aesthetics was given its modern meaning by a German philosopher in 1750.[33] Philosophy gained independence from religion and aesthetics became a separate discipline, dealing with beauty and taste. In the ancient world, 'how things should look' was determined by religion, function and convention, not by personal taste. Confucius' aesthetic views (c.500 BCE) were utilitarian in the sense that he wished the arts to convey moral ideas. The Buddha (c.500 BCE) founded a faith without a devotional god. He preached meditation, not worship, and as a constant traveller had no place for religious imagery in his life or work. The following brief history of aesthetic theory in the ancient world is intended only to set garden design in a wider context. It is written without references and without cautionary qualifications ('may have', 'could have', etc.) because so many would have been necessary.

Asian aesthetics

The cuneiform tablets of Sumer, which are the world's oldest literature, say little about aesthetics but give much information about gods and goddesses. Inanna, associated with the planet Venus, is equated with the Akkadian goddess Ishtar, the Semitic goddess Astarte, the Egyptian goddess Isis, the Greek goddess Aphrodite and the Roman goddess Venus. Inanna means 'Lady of the Sky'. In Sumer, she was a goddess of both love and war. Isis means 'Lady of the Throne'. Often depicted breast-feeding a pharaoh, Isis was the goddess of love, the wife of Osiris and the mother of Horus (see p. 40). Aphrodite was the goddess of love, lust, beauty and sexuality. Her name probably means Morning Star and the Romans called her Venus. In Western countries she remains the most popular garden deity with innumerable new statues of her manufactured each year. Her name produced the Latin word *venustas*, meaning loveliness, charm, attractiveness and beauty. Venus' personal qualities became gifts to the human race; she gave girls their loveliness, cities their elegance, gardens their delight. The underlying aesthetic theory is that beauty is transmitted from the world of the gods to our world – and to the things we make. Saying that beauty derives from 'the faculty of imagining' contributes little more to our understanding of its nature.

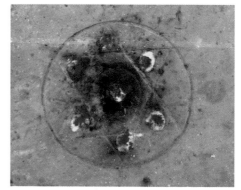

Hindu aesthetic theory was founded on belief and the oldest information comes from the *Rig Veda*. Archaeologists have not found any Vedic art but it is evident from the hymns that the authors had a keen appreciation of aesthetic quality. They associated it with natural phenomena, with the gods and with women. Indra was the storm god, cognate with the European thunder-god, Thor.

> *None with more ardour offers all her beauty to her lord's embrace. Supreme is Indra over all. HYMN LXXXVI. Indra.*
>
> *Thou, being born, art Child of Earth and Heaven, parted among the plants in beauty, Agni! HYMN I. Agni.*
>
> *Thou shinest out from beauty fair to look upon: thou leadest us to conquering power. HYMN CXL. Agni.*
>
> *Dawn, like a loving matron for her husband, smiling and well attired, unmasks her beauty. HYMN CXXIV. Dawn.*
>
> *In pride of beauty like a maid thou goest, O Goddess, to the God who longs to win thee. HYMN CXXIII. Dawn.*

1.24 Mandalas were used to plan *stupas*, often with lotus ponds (Piprahawa, India), and set into pavements as religious symbols (Kirtipur, Nepal) (**Figure 1.25**).

The *Rig Veda* is divided into ten Mandalas ('cycles') containing 1,028 hymns. Because the hymns were recited on ceremonial occasions, the Sanskrit word 'mandala' came to mean 'ritual' (see p. 149). At a later date, when the people who composed the *Vedas* had settled in North India, a ritual developed for the inauguration of building projects. This too became known as a mandala and it included drawing a square on the ground. The four sides of the square faced the four cardinal directions of the natural world: north, south, east and west. A square is also of practical use in setting out a building. Every town, palace, temple and garden was begun with a mandala, though the squares may have been more theoretical than mathematical. Sacred rituals could also be described as mandalas. Modern builders hold less dignified ceremonies for breaking the turf, topping out and opening projects.

A significant difficulty in understanding the use of mandalas in design is that no ancient Hindu buildings survive, because the construction materials were timber and mud. It was Buddhism which brought the art of stone building to India and it is thought to

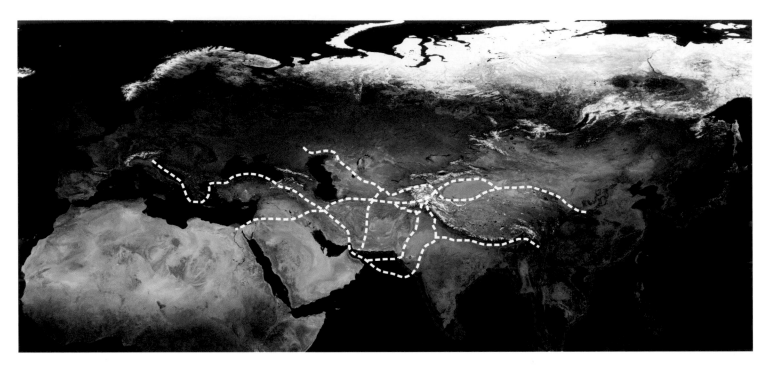

1.26 The 'Silk Routes' inter-linked zones of garden development in East, West and Central Asia.

have come, via the Silk Road, from Greek colonies in West Asia. Buddhist construction projects were executed by Hindu-trained craftsmen, continuing the use of mandalas to inaugurate projects and guide their design. The best-preserved ancient example is the Great Stupa at Sanchi, which uses circles and squares. When Buddhism travelled the Silk Routes to China, the idea of combining circles with squares travelled with it. Circles symbolize heaven; squares symbolize earth. The primary geometrical forms became visual symbols of the way nature was understood. Coomaraswamy summarized the point as follows:

> Because theology was the dominant intellectual passion of the race, oriental art is largely dominated by theology. We do not refer here only to the production of cult images, for which India was primarily responsible, but to the organization of thought in terms of types of activity. Oriental art is not concerned with Nature but with the nature of Nature; in this respect it is nearer to science than to our modern ideas about art. Where modern science uses names and algebraic formulae in establishing its hierarchy of forces, the East has attempted to express its understanding of life by means of precise visual symbols.[34]

Early Chinese art was influenced by the belief that objects, including rivers and mountains, can be 'animated' by spirits and energy. The belief is called animism and no boundaries were drawn between body and soul or between spirit and matter. The natural world was seen as a manifestation of the *Dao* ('The Way of Nature'). Heaven, Earth and Humanity have a single source of energy, the *qi* ('The Breath of Life) because

1.27 Mount Hua (Huashan) retains its religious significance and continues to attract pilgrims. A painter explained: 'In short, till I knew the shape of Hua Mountain, how could I paint a picture of it? But after I had visited it and drawn it from nature, the "idea" was still immature.'*

Note: *Waley, A., 'Chinese philosophy of art-IV', *Burlington Magazine for Connoisseurs*, vol, 39, no. 221 (August 1921), pp. 84–9.

they are a single entity: the cosmos. It was a theory of everything. The forces of nature (wind, sun, etc.) embody the *qi* and the *qi* gives individuality (spirits) to places. Early Chinese art evoked the spirits of natural phenomena: it was symbolic. Later Chinese art, influenced by Buddhism, became more devotional. Some of the devotion went to images (Buddhist and Daoist) and some went to artistic representations of generalized natural scenery. This is the origin of the aesthetic principles employed in Chinese garden design and landscape painting. Artists and designers sought to merge their spirits with the Dao. They 'entered' a tree, a river or a mountain, seeking to know the 'nature of its Nature' before representing it in a painting or a garden design.

The traditional religion of Japan (Shinto) was animistic. When the oldest Japanese gardens were made, in the Heian Period, art and design were influenced by Shinto and by the Chinese attitudes described above. As Buddhism waned in India and China, it waxed in Japan. Mountains, lakes and trees came to be viewed as symbols of the

1.31 Diagrams showing the evolution of Asian sanctuaries, parks and gardens through five millennia.

Egyptian sanctuaries

Egyptian gardens

Hindu and Buddhist enclosures

Islamic gardens

Daoist-Buddhist parks and towns

Daoist-Buddhist gardens

Shinto-Buddhist gardens

CHAPTER 2

Polytheist gardens

2.1 As nomads became settlers they appreciated both wild landscapes and the benefits of living in cities (Bilad Sayt, Oman).

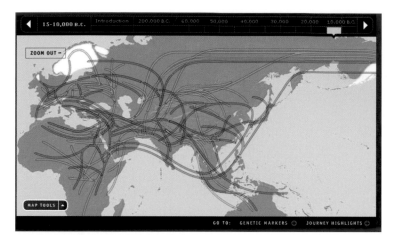

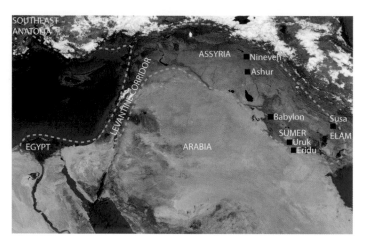

2.2 The Genographic Map shows that Homo sapiens evolved in Africa and migrated through West Asia to Central Asia and beyond.

2.3 The Fertile Crescent, shown by a green dashed line. The earliest evidence for cultivation and settlement comes from the Levantine Corridor.

The Genographic Map, by the National Geographic Society,[1] shows humans migrating 'out of Africa' from the north-east segment of the mother continent. They settled in the Fertile Crescent and developed the technologies of farming and city building. It is an arid zone where the cultivation of fields and gardens depends, even today, on water brought from distant mountains by great and lesser rivers, including the Jordan, the Nile, the Tigris and the Euphrates. Irrigation was a fundamental aspect of these societies and their gardens.

Other human groups pushed beyond the Fertile Crescent. They migrated along coasts to South and East Asia and through mountain passes to Central, North and East Asia. Some of their descendants turned back, bringing fresh ideas and technologies to the Fertile Crescent. It became a junction for migration paths, a centre of civilization and a zone of conflict, as it is today. Relations between the 'steppe and the sown' were both symbiotic and combative.[2] Some nomads lived in peace with settlers, exchanging wool and leather for craftwork. Others felt entitled to hunt and gather whatsoever they found, including herds and crops. Settlers believed they had rights to the lands, herds and crops they cared for. City-states fought with nomads and with each other. This led to the development of walled cities, walled gardens, legal systems, religious concepts, and empires.

By 3,000 BCE, West Asia had two superpowers, one at each pole of the Fertile Crescent and both polytheist. We call them Egypt and Iraq. 'Egypt' derives from a Greek word meaning 'below the Aegean' and 'Iraq' is thought to take its name from the Sumerian city of Uruk. The Sumerians called their territory 'the land of the civilized lords' (*ki-en-gir*), thus distinguishing it from the land occupied by nomads. The ancient occupants of the Nile Valley called their country 'the black soil' (*km.t* or *kemet*) to distinguish it from the surrounding desert, which they called 'the red soil' (*deshret*).

Possibly, the art of making aesthetically designed gardens originated with the civilized lords; probably, it began in several places; definitely, it flourished on Egypt's black soil. Invaders and migrants carried ideas and techniques in every direction. Rivers and shorelines facilitated their transit in some directions. Mountains blocked their passage elsewhere but the Silk Routes facilitated communications on the fringe of Central Asia. Discovering what happened is like investigating earthquakes without instruments: one can find the results but not the epicentres.

In West Asia and Europe, the period of polytheist gardens extends from the earliest historical information about gardens (*c.*3,500 BCE) to the time of the region's dominance by the God of the Jews, Christians and Muslims (*c.*650 CE). The fall of the Western Roman Empire in 476 CE marked the political end of the Ancient World but for religion and design, it was the monotheistic religions which brought down the curtain on polytheism and its gardens.

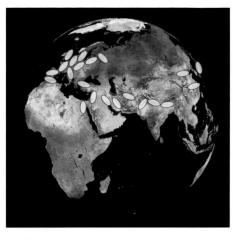

2.4 The main zones of garden development were on the fringes of the Eurasian continent.

Mesopotamian gardens

The land in and around the Rivers Tigris and Euphrates now falls within Iraq, Kuwait, Eastern Syria, South East Turkey, and South West Iran. To the Syrians, it was Beth Nahrain ('the house of the rivers'); to the Greeks, it was Mesopotamia ('the land between the rivers'); to the Arabs, it was Bayn Nahrain ('between two rivers') or Al Jazeera ('the island'). Being European, I use the Greek word. The American archaeologist, James Henry Breasted (1865–1935) coined the term 'Fertile Crescent' to describe the arc of land which stretches from the Gulf to the Mediterranean. Western civilization was once thought to have begun at the Egyptian end of this arc but priority is now given to the eastern section of the arc. Within Mesopotamia, formerly nomadic tribes, including the Semites and Aryans, seized power and introduced new languages. This caused the centre of power to shift north and west. The Mesopotamian civilizations included:

- *Sumer* (*c.*3100–*c.*2400 BCE) the main cities were Uruk and Ur; the language has no known relatives.
- *Elam* (*c.*2700–539 BCE) included the city of Anshan, on the Iranian plateau and the city of Susa on the plain of Mesopotamia; the language was Elamite, which might be related to the ancient language of India (Dravidian).
- *Akkadia* (*c.*2400–2200 BCE) the capital was Akkad; the language belonged to the Semitic group; the culture and technology of Sumer were absorbed.
- *Babylonia* (*c.*2000–1600 BCE) the capital was Babylon; the language belonged to the Semitic group; the territory was that of Sumeria and Akkadia.

- *Assyria* (*c.*1350–612 BCE) the capital was Ashur (or Assur); the language belonged to the Semitic group; the territory reached to Egypt; the culture gave rise to Judaism and Christianity.
- *Persia* (*c.*550–330 BCE) the capital was Parsa (or Persepolis); the language was Indo-European; the territory extended from the Iranian plateau to include Elam, the Fertile Crescent and Anatolia.

Garden origins, 3500–2500 BCE

Sumer, on the fringe of the Persian Gulf is 'where history began'[3] in the limited sense that it is where the oldest known texts have been found. Writing was invented *c.*3500 BCE. Scribes used a blunt reed on damp clay to produce cuneiform ('wedge-shaped') marks. Sumer is also where garden history begins. The Sumerian word *sar* is translated as 'orchard garden'. The Akkadian word *kirum* has two elements: *ki* meaning 'place' and *rum* meaning 'to send forth shoots, buds or blossoms'.[4] *Kirum* is translated as 'orchard', 'garden' or 'palm grove' and is distinguished from *agar*, meaning a field or communal meadow. A *kirum* was enclosed. An *agar* was open, cultivated with oxen and used for barley and wheat – which do not produce blossoms.

2.5 This is one of the world's oldest maps. The rectangle in the top half of the circle is Babylon and the lines running through it are water courses. The circle represents the primeval ocean, labelled Salt-Sea. Cuneiform text describes the regions of the world, shown as triangles touching the outer circle.*

Note: *Wellman, J.K. (ed.) *Belief and Bloodshed: Religion and Violence across Time and Tradition.* Lanham, MD: Rowman & Littlefield, 2007.

The king-list of the Sumerians identifies Eridu as the world's first city. It was built before the Flood: 'After the kingship descended from heaven, the kingship was in Eridu(g).'[5] Eridu means 'Good City' and it was a temple city. According to Leick, it was built at the meeting point of three ecosystems and supported three lifestyles: agriculture, nomadic pastoralism and fishing.[6] The brick temple complex at Eridu was surrounded by fresh water and therefore by vegetation. In the cosmic geography of Mesopotamia, the Earth was an island surrounded by bitter waters, with dark depths below and heaven ('On High') held in position by great mountains.[7] As a composition of sky, buildings, landform, water and vegetation, Eridu would have symbolized the creation.

2.6 Cuneiform script was originally pictographic, with the symbol for orchard or garden representing trees and an enclosure, shown above in the script of Uruk IV (*c.*3100 BCE) and Sumerian (*c.*2500 BCE). An orchard garden was *sar* in Sumerian and *kiru* in Babylonian and Assyrian.

The world's oldest literary work, *The Epic of Gilgamesh*, has references to gardens. It was written in cuneiform script and translated into many languages. The fullest surviving set of tablets is in Akkadian and dates from *c.*700 BCE. The *Epic* tells the story of King Gilgamesh, who ruled the city of Uruk *c.*2700 BCE, 10 km north-east of Eridu. Several English translations of the epic are available and they differ. The following excerpt is given in two versions, hoping to throw more light on the original.

> *Go up on the wall of Uruk and walk around,*
> *examine its foundation, inspect its brickwork thoroughly.*
> *Is not (even the core of) the brick structure made of kiln-fired brick,*
> *and did not the Seven Sages themselves lay out its plans?*
> *One league city, one league palm gardens, one league lowlands, the open area(?) of the*
> *Ishtar Temple, three leagues and the open area(?) of Uruk it (the wall) encloses.*
>
> (Excerpt from Tablet 1, trans. Maureen Gallery Kovacs, 1998)

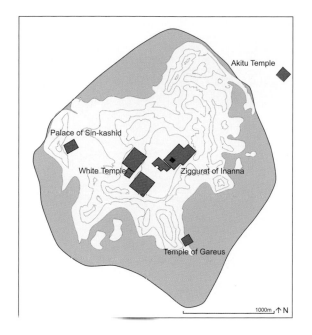

2.7 Gilgamesh reigned *c.*2600 BCE and Uruk survives as a dry tell. The green area on the plan indicates low land between the city wall and the city mound (tell) which probably contained ponds, canals and orchard gardens. The course of the Euphrates used to run beside the town but is now 12 km away.

2.8 Ur was formerly a coastal city near the mouth of the Euphrates.

Go up on the wall of Uruk and walk around!
Inspect the foundation platform and scrutinize the brickwork!
Testify that its bricks are baked bricks,
And that the Seven Counsellors must have laid its foundations!
One square mile is city, one square mile is orchards, one square mile is claypits, as well
as the open ground of Ishtar's temple.
Three square miles and the open ground comprise Uruk.
    (Excerpt from Tablet 1, trans. Stephanie Dalley)

The land use plan, as recommended by the Seven Sages, was:

- one-third for city (probably houses and temples);
- one-third for gardens (within the city walls);
- one-third for 'lowlands' or 'claypits' (possibly water-filled, used for animals and for washing clothes).

Gazing inwards from the battlements, we would have seen buildings, trees and open space round Ishtar's temple. Gazing out from the battlements, though the text does not say so, we would have seen fields of wheat and barley cultivated by oxen.

Archaeology confirms the layout of Uruk as described in *The Epic of Gilgamesh*. There is a mound (a tell) with centrally placed buildings. Changes in the climate and the

2.9 a, b The citadel of Erbil, 80 km east of Nineveh and one of the oldest continuously inhabited cities, retains the structure of a fortified tell though it has been repeatedly destroyed and rebuilt. The 'Hanging Gardens of Nineveh' were made by irrigating a bank below a citadel.

river course have left it dry. A wall ran at the foot of the mound on three sides and enclosed some low land. The 'gardens' mentioned in *The Epic* are likely to have been orchards on the low area. Greek and Roman historians reported that gardens inside city walls helped the Mesopotamians withstand a siege.[8] The date palm was the most important tree, with fruit trees and vegetables grown in their shade.[9] The buildings on the mound are often described as 'temples' but, Leick argues, are more likely to have been multi-functional civic buildings with religious, economic and administrative uses. She believes the open courtyards were as important as the roofed areas and notes 'the possibility that some of the spaces, supplied with cisterns and conduits, could have been planted and might have served as gardens'.[10] Cuneiform records of commercial transactions show that Uruk was a great trading centre.

According to *The Epic*, the Seven Sages were sent by Enki to teach mankind the arts of civilization. The English word 'civil' derives from the Latin word *civis*, meaning citizen, and the key arts were writing, building and agriculture. Cities in West and Central Asia were walled until modern times and there are still cities where one can walk round the battlements, looking inward to housing and outward to agriculture. The walls of Uruk were constructed with fired brick. Other cities used rammed mud (*pisé*). No houses have been found at Uruk but there are many dwellings at Ur. They are small partly-roofed compounds with outdoor yards.[11] The yards were used for cooking and are not likely to have contained plants or to have been described as orchards.

2.10 Khiva, now in Uzbekistan, survives as an example of a classic West Asian walled city – with the land immediately outside the walls still used for crops.

2.11 Ishtar was the goddess of love and of war.

Polytheist sanctuaries

The Epic of Gilgamesh records that Uruk had an Ishtar temple (Inanna in Sumerian), as did other Mesopotamian cities. Ishtar was a mother goddess with the power to influence love, fertility and war. Her image appears on statuettes, monuments and seals. The names of the gods were written with a star, signifying heaven, as a determinative.[12] Ishtar's name means 'star' and she was represented in the night sky by the planet Venus. Her priestesses were temple prostitutes (*hierodules*). Gilgamesh was two-thirds god and one-third human. He resisted Ishtar's advances, deciding that he could best achieve immortality by great deeds, including city-building. Other Mesopotamian kings had a holy marriage (*hieros gamos*) with a priestess, its consummation taking place in a house of god (a temple). New temples were built on the remains of old temples, the work of generations lifting structures nearer to god. Rising platforms are thought to be the physical origin of ziggurats. Images of gods were anthropomorphic and gods behaved like humans, though in control of the forces of nature. A king was seen as 'the human executive of the divine king'.[13]

The *Enuma Elish* is the creation epic of Mesopotamia, with the surviving version dating from the eighth century and written in Akkadian. The original is thought to have been much older. The text gives a creation story which compares to the account in Genesis. Marduk was the patron deity of Babylon. He is described as the Bestower of Planting, the Founder of Sowing, the Creator of Grain and Plants. The *Enuma Elish* reports him saying:

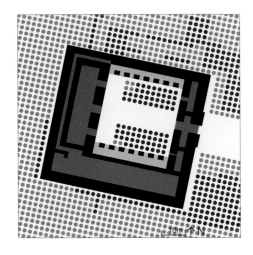

2.12 Excavations have revealed that the Temple of Ashur was set among trees. Actual planting pits are shown in dark green and conjectural pits in light green.

My blood will I take and bone will I fashion

...

I will create man who shall inhabit the earth,
That the service of the gods may be established, and that their shrines may be built.[14]

Babylonian kings were intermediaries between gods and men, able to lead their people, make laws and administer justice. It was believed that at one time 'the king had lived in fellowship with the gods in the fabulous garden that contains the Tree of Life and the Water of Life'.[15] These beliefs have parallels with the creation stories of Egypt and Israel. There are some references in Mesopotamian texts to planting in sanctuaries and tree pits have been found around the Temple of Ashur in the Assyrian capital. An official wrote that at a festival in Nimrud, 'The god will come out from the dark shrine of the palace; when he goes from the shrine of the palace into the park, a sacrifice will be offered there.'[16] Nimrud is 30 km south of Mosul, in Iraq.

Plans for temples, cities and gardens, like the right of kings to reign, were taken to have had a pre-existence in the sky before they could exist on earth. Mircea Eliade comments that:

> *The belief in the pre-existence of words and institutions will have considerable*
> *importance for archaic ontology and will find its most famous expression in the Platonic*
> *doctrine of ideas. It is attested for the first time in Sumerian documents, but its roots*
> *presumably reach down into prehistory.*[17]

Eliade's comment provides a link between the history of Asian art and that of the European art which derives from Plato's Theory of Forms (see p. 24). In philosophical terms, it can be described as the theory that universals come before particulars. One cannot make a garden, or any other thing, unless there is a pre-existing idea or form. There are various ways of expressing the point: ideas are categorically different from objects; ideas have primacy over objects; ideas are immaterial; ideas are divine; the appreciation of ideas requires consciousness.

The Garden of Eden

Abraham was born, *c.*2000 BCE, in or near the city of Ur (65 km south-east of Uruk) and migrated west to Palestine. Since the Bible describes the Garden of Eden as being 'eastward', it is often thought to have been in the marshlands of Sumer. The Book of Genesis (2: 8–11) has the following account:

> *And the Lord God planted a garden eastward in Eden; and there he put the man whom*
> *he had formed.*
> *And out of the ground made the Lord God to grow every tree that is pleasant to the*
> *sight, and good for food; the tree of life also in the midst of the garden, and the tree of*
> *knowledge of good and evil.*

2.13 The marshlands of the Tigris and Euphrates may be the type of scenery which shaped the Biblical account of the Garden of Eden.

2.14 Athanasius Kircher's drawing (1765) places the Garden of Eden west of the Persian Gulf and between the rivers Tigris and Euphrates. This remains the most common theory.

And a river went out of Eden to water the garden; and from thence it was parted, and became into four heads.

Abraham became the founding father of Judaism, Christianity and Islam, described, initially by Islamic scholars, as the Abrahamic faiths. His Sumerian origin confirms the importance of Mesopotamia in the generation of religious ideas. The Biblical account of the Garden of Eden tells us something about the context in which ethical principles developed. Initially, Adam and Eve were told to dress and keep the Garden from which they could eat freely (Genesis 2: 15–17):

*And the Lord God took the man, and put him into the Garden of Eden to dress it
and to keep it.
And the Lord God commanded the man, saying, Of every tree of the garden
thou mayest freely eat.*

After The Fall, when Adam and Eve had gained knowledge of good and evil by eating fruit from the forbidden tree, they were sent forth to engage in gruelling agricultural labour (Genesis 3: 17–20, 23):

*And unto Adam he said, Because thou hast hearkened unto the voice of thy wife,
and hast eaten of the tree, of which I commanded thee, saying, Thou shalt not eat of it:
cursed is the ground for thy sake; in sorrow shalt thou eat of it all the days of thy life;
Thorns also and thistles shall it bring forth to thee; and thou shalt eat the herb
of the field;
In the sweat of thy face shalt thou eat bread, till thou return unto the ground;
for out of it wast thou taken: for dust thou art, and unto dust shalt thou return.*

2.15 Returning from a day in the fields (in the Nile Valley).

Therefore the Lord God sent him forth from the Garden of Eden, to till the ground from whence he was taken.

Placing a socio-economic interpretation on this magnificent prose feels insensitive. Yet the story can be used as a source of information about the relationship between nomads and farmers. When humans first reached the Fertile Crescent, it must have been a veritable Garden of Eden. Food-bearing plants would have required only care and respect. But as knowledge of agricultural techniques advanced, it became necessary to sweat in the fields before one could make bread. Legal and ethical codes then became necessary, so that those who dig ditches, sow seeds and pull weeds can reap a just reward for their toil. On returning home in the evening, it must have been pleasant to find ripe fruit in an orchard and to dream of a time when the whole world had been a paradise garden.

Palace gardens

Uruk, Ur and other cities in the valley of the Tigris and Euphrates are described as tells ('hills'). They are mounds created by human occupation over long periods of time. Decayed mud brick is one of their main constituents and the higher the tell, the better the protection against floods and armies. City walls were built round tells. Palaces and temples were located at high points. Most of the annual rainfall now falls between December and April. It may once have been within the South Asian monsoon region but horticulture was always dependent on irrigation and dry tells were not good places to grow flowers, fruit or vegetables. Palace courtyards may have had plants for shade and decoration but planting was not of their essence. The primary role of courtyards was outdoor rooms for living, eating and working. In Babylonia, courtyard planting would have required irrigation. In Assyria, plants would have received sufficient rainwater to survive.

There is good textual evidence for ancient cities having had horticultural gardens – and a number of reasons for believing they were on low land inside and outside city walls. First, the region was famed for its irrigation system, which would have watered the lower land. Second, cities had water available within their walls. Third, the plants grown in ancient gardens were primarily food plants. Fourth, if we look at the earliest known gardens in Egypt and Iran, they were mud-walled enclosures in which choice fruits were grown. Fifth, the area ascribed to gardens was proportionally large (one-third of Uruk). Sixth, the history of garden design has many examples of gardens having been made just inside and just outside city walls.

My hypothesis is that the palace gardens of Mesopotamia were mud-walled enclosures with irrigation channels, on flat land between the tell and the city walls. One can imagine a young couple leaving a palace to visit such a garden in the cool of the evening. Servants open a private gate in the city wall. They descend a stepped path, on the slope of the tell, to a door in the garden wall. The gardeners have retired to cook their evening meals. Irrigation channels and paths divide the space into compartments. Apples, plums, dates and grapes are grown with sweet-smelling flowers. They pick the ripest fruits for each other, sit under a canopy, listen to the frogs, watch the egrets and kiss.

'The Hanging Gardens of Babylon' may have been of this type. According to the Greek historian Diodorus, quoted below, who lived in Sicily, they were made by a king to re-mind a beautiful girl of her mountain homeland. According to a modern scholar, whose views have not received general support, the Hanging Gardens may have been in Nineveh with an Archimedes screw acting as a 'machine' to supply water. The Nineveh garden, shown on a relief in the British Museum, is most likely to have been supplied by an aqueduct and, apart from the slope, has the use and character of an orchard garden. Diodorus the Sicilian described the Hanging Gardens of Babylon as follows:

2.16 a A mud-walled orchard garden (in Iran).

2.16 b Mesopotamian gardens were probably mud-walled enclosures with a canopy of date palms and an under-storey of other fruiting plants, flowers and vegetables.

There was likewise an hanging garden (as it is called) near the citadel, not built by Semiramis, but by a later prince, called Cyrus, for the sake of a courtesan, who being a Persian (as they say) by birth, and coveting meadows on mountain tops, desired the king by an artificial plantation to imitate the lands in Persia. This garden was four hundred feet square, and the ascent up to it was as to the top of a mountain, and had buildings and apartments out of one into another, like unto a theatre. Under the steps to the ascent, were built arches one above another, rising gently by degrees, which supported the whole plantation. The highest arch upon which the platform of the garden was laid, was fifty cubits high, and the garden itself was surrounded with battlements and bulwarks ... The roof over all these was first covered with reeds, daubed with abundance of brimstone; then upon them was laid double tiles pargeted together with a hard and durable mortar, and over them after all, was a covering with sheets of lead, that the wet which drenched through the earth, might not rot the foundation. Upon all these was laid earth of a convenient depth, sufficient for the growth of the greatest trees. When the soil was laid even and smooth, it was planted with all sorts of trees, which both for greatness and beauty, might delight the spectators. The arches (which stood one above another, and by that means darted light sufficient one into another) had in them many stately rooms of all kinds, and for all purposes. But there was one that had in it certain engines, whereby it drew plenty of water out of the river through certain conduits and conveyances from the platform of the garden, and nobody without was the wiser, or knew what was done.[18]

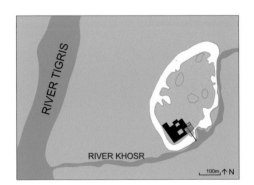

2.17 a, b The 'Hanging Gardens' shown on a tablet in the British Museum (left) may have been outside the palace at Nineveh (right).

The Hanging Gardens of Babylon date from *c.*700 BCE and the above account by Diodorus was written *c.*50 BCE. It was based, one hopes, on older sources and cannot be relied upon for technical details.

Egyptian gardens

Ancient Egypt was the south-west pole of the Fertile Crescent. It is joined to the Asian land mass and forms part of the same tectonic plate. Linguistically and genetically the Egyptians belong to the Afro-Asian group. At all periods, the Genographic Map[19] shows migration routes from West Asia flowing along the coast of North Africa. Migrant hunter–gatherers settled in the Nile valley between 9000 and 5000 BCE, probably because the Sahara was becoming drier. By the Gerzean Period (*c.*3500 BCE), Lower Egypt was in contact with Mesopotamia and, as in Sumer, the organization of an agricultural society was found to require kings, priests, scribes and soldiers. The strategic difference between the two regions was that while Mesopotamia was always liable to invasion, Egypt was comparatively protected: by the Sahara Desert, the Eastern Desert, the Sinai Peninsula, the Mediterranean and the Red Sea. Linguistics indicates that cities were used for trade, for livestock protection, for flood protection and as sacred sites.[20] In Egypt's hieroglyphic script the determinative for a named city is a circle with a cross (*niwt*). It has been variously interpreted as a view of the ordered cosmos,[21] as a village with a crossroads and as a basin with crossing channels.[22] I see it as a symbol which identifies cities and their gardens as places requiring both linkage and protection.

2.18 a, b The determinant for city (*niwt*) seems to represent the need for cities and palaces to have both linkage and protection.

Origins

Egypt's creation myth is explained in different ways in different texts and, like all aspects of Egyptian culture, evolved over a long period of time. Since they formed a family, gods could take on each other's forms, characteristics and names. The following outline aims to explain the context in which garden designers worked, but suffers from the inexactitudes of all generalizations.

The world began as nothingness, wetness and darkness. When the primeval waters began to ebb, a mound emerged. A lotus grew in the water and sunlight gleamed from its stamens. This was the First Light, the First Land and the First Life. A bird landed and the sun god, Ra (Atum), came to live on earth. Another version of the story has a 'bird of light' emerging from a primordial egg.[23] The First Land, a mound surrounded by water and bearing a god's house, became a sacred symbol. The coming of light was re-enacted each dawn and the creation of land was re-enacted each year as the Nile flood receded to leave smooth black mounds which became re-vegetated and attracted birds. The creator was reborn in each pharaoh.

2.19 a, b The Sacred Ibis, *Threskiornis aethiopicus*. According to an Egyptian creation myth, the Ibis laid an egg on a mound in the primeval waters which hatched to become the sun god.

2.20 The sycomore (*Ficus sycomorus*) can produce figs on bare wood even when the tree has no leaves. It was one of the first trees to be cultivated and was planted in gardens and by tombs.

Atum was the creator god. Having no wife, he masturbated to produce Shu and Tefnut, who copulated to produce Geb and Nut. Geb was the god of the earth – when he laughed, there was an earthquake. Nut, his wife, became goddess of the sky. Their children were born of the earth and the sky. Osiris, their son, became god of life and death. During his earthly life, a pharaoh was an incarnation of Horus, the son of Osiris, with Hathor his wife or mother. During his afterlife, a pharaoh was an incarnation of Osiris himself. Osiris was buried in a mound, surrounded by symbolic water and planted with the sycomore fig (*Ficus sycomorus*) which fruits on bare wood. As god of the underworld, he decided the fate of the dead. Souls were weighed against a feather, representing the goddess of truth and justice (Ma'at). Only the good were allowed to start the long journey to a land of eternal pleasure (Aaru). Knowing that a pharaoh would one day be their judge encouraged obedience. As a god of life, Osiris was married to Isis. He caused the Nile to flood and vegetation to grow.

The word pharaoh originally meant 'great house' and came to mean 'majesty' in the New Kingdom period. The hieroglyph for a pharaoh's Horus name (*serekh*) was written with a symbol for a palace with a falcon standing on top. The falcon is Horus. A royal palace was a home for a worldly god and a royal tomb was a dwelling for his other-worldly afterlife. A pharaoh's body had to be preserved, by mummification, and he required grave goods, including furniture, clothes and gardens, for use in his afterlife. Some of these items were provided as objects, others as paintings on tomb walls. This is where most information about Egyptian gardens originates. Tomb paintings show the types of garden which pharaohs enjoyed on earth.

2.21 A *serekh* gives the Horus name of a pharaoh. The lower section of the rectangle represents the façade of a palace. The middle section is a plan of a courtyard with, in this example from the Metropolitan Museum, the name Raneb. Horus, represented by a falcon, stands above.

2.22 The Ancient Egyptians called the Nile Valley the Black Land to distinguish it from the surrounding Red Land.

The Domain of Amun

Herodotus wrote: 'The Egypt to which the Hellenes come in ships is a land which has been won by the Egyptians as an addition, and that it is a gift of the river.'[24] The northern section of the longest river in the world runs in a narrow valley (Upper Egypt) and opens into a broad delta (Lower Egypt). When the two kingdoms were united, the

2.23 a, b A mortuary temple was a home for a god whose earthly life had concluded. David Roberts' drawing and the photograph show the site before it was flooded by the Aswan High Dam. Access was from the Nile and the temple stood at the meeting point of the Red Land and the Black Land. The Kalabsha temple was moved to a new site in 1970.

2.24 a, b Dier el-Medina was built for craftsmen and is the best surviving example of an Egyptian settlement. Dwellings were small enclosures part-open and part-roofed. The temple, dedicated to Hathor, dates from *c.*220 BCE.

city became the capital of Egypt. It was called Thebes by the Greeks and Waset ('The City') by the ancient Egyptians. 'Luxor' is an Arab name, meaning 'The Palaces'. The sun rises over the east bank of the Nile and sets over the west bank, so the land of the setting sun became the land of the dead. The pharaohs, whose family brought light and life to earth, built homes for their earthly lives on the east bank and for their after-lives on the west bank. The Domain of Amun is the royal and sacred estate which spans the east and west banks of the Nile. Amun was a god of air who merged with Ra, who merged with Atum, to become the creator-god Amun-Ra. The Domain of Amun is a sacred landscape of the first importance. In many respects it is the prototype for the aesthetically designed landscapes and gardens made in Europe at later dates.

Egypt was in close contact with Mesopotamia and an exchange of ideas took place. Both countries regarded cities as sacred and both built temples on symbolic mounds. Significantly, the diplomatic correspondence between the two superpowers, found at Amarna, is written in the cuneiform script of Mesopotamia. Since there were older cities in other parts of West Asia, it seems probable that any ripples of garden influence were more westward than eastward. But since so much less is known about gardens in Mesopotamia, Assyria and Palestine, one can get a better appreciation of ancient gardens from Egypt.

Domestic gardens

Egypt had both rich and poor people. Agricultural workers, like their nomadic predecessors, lived in makeshift shelters. Timber was in short supply and the simplest way of making a shelter was to build a circular mud wall with a roof of palm fronds and

2.25 a, b One can imagine the type of house represented by the tomb model set in what is now a deserted village (in Siwa Oasis, West Egypt).

43

2.26 a, b, c Hollyhocks, poppies and papyrus were used in Egyptian gardens.

grass. It is a building type still found in Africa. Egypt's labourers owned no valuable property and their shelters could be between fields. For obvious reasons, none survive. Craftsmen, who owned tools and other possessions, required more security and lived in settlements. The best surviving example of a village is Dier el-Medina. It was used by the men who built tombs for kings and nobles, on the west of the Domain of Amun. The layout of Dier el-Medina resembles the hieroglyph for a city (*niwt*). It is a cluster of dwellings with a defensive outer wall. Craftsmen had valuable tools and materials which required protection. By modern standards, they were upper middle class – but their dwellings were the size of animal sheds. Some food and shade plants may have been grown within the village but it is difficult to see how there can have been ground-level space for shrubs, vegetables or herbs.

Evidence for the design of aristocratic dwellings comes from models in tombs and from papyrus drawings. They have similarities with the vernacular mud houses which survive in Iran, Turkey, Yemen and other parts of West Asia. Typical features of Egyptian tomb models include mud walls, outdoor steps to flat roofs, vents to catch the breeze and roofed outdoor space. The only Egyptian model to show both a roofed area and a garden has one quarter of the space covered and the rest planted with shade trees. Climatically, this is a good arrangement. Evaporation from leaves uses latent heat which cools the surface of the leaf and then the surrounding air. Cool air, being heavier than warm air, falls to the ground and produces a breeze which helps perspiration evaporate. It is a natural air-conditioning system. The largest group of dwellings was found at Amarna where villas had 'a large square plot of ground with the main house centered in a walled enclosure'.[25] Though often regarded as typical, Lacovara regards this opinion as incorrect. He believes the typical house was a divided-court – a rectangular enclosure, part-roofed and part-open.[26] The form resembles that of Mesopotamian dwellings but in Egypt they were normally built on agricultural land, instead of on dry tells. When large enough, the open sections of Egyptian courtyards could therefore be planted, mainly with food plants but also with symbolically important flowers.

Palace gardens

The palaces and gardens of living pharaohs were built with mud brick. Since they were required only for an earthly life, there was no need to build in stone and no examples survive in Egypt's intensely farmed, and now urbanized, riverside zone. It was, however, the practice for living pharaohs to visit the afterlife homes of their ancestors on the west bank. These visits took place during festivals and, because they were annual events, the pharaohs had need of short-stay palaces on the west bank. They are known as 'temple palaces' and the best example is at Medinet Habu.[27] The temple itself is in good condition, because it was built in stone for a god's life ('millions of years'). The mud-built palace has decayed, but the general layout of rooms and courtyards can be seen. The sizes of the two types of space are similar and one can guess that the courts were planted with trees like the house model (see p. 43). Courts would have functioned as light wells for adjoining rooms and as places to sit or sleep when it was more comfortable to be outside than inside. Trees would have survived

2.27 The stone-built mortuary temple at Medinet Habu survives. The mud-built palace to the left of the pylons has decayed to its foundations. It has courtyards which might have contained palm trees.

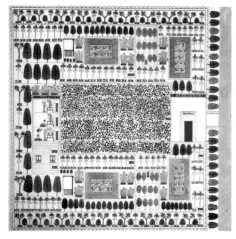

2.28 The central space of 'Sennufer's garden' was a vine pergola. It also had rectangular pools and orchards. This plan could and should be used for a re-creation of the garden in Luxor.

2.29 During the season of inundation (*akhet*) villages became islands.

with minimal irrigation but since mortuary palaces are at the juncture of the desert and agriculture, the land was not suited to productive horticulture. The soil would not have been rich and water was probably brought by carriers.

The best information about the layout of palace gardens on the east bank at Luxor comes from a famous painting found on the ceiling of a west bank tomb. The original has been destroyed but an excellent copy survives. It is described as Sennufer's garden because, as Mayor of Thebes, it was under his care. But the painting was not in his tomb and the garden is not likely to have been in his ownership. As shown in Figure 2.28, it had several pools and was well planted. There is a canal on one side of the garden wall but no channels within the garden boundary.

In Egypt, floods were welcome and predictable annual events. The season of inundation (*akhet*) lasted from June to September, which was a good month for planting. In Mesopotamia, the annual flood arrived at a less convenient time, in spring, when the crops were ripening, making great floods a catastrophe. Mesopotamian palaces were built on dry mounds (tells), above flood levels, and their orchard gardens are likely to have been on the irrigated land below. In Egypt, receding floods left uneven silt deposits which grew from year to year. The Nile was confined to its channel for most of the year but spread over the agricultural land once a year to become a braided river with raised bars. Currents slowed when they passed through vegetation or over mounds and less

silt could be held in suspension. Mounds therefore grew and the higher land provided better sites for permanent dwellings. Perimeter walls of straw-reinforced mud give additional protection. Pre-Aswan Dam paintings and photographs of Egypt in the flood season show mud villages with tree canopies resembling islands in a great lake. Sailing boats were used for travel between villages. Sennufer's garden could have been on a mound with the walls helping to keep out the flood. This could explain the absence of canals from Egyptian gardens and their presence in Mesopotamian gardens. Nile floods can still be seen in the Sudan, south of the Aswan Dam.

The central rectangle in Sennufer's garden is bounded by an inner wall and 'roofed' with grape vines. Vines also appear on the beautiful painted roof of Sennufer's tomb. The treatment of the land beneath the pergola is not shown but conclusions can be drawn from the fact that the area is walled and between two buildings: it must have been living space, not horticultural space, and the surface must have been mud, not stone – because this was the construction material used for domestic architecture. The pavement is likely to have been painted so that it could be kept clean. Verandah floors are still painted in Indian villages and examples of painted pavements have been found in Egyptian palaces:

> *Pavements were ornamented with marsh and water scenes, palm or lotus columns, and ceilings with birds or stars, as found in the palaces of Merenptah at Memphis or Amenhotep III at Malkata. Bound captives were shown underfoot on the Windows of Appearance, throne bases and stairways; and scenes of armed men or hunters in the desert evoked the king's symbolic mastery over the forces of chaos, as is found on the exterior of temples.*[20]

Amarna was a town 400 km north of Luxor, on the east bank of the Nile. The layout has survived because it was outside Egypt's black (agricultural) land and occupied for only twenty years. There are large courtyards within the king's and queen's palaces. In the absence of information about their design, the best that can be done is to assume it resembled the painting of Sennufer's tomb. This would make it a place where one could sit in the shade, pick fruit and sit in shady arbours to watch fish swimming among lilies in garden ponds. When the palace was excavated, it had a beautiful painted pavement which became a tourist attraction. Local farmers, understandably annoyed by visitors walking across their fields, destroyed it.

Temple gardens

More is known about Egyptian temples than about Egyptian palaces. Their layout was derived from the creation myth outlined above and their components, actual or symbolic, included a mound, a house for a god, a sacred lake and a sacred grove. Since the use of open space around temples was symbolic and ceremonial, one might want to call them temple landscapes instead of temple gardens. At Luxor, they formed part of

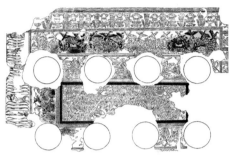

2.30 a, b A painted pavement (*rangoli*) in India (top) and Petrie's drawing of a painted pavement in Amarna (above). The circles are columns.

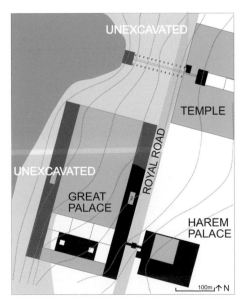

2.31 Akenhaten's palace at Amarna. It is possible that the palace courtyard was treated like Sennufer's garden (p. 46).

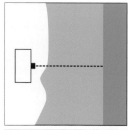

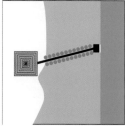

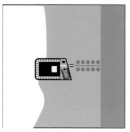

2.32 Evolution of the Egyptian sanctuary: Predynastic Enclosure (top), Old Kingdom Pyramid (centre), New Kingdom Mortuary Temple (bottom).

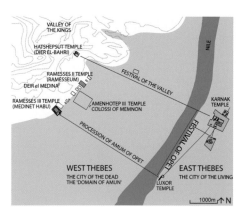

2.33 Domain of Amun, with the land of the living (East Thebes) and the land of the dead (West Thebes).

the Domain of Amun. Each temple was part of a sanctuary from which the public was excluded. The users were priests, either resident or visiting, and royal processional parties.

The evolution of Egyptian temple gardens is shown in Figure 2.32. In the Old and Middle Kingdoms the features of a sanctuary were:

● a significant location in the wider landscape;
● a protective wall, often wavy in plan to symbolize the primordial waters;
● a sacred mound, or pyramid, to symbolize the land which emerged from the waters;
● a sacred walk, or processional path, from water (the Nile, or a canal) to the temple site.

The New Kingdom was established after an Intermediate Period in which the Nile Delta had been ruled by an Asiatic people, the Hyksos. They probably came from Palestine and introduced war chariots to Egypt. A 'standard' temple layout developed, deploying the above symbolic elements as follows:

● a small 'valley temple' stood beside the water. It housed a barge, used for the pharaoh when he died and by visiting gods at subsequent festivals;
● a ceremonial route from water, in the form of a river, a pool, or a T-shaped canal-end, to the temple site. Gardens could be made along the route;
● an outer wall of mud-brick, bounding the temple compound with its sacred lake, sacred grove, god's mansion food stores;
● a pylon gateway marked by flagpoles and leading to the mansion itself;
● an open peristyle court to admit the sun;
● a hypostyle hall, symbolizing the created world;
● the holy of holies (an inner sanctuary with a plinth for the god's statue).

Later temples were placed at the margin of life and death: the edge of the floodplain. Ceremonial routes were then walled, roofed, planted, lined with sphinxes, or given significance by colossal statues. Pylon gates were positioned so that the sun rose between the towers, creating the hieroglyph for horizon. A sacred lake and a sacred grove were contained within the sanctuary. The sacred grove was planted with the sycamore fig, native to water margins, and with tamarisk, native to desert margins. A flight of steps descended from the temple to the lake. The lake was used by priests, for ritual bathing at dawn, as *ghats* continue to be used in India. At Karnak, the sacred lake had a tunnel from which geese, symbolizing Amun, could emerge onto the water surface, as Amun himself had done at the beginning of time. The pharaoh, an incarnation of Amun and of Horus, was rowed on the lake.

At Malkata, near Medinet Habu, Amenhotep III made a ceremonial lake (2 km by 1 km) and shaped the spoil into 'rows of artificial hills'.[29] Kemp describes Malkata as 'Egypt's largest earthwork' and the mounds as an 'early example of landscaping'. They stood at the meeting point of the Nile floodplain and the desert. The lake was traversed by Morning and Evening Barges, representing the journeys of the sun-god at royal jubilees (Sed festivals). A New Kingdom temple was a symbol of the created world. The ceiling represented the sky; the columns represented plants; the floor, occasionally flooded by the Nile, represented the primordial waters from which land emerged. The processional axis lay along the sun's daily path from east to west. The inner sanctuary

2.34 a, b (top) Views from East Thebes of the Festival of the Valley processional route to Hatshepsut's temple. The electricity pylons and modern buildings should be removed.

2.35 a, b (below) The sacred lakes at Medinet Habu and Karnak.

was at the west, near the place where the sun set. The temple compound was the meeting place of heaven, earth and the underworld. It was a gate. It allowed gods and kings to move between the here-now and the here-after. Blank doors defined entry–exit points. Many temples were tombs and many tombs were temples. Temple compounds symbolized the creation with what became the compositional elements of garden and landscape design: land, water, vegetation, paving and buildings.

Greece and Rome

A ripple of influence from Egypt and Mesopotamia spread north and west from the Mediterranean. It inspired the sanctuaries and the stone architecture of Ancient Greece, from which the villa gardens of Rome developed. The consequences of this ripple, traced through 4,000 years in *Garden History: Philosophy and Design 2000 BC to 2000 AD*, are summarized below.

Mycenaean towns (1600–1100 BCE) were fortified, and, as in Mesopotamia and Egypt, had productive gardens in the fields below their walls. Homer makes reference to three types of designed outdoor space in *The Iliad* and *The Odyssey*:

- productive gardens, outside cities;
- palace courtyards, within walled cities;
- sacred groves (sanctuaries), outside cities.

Classical Greek towns (500–300 BCE) had outdoor space types which relate to those in Mycenaean towns. There were dwellings with peristyle courtyards inside towns, which may have contained pot plants. Outside city walls there were productive gardens. Sacred groves and gymnasia, also outside city walls, provided for the educational and recreational needs of town dwellers. They were communal facilities, available for general use. The making of private villas with private groves began in Northern Greece (Macedonia) and may have been stimulated by Alexander the Great's expedition into Asia. His generals are thought to have returned home with memories of lavish palace gardens seen in Mesopotamia and Persia. The private villas of Rome took Macedonian villas as their starting point and included gardens which were, in effect, privately owned sacred groves and gymnasia. They also had peristyle courts, bathing pools, hippodromes and grottos.

A second ripple of influence travelled round the eastern shore of the Mediterranean with Christianity, bringing disapproval of the luxury and polytheist idolatry of Graeco-Roman villa gardens. This became joined to an enthusiasm for a particular type of religious outdoor space: the cloister court. The best surviving examples of European cloisters are attached to monasteries but it is known that the two greatest churches

2.36 Mycenae is likely to have had productive gardens in the valley below the citadel.

2.37 The temple in the Sanctuary of Olympian Zeus, begun in 520 BCE and completed by Hadrian, was outside the walls of Athens.

2.38 a, b, c An image of how the *chahar bagh* at Pasargadae (top) might have looked can be assembled by adding flowing water and orchard-type planting (centre and bottom). The lower image is from the Bagh-e Fin, made 2000 years later and furnished with paving stones in the twentieth century.

in the Roman Empire both had peristyle courts: Old St Peters, in Rome, and Hagia Sophia, in Constantinople (Istanbul). The internal layout of these courts is unknown but there is evidence that some courts in Constantinople had crossing paths and a central feature. This is the arrangement shown on the famous St Gall plan which was drawn by Haito after visiting Constantinople and studying the design of 'all monasteries in the bosom of France and Italy'.[30]

Persian gardens

Achaemenid gardens

Another ripple of influence from the Fertile Crescent may have spread north, to Persia and beyond. The main influences on the civilization of Ancient Persia were:

- Aryan culture from the steppes, mountains and oases of Central Asia, established in Persia's Achaemenid Empire (558–330 BCE);
- Mesopotamian culture from the river valleys of the Fertile Crescent on Persia's southern flank.

They came together at Ilam and Fars in Iran. Fars Province, on the high plateau of Persia, takes its name from the language known as Farsi or Persian. It travelled with the Aryans from Central Asia and is related both to Proto-Greek and the language of the Vedas (see p. 112).

Ilam Province is in South West Iran. Its ancient name, Elam, means 'highland' but the Elamites held land both on the plateau which became Persia and on the low land of the Mesopotamian valley, which was the dominant cultural influence. Elamite was unrelated to the other languages of Mesopotamia but may be related to the ancient languages of East and South India, including Dravidian, or to an Afro-Asian language group.

Persia was a crossing point, geographically and culturally. The people who gave the name Aryan (meaning 'noble') to Iran spoke an Indo-European language. Information about their culture comes from languages deriving from Proto-Indo-European (PIE) and from texts in these languages, including Persian and Sanskrit. This has led to the following theories about the Aryan people, *c.*2500 BCE: they were pastoralists and nomads; they were warriors; they had horse-drawn carts and chariots; they composed heroic poetry; their religion had a sky father and an earth mother; fire was central to their beliefs; horse sacrifice was important. Since the Aryans left no architecture or gardens, the early development of building construction in Persia is more likely to derive from Mesopotamia.

2.39 A water channel and basin in an Uzbek farmhouse, used for drawing water. A former resident of this type of dwelling told the author that washing in the channel was considered bad manners, because the debris flowed to the neighbour's garden. Washing was therefore done in bowls and the slops were used for irrigation.

Palace gardens

By 700 BCE, a group of Aryans had settled around Lake Urmia (in North Iran) under the leadership of Achaemenes (Haxamanis in Old Persian) who gave his name to the empire. Cyrus the Great claimed Achaemenes as an ancestor[31] and founded the Achaemenid Empire (550–330 BCE), on land around Shiraz formerly occupied by Flamites. The first Achaemenid capital was founded by Cyrus the Great (c.546 BCE) at Pasargadae and has a pivotal importance in garden history. David Stronach, who excavated the palace garden, wrote:

> *Recent excavations at both Pasargadae and Susa suggest that the history of the chahar bagh begins in the Achaemenid period. The clearest evidence comes from the Palace Area at Pasargadae. There the surviving elements of several stone water channels help to define the plan of a major garden, which was founded in the later years of the reign of Cyrus the Great (559–30 b.c.).*[32]

If we follow Stronach, a *chahar bagh* is a type of garden in which canals have 90 degree intersections in square basins. The development of the *chahar bagh* in Islamic gardens will be discussed in the next chapter (p. 73), but where did the idea come from? There are two possible sources in Persia's antecedents. First, it might have been an Aryan invention. Given the relative lack of a settlement history and the absence of archaeological evidence, this seems unlikely. Second, the idea might have come from

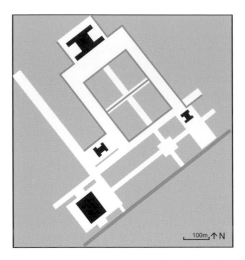

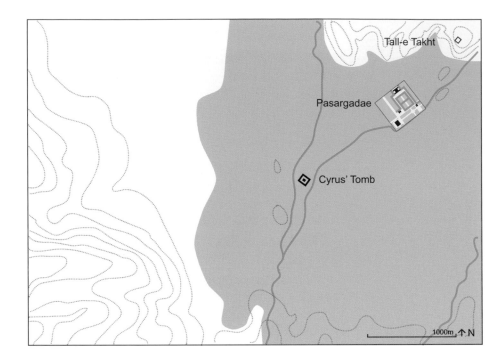

2.40 a, b Cyrus' tomb (assumed) and his palace at Pasargadae are in a valley protected by a fort (Tall-e Takht). The modern version of the name Pasargadae is of Greek origin and may derive from a word meaning 'the garden of Pars'. The palace garden is likely to have had the character of an orchard in Cyrus' time and is assumed to have been walled.

Mesopotamia. If correct, the *chahar bagh* at Pasargadae is the only known example of an ancient garden culture based on irrigation channels.

The first recorded use of the term *chahar bagh* in connection with gardens was over a thousand years after the construction of Pasargadae, and the Mughal gardens of sixteenth-century India, created 2,000 years after Pasargadae, are often cited as the best examples. Mughal gardens do have water channels dividing squares into quadrants but the idea of crossing canals should be kept separate from their use to make perfectly symmetrical gardens. Two functions of a *chahar bagh* are possible: (1) when four channels meet at 90 degrees, floating material is caught and the channel is blocked. An open square at the meeting point allows the blockage to clear, giving an opportunity to see the water and create a beautiful design feature; and (2) in an encampment garden, a square basin can be used for washing and for drawing water. The *chahar bagh* at Pasargadae is lined with stone and surrounded by dry hills. In Mesopotamia, building stone had to be brought from afar and, because gardens were on low-lying farmland, there was no need to line water channels with stone. This explains why what may be the oldest surviving example of Mesopotamian garden design is in Persia. Mud channels would also have required basins at intersections and if the basins were stone-reinforced, it is possible that one will be found.

There may also be an Aryan influence on the layout of Pasargadae, making it more than a stone-built Mesopotamian garden. The site is ringed by hills and must have had the character of an oasis when first settled. With plentiful water, rich soil, ripe fruit, a

2.41 a, b Persepolis is on a platform overlooking a fertile plain. Bas reliefs in the palace imply lines of trees marking paths used by tribute bearers from distant parts of Darius' empire.

supply of firewood and grazing for the herds, it would have been an attractive place for nomads to settle as winter approached and the northlands froze. A network of water channels would create an excellent site for an encampment, as in Timurid and Mughal gardens two thousand years later (see p. 74). Pasargadae was suited for use as a temporary encampment and could then have been settled at a later date.

Cyrus the Great founded an empire which embraced much of the land between Egypt, Turkey, and India. This required a ceremonial capital, which was built 85 km south of Pasargadae. The old name was Parsa (or Farsa) and it is now known by the Greek name of Persepolis ('City of the Persians'). Cyrus might have selected the site but the king who led its construction was Darius I (522–486 BCE). It sits below a hill and has a great terrace overlooking a fertile plain and barren mountains to the south. Wall carvings show envoys bringing tribute from distant parts of the empire. Their customs, clothes, languages and religions were respected and this principle is embodied in the architecture of Persepolis. It is an admirable principle but has the consequence that Persepolis tells us less about ancient Persian gardens than Pasargadae. One can speculate that the land below the palace was used as an orchard garden but there is no evidence of that.

Tomb gardens

The tomb at Pasargadae is believed to be that of Cyrus the Great, and there is a story that it was once surrounded by a rectangular garden. Neither theory has been

2.42 This may be the tomb of Cyrus the Great, at Pasargadae.

2.43 a, b The presence of a fire temple at Pasargadae shows the Persian kings to have been at least sympathetic to Zoroastrianism (above, looking from Tall-e Takht to the fire temple and right, looking from the fire temple to Tall-e Takht).

2.44 a, b Burial mounds are found across Asia, from Sweden to Japan. The photograph is of *kurgans* at Uppsala and the painting (by Viktor Vasnetsov, 1899) shows Oleg of Novgorod's warriors holding a feast beside his *kurgan*. He died in 912.

confirmed by archaeology. Darius I was buried 3 km from Persepolis in a cliff-hewn tomb, at Naqsh-e Rustam, which has a Zoroastrian fire temple nearby. There is also a fire temple at Pasargadae. Their presence suggests that Cyrus and Darius were Zoroastrians. But since Zoroastrians did not bury their dead, it raises the wider question of Central Asian burial customs. There may have been a polytheistic diversity.

Burial of the dead involves practical and conceptual issues. Shamanism led to the belief that the dead should merge with the spirit world. To join with the earth mother, a body could be buried. This was difficult if the land was frozen or stony, which may be the origin of burial mounds (now called *kurgans,* from a Russian word). To join with the sky father, a body could be cremated or, if there was a shortage of wood, exposed to carnivorous birds. The Vedic-Aryans used cremation and the Zoroastrians, believing that burial would pollute the earth and cremation would pollute the sacred fire, built 'Towers of Silence' in which bodies were exposed to vultures. Zoroastrians stressed the contrast between good and evil, associating good with cultivators and evil with marauding nomads from the steppes. They also introduced the concept of paradise, not as a place where man lived before the fall, but as a place where the good will live hereafter. As a metaphor, the paradise garden had such a profound influence on the subsequent history of gardens that it is tempting to believe that the tomb at Pasargadae

2.45 Zoroastrians offer their dead to the sky and the vultures in Towers of Silence (outside Yazd).

2.46 a, b Hindus cremate their dead and cast the ashes into rivers. It is a sacrifice to Agni, believed to assist passage to another life, and takes place at special locations in the landscape (Pashupatinath, in Nepal).

did belong to Cyrus and *was* set in a garden. We can, in any case, remember him as 'Cyrus the Great Gardener', for having made the *chahar bagh* at Pasargadae.

Sassanian gardens

Persia came under Greek influence after Alexander the Great overthrew the Achaemenid Empire in 323 BCE. This lasted until the Sassanids, after 226 CE, rejected Greek influence and re-established Persian culture, including the Zoroastrian religion. The Sassanid Empire prospered and its kings built palaces at Firuzabad and Bishapur. Firuzabad had a circular plan with a Zoroastrian fire temple at the centre. Bishapur was laid out by King Shapur I in 266 on a Graeco-Roman grid and was built with the help of captive Roman soldiers. The arched *iwans* of these palaces survive but the garden fragments are insufficient to determine their layouts, which could have drawn upon both Roman and Achaemenid precedents. An *iwan* is a vaulted hall, walled on three sides, and open on a fourth side which may have overlooked a pool or garden. When archaeology has revealed more about Persian gardens, it will be interesting to discover if, and how, they influenced the Islamic gardens discussed in the next chapter.

The rise of Islam overwhelmed Zoroastrianism, partly because the priests required a Zoroastrian king and partly because Islam shared key beliefs with Zoroastrianism. In the belief that 'world history was leading to the Day of Judgement to be followed by eternal life of beatitude for the righteous, Islam presented a path to salvation that was familiar to Zoroastrians.'[33] David Stronach comments on the cross-over between pre-Islamic and post-Islamic Persian gardens:

2.47 Ctesiphon was the capital of the Parthian and Sassanid Empires. The Taq-i Kisra, now in Iraq, was part of the palace complex. The garden is lost.

In view of the previously unsuspected antiquity of the quadripartite garden plan it is certain that such gardens (and even the sequence of two such gardens along the principal axis) were familiar to the Sasanians, energetic builders who particularly delighted in the creation of very elongated garden designs. The Koranic conception of the 'eight gardens of Paradise' may thus have been partly connected with an evolved, formal garden of this type with eight plots that was already well represented in the Near East at the beginning of the Islamic era.[34]

Sassanian gardens were rectangular and are known to have had long pools and pavilions.[35]

The end of the Ancient World

The advent of Judaism and Christianity and, as outlined in the next chapter, of Islam, wrought many changes in West Asia and Europe: the Zoroastrian fires were extinguished; monotheism replaced polytheism; the graven images of Mesopotamia and Egypt were buried in the sands; sacred groves were de-consecrated; sacred trees were felled; the pagan deities of Greece and Rome were smashed or buried; temple gardens were destroyed or abandoned. Monotheistic art and design took their place, with brilliant results but with an end to the period we call the Ancient World. As when DNA cascades down the generations in a single family, one mourns the old and welcomes the new.

2.49 The famous story of St Boniface felling Thor's oak symbolizes Christian suppression of European polytheism. The Thunder God, Thor, is cognate with India's Storm God, Indra. The painting (1737) is in St Martins-Kirche in Westenhofen.

CHAPTER 3

Islamic gardens

3.1 Islam arose in Arabia; green became the colour of Islam.

Islam arose in the deserts of Arabia. In the pre-Islamic 'time of ignorance' (*jahiliyyah*), Arabia had a warlike and feuding society. After 610, Muhammad founded a community on faith and laid upon each individual the duty of creating a just society. Islam means 'submission' – of the self to the will of God. The prophet lived and preached in an enclosed outdoor space. It is not known whether it contained plants but green became the colour of Islam and Muhammad's courtyard home became the first mosque. It was partly covered by a sun-shade and on one side had a row of small rooms for his wives.[1] Muhammad was a merchant until, at the age of 40, he was visited in a cave by the Archangel Gabriel and commanded to recite verses sent by God. This created a new faith and a new culture, related to the context in which they grew. But Islam focused on relationships between man and god. Holy places were revered and worship was not tied to specific locations. The polytheist idolatry of the ancient religions was entirely rejected but aspects of the older monotheist faiths, including Judaism and Christianity, were accepted. This included congregational worship and references to the garden as a symbol of paradise.

Adherents of the Mesopotamian religions believed their gods lived in a 'fabulous garden that contains the Tree of Life and the Water of Life'.[2] We would call it a 'paradise' but this word comes from Persian and had a different meaning (see p. 57). The Persian (Zoroastrian) idea was that heaven is a state of mind reached by the virtuous after death, as a reward for having defended order, been kind to animals, led the good life and crossed the bridge (Chinavat). The Biblical conception was that Adam and Eve had been born in paradise but were cast out because they had sinned. Muslims believe that God promises an afterlife in paradise as a reward for keeping the faith. The Quran states:

> *To the faithful, both men and women, God promiseth gardens beneath which the rivers flow, in which they shall abide, and goodly mansions in the gardens of Eden. But best of all will be God's good pleasure in them. This will be the great bliss.*[3]

This passage may have misled garden historians, who are over-enthusiastic in interpreting Islamic gardens as four-square symbols of paradise. The *Oxford Companion to Gardens* has the following entry:

> *Chahar bagh, literally 'fourfold garden' (chahar, 'four'; bagh, 'garden'). The earliest Persian gardens, dating back to 2000 BC, were square enclosures divided into four equal parts by intersecting water channels. Throughout the centuries this pattern has been the basis for all gardens designed in the Persian tradition, wherever they may be.*[4]

This is a view I have held for many years and its simplicity remains tempting. Khansari and Minouch, in a book entitled *The Persian Garden: Echoes of Paradise,* note that the four-square pattern can be found on ceramic tiles dating from *c.*700 BCE.[5] But the evidence for gardens having been made on this pattern comes from another place and

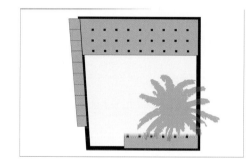

3.2 Muhammad's House, which became the first mosque, was a partly-roofed courtyard. It is not known whether it contained plants. As the plan suggests, it might have had a date palm.

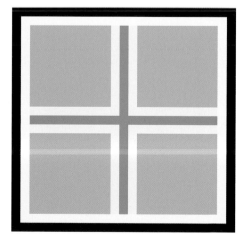

3.3 The 'classical' quadripartite garden plan, symbolizing the Four Rivers of Paradise, is a theoretical garden type which may not have existed in ancient times.

3.4 The term *chahar bagh* is applied to several different types of garden: **b** the Achaemenid palace garden; **c** the Persian orchard garden; **d** the Mughal tomb garden; **e** the Mughal canals garden; **f** the Islamic courtyard garden. From these known types it is possible to make a tentative hypothesis concerning the layout of the vanished gardens of Mesopotamia: **a**.

Typically, these garden types used water brought by irrigation canals to make gardens in oases.

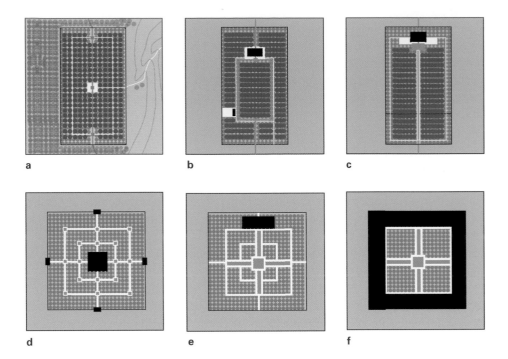

another time: the mausoleum gardens made in India after the Mughal conquest of 1526 are square enclosures and are properly interpreted as representations of paradise. There is a marked lack of evidence for either the four-square pattern or the paradise symbolism having been used before the sixteenth century. Spain is a possible location but after a careful study, Ruggles states: 'I have found no explicit conceptual link between the gardens of the *munyas* [suburban estates] of Cordoba and the Quranic concept of paradise as a garden of shade-giving trees and flowing rivers.'[6] Gardens do, however, have more significance in Islamic culture than in Christian culture, which associated tree worship with pagan idols and gardens with Roman orgies.

The origin of the four-square canals idea was discussed in the previous chapter (p. 53) and the earliest known use of the term *chahar bagh* is from tenth-century Uzbekistan. The term travelled to India with the Mughals in the sixteenth century but 'After Babur, the Mughals did not employ the term *chahar bagh* very much.'[7] Its use revived when Babur's memoirs were translated into English and read by garden historians, including Constance Villiers-Stuart. The term was then applied retrospectively, by David Stronach, to the layout of Pasargadae. These uses are related and may derive from the lost gardens of Mesopotamia but this should not blind us to the differing layouts, functions and design intentions of the gardens in which rectilinear canals have been used.

The account of Islamic gardens in this chapter is partly geographical and partly dynastic. It does not attempt to distinguish between the gardens made by different Islamic sects (Sunni, Shia, Sufi, etc.) and I do not know if this should be done. The evolution of Islamic garden types from a hypothetical Mesopotamian prototype and its Persian cousin are shown in Figure 3.4.

Arabian gardens

The Arabs of old lived in the Arabian Peninsula and surrounding territories. Today there are many Arabized peoples who speak Arabic but whose ethnicity is Mesopotamian, Levantine, Egyptian or North African.

3.4 g A desert encampment in an oasis.

Pre-Islamic Arabian gardens

According to the Quran and the Bible, Arabs and Jews descend from Noah's son, Shem, from whom the word 'Semitic' derives. Arabic belongs to the Afro-Asian family of languages and was spoken in the countries which are now Saudi Arabia, the Gulf States and Jordan. Using the word 'Saracen' in the Greek sense of 'easterner', a Byzantine scholar born in Palestine wrote: 'This coast immediately beyond the boundaries of Palestine is held by Saracens, who have been settled from of old in the Palm Groves.'[8] His observation provides documentary evidence for the intuitively obvious point that tree orchards, also called tree gardens, provide the best living conditions in hot arid climates. A Roman author (c.380) attests to the Arabs having had a predominantly nomadic lifestyle:

> All the men are warriors of equal rank; half naked, clad in colored cloaks down to the
> waist, overrunning different countries, with the aid of swift and active horses and speedy
> camels, alike in times of peace and war. Nor does any member of their tribe ever take
> plow in hand or cultivate a tree, or seek food by the tillage of the land; but they are
> perpetually wandering over various and extensive districts, having no home, no fixed
> abode or laws; nor can they endure to remain long in the same climate, no one district or
> country pleasing them for a continuance.[9]

The oldest-known written work in Arabic (sixth century CE) is called a 'Hanging Poem' (*Mu'allaqat*) because it was hung on the Kaaba in Mecca. It gives a poetic glimpse of Ancient Arabia:

> Stop, oh my friends, let us pause to weep over the remembrance of my beloved.
> Here was her abode on the edge of the sandy desert between Dakhool and
> Howmal. The traces of her encampment are not wholly obliterated even now.
> For when the South wind blows the sand over them, the North wind sweeps it
> away. The courtyards and enclosures of the old home have become desolate;
> the dung of the wild deer lies there thick as the seeds of pepper. On the morning
> of our separation it was as if I stood in the gardens of our tribe. Amid the

3.5 The Arabs had a nomadic lifestyle but also had mud-walled enclosures in palm groves (Najran Province, Saudi Arabia).

3.6 The Kaaba in the courtyard of the al-Haram Mosque. The desert hills can be seen outside the city of Mecca (1910).

acacia-shrubs where my eyes were blinded with tears by the smart from the bursting pods of colocynth.[10]

The 'gardens' were probably groves of date palms and the 'courtyards' are most likely to have been outdoor yards enclosed by mud brick walls. Walls provide shelter for plants and people. Ptolemy mentions palaces in coastal areas and ancient Arabia had temples resembling those in Mesopotamia.[11] The most famous survival is the Kaaba (or Ka'ba), now the centrepiece of the Sacred Mosque (Al-Masjid al-Ḥarām) in Mecca.

Precursors of Islamic gardens

The Fertile Crescent was under the influence of the Roman and Persian (Sassanid) empires in the seventh century. Islam was tolerant of Zoroastrianism and sympathetic to Jews and Christians, seeing them as 'people of the book' who followed the 'religion of Abraham'. Zoroastrian fire temples, Jewish synagogues and Christian churches were not destroyed, as Timurid and Afghan conquerors boastfully destroyed the 'idolatrous' temples of India at a later date. In the seventh century, Jews, Christians and Muslims shared a deep hostility to the polytheism of the ancient Akkadians, Assyrians, Arabs, Hebrews and others.

The Arabs who took control of the Fertile Crescent were in many ways receptive to the old civilizations of the region: Egyptian, Persian, Byzantine and Mesopotamian. Though innovative in many ways, the art and architecture of Islam were born of the older civilizations. This can be seen in the first great Islamic building, the Dome of the Rock on the Temple Mount in Jerusalem:

3.7 The Dome of the Rock, set in the ancient Jerusalem landscape, illustrates the relationship between Byzantine and early Islamic architecture.

Islamicists consider both the Iranian and the Byzantine impact to be essential to the unfolding of early Islamic architecture in general and the Dome of the Rock in particular. As Grabar has pointed out in perceiving a link between the Dome of the Rock and the Ka'ba, the all but forgotten Arab heritage may be more critical to this early phase of Islamic architecture than has heretofore been suggested or accepted.[12]

Conversion to Islam was not encouraged in the years immediately after the prophet's death but this policy changed as Islam began to spread rapidly, with help from the sword, into Mesopotamia, Persia, Afghanistan, Egypt, North Africa, Spain and Portugal. The Umayyads led the advance but were overthrown by the Abassids in 750. Both were Sunni. The south of Spain remained in Umayyad control until 1031. It was then ruled by a succession of Islamic Berber dynasties (Almoravid, Almohad, Marinid and the Emirs of Granada) until the Christian re-conquest of 1492.

There are few garden survivals from the six centuries between the founding of Islam (622) and the defeat of the Abassid Caliphate by the Mamelukes (1258). This makes it difficult to write about the characteristics of early Islamic gardens – and doubly difficult

3.8 No ancient gardens survive in Mesopotamia but an aerial view of the Tigris Valley near Nineveh shows the environment in which they were made. One can imagine orchard gardens with canal irrigation.

to write about the origin of the *chahar bagh* and other features. Yet an indisputably Islamic style of garden design developed and it is necessary to consider its origins. The pattern of cultural influence outlined above suggests the possible antecedents listed below.

Mesopotamian palace towns
Nineveh, like other Mesopotamian towns, had a palace within its walls and a royal garden with water channels outside its walls (see p. 38).

Persian palace gardens
The best evidence for the layout of ancient gardens comes from Pasargadae (see p. 53). It can be described as a *chahar bagh* design but it is *neither* symmetrical *nor* quadripartite (see p. 61). The Sassanians also made palace gardens. Little is known about their design but they are believed to have been an influence on Islamic gardens (see p. 73).

Byzantine palace gardens
The palace gardens of Byzantium were destroyed after the Ottoman conquest. The Great Palace, already in decay, became the site of the Sultan Ahmet Mosque and other buildings. The section of the palace which has been excavated suggests its character was that of a classic Roman garden. A fragment of the Blachernae Palace also survives but not its garden.

Christian cloisters
A cloister court, surrounded by an arcade is the only type of Christian outdoor space which survives from late antiquity. It derives from the classical peristyle courts made throughout the Greek and Roman worlds. Monastic cloisters were unplanted, except

3.9 a, b A courtyard from the Emperor's Palace in Constantinople has been excavated and is now the Great Palace Mosaic Museum. Right, a reconstruction of the Great Palace based on Albert Vogt.

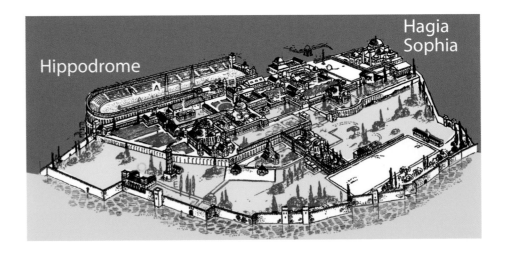

3.10 The Emperor's Palace in Constantinople extended from the sea to the site of Sultan Ahmet Mosque, marked by the four minarets on the left. Hagia Sophia, on the right, has the two minarets added by the Ottomans.

with grass, but there is some evidence that early Christian courtyards contained shrubs and herbs. The best information is from the St Gall plan, drawn after the designer had visited a number of monasteries in Constantinople. It shows a cross of paths with juniper plants near the crossing point. The pattern is quadripartite, like later Islamic gardens, but there is no evidence for the pattern being formed with canals.

This imperfect information will be used to try and explain the character of the early Islamic courtyards and palace gardens.

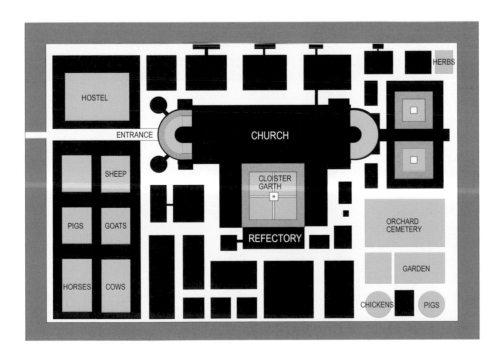

3.11 The St Gall plan (*c.*820 CE) is the best evidence of how medieval Christian cloister gardens were designed in the Early Middle Ages.

3.12 Gathering to pray was the primary role of a mosque court (*sahn*). The maidan, beyond, was a multi-purpose space for markets, games and other gatherings (see the Masjed-e-Shah in Isfahan, Figure 8.28b).

Islamic courtyards

The first outdoor spaces made under the influence of Islam were mosques. In early mosques, the *sahn* was a place of congregation where the faithful gathered to pray under an open sky, equal before God. The same word (*sahn*) is used for a yard in a private house. The Grand Mosque of Damascus (the Umayyad Mosque) was, in succession, an Akkadian temple, a Roman temple and a Christian church before it was rebuilt as a mosque. Some of the building materials were re-used and 200 workmen were sent from Byzantium to help with the work. The ornamentation looks Byzantine and the courtyard is enclosed by a covered walk, like a peristyle garden or cloister court. Mosque courts had a different role to Christian cloister courts. They were places for the faithful to gather and pray. Few mosque courts are planted, but it became common for holy shrines and madrasah courts to be treated as gardens. A madrasah is a theological college, often with courts surrounded by student bedrooms. Use of

a

b

c

d

e

f

g

these courts was both scholarly and domestic, giving them a functional relationship with monastic cloisters. *Caravanserai* courts were planned in a similar way but can have had few plants when used as places of protection for men and animals.

Islamic palace gardens

The pre-Islamic Arabs were nomads and herdsmen who met in sanctuary towns to engage in trade and worship in temples. Cities like Mecca were occupied by merchants and holy men. When Islam expanded into the Fertile Crescent, which already had a palace-building tradition, it did not take long for the Commanders of the Faithful (*Amir al-Mu'minin*) to appreciate the delights of palace gardens. A few remnants of early Islamic gardens survive: in Palestine, Iraq and Southern Spain. They were made by separate dynasties (Umayyad, Abassid, Almoravid) but within a single cultural tradition. Taken together, they cast some light on the origins of what, between the seventh and seventeenth centuries, became a unique and distinctive approach to the design of gardens.

The best early example of an Umayyad palace garden is Khirbat al-Mafjar, 5 km from Jericho in the Jordan valley. Designed between 724 and 743 as a hunting lodge, for either Hisham or Walid II, the palace had a paved court, a fountain court and a

h

3.13 a–h Mosque courts are generally open and unplanted, because they are places to pray. The entrance to a mosque court is a place to receive alms. The pools (*hauz*) are for ritual ablution (*wudu*). The courtyards of madrasahs, holy shrines and *caravanserais* were more likely to contain plants: **a** mosque, Damascus **b** madrasah, Shiraz **c** holy shrine, Shiraz **d** mosque, Yazd **e**, **f** and **g** mosques in Srinagar **h** *caravanserai*, Shiraz.

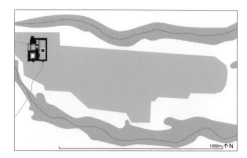

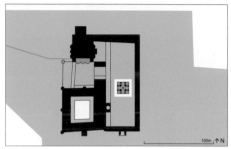

3.14 a, b The Khirbat al-Mafjar, also known as Hisham's Palace, is an early example of a Muslim palace. It is north of Jericho and was set in a hunting park.

3.15 Mosaic of a hunting scene in the audience room of the bath house at Khirbat al-Mafjar.

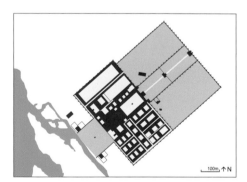

3.16 The Balkuwara Palace is in the desert south of Samara, beside the River Tigris. The layout of the courtyards is not known. They are likely to have been planted with date palms.

3.17 The Abu Dulaf Mosque, 35 km north of the Balkuwara Palace, was built in the same period and survives in better condition. Mosque courts are unlikely to have been planted.

60-hectare *hayr* (walled enclosure) containing, like a Persian *paradiso*, plants and animals. The fountain court may have been a garden but the details of its layout have not survived.

The best example of an Abbasid palace garden is near Samara, 125 km north of Baghdad. The Balkuwara Palace was designed in 833 as a new capital for the Abbasid Caliphate, in succession to Baghdad. The move from Damascus brought Islam under the influence of Persia. While the culture remained cosmopolitan, Persian court customs were adopted and Persian designers were employed. Baghdad had been planned on a circular plan, like Firuzabad. Ettinghausen and Grabar describe the Balkuwara as 'a palace the size of a city' and state that 'the ancient Near Eastern tradition of the royal "paradise" was adopted by the Abbasids and sung by their poets'.[13] The palace had a series of courts on an axis with elaborate doorways leading from one court to another. The plan is often drawn with paths connecting the doors to form a cross but their existence has not been confirmed by excavation.[14]

The best example of an Umayyad palace and garden is Madinat al-Zahra, 6 km west of Cordoba in Southern Spain. The complex was built between 936 and 976 as a new town with a palace at its heart. Analysis of the layout suggests the design was modelled on Samara – because Abbasid culture was then the 'standard against which all Islamic kingdoms measured themselves'.[15] Ruggles quotes an account of the Byzantine ambassador's visit to Baghdad:

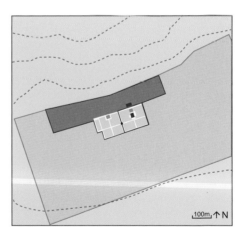

3.18 Madinat al-Zahra, below the hills outside Cordoba, was modelled on the plan of Samara.

3.19 Madinat al-Zahra had an axial layout and walkways with water channels.

3.20 a, b, c Girault de Prangey's paintings of
the Alhambra (1842) show its earlier character,
but not its original character. Granada has the
classic Islamic plan of a fortress on the edge of
a walled town.

3.21 Sikandra: 'These are the gardens of Eden:
enter them to dwell therein eternally' (see p.88).

They were taken to the Court of the Horses and passed by the Park of Wild Beasts. They proceeded next to the New Palace, which was an enclosure between gardens with a central pool surrounded by four hundred palm trees dressed from top to bottom in painted cloths hung with golden rings. Then they went to the Tree Court, a palace called Paradise, and on and on until they were finally brought before al-Muqtadir.[16]

Al-Muqtadir was the Caliph of Baghdad (908–932). The earliest use of the term *chahar bagh* is from about this time but comes in a history of Bukhara written in 944. Pinder-Wilson suggests that it may derive from the Soghdian *s'r'b'gh*, meaning 'tower', rather than from *chahar*, meaning 'four'.[17]

The best example of an Almoravid palace garden is in Granada. From without, the Alhambra looks like what it is: a fortress. Though built in stone, the overall visual impression relates to the Mesopotamian forts from which, directly or indirectly, the design idea derives. The Alhambra has internal courts, like a Mesopotamian or Roman palace, and an abundant supply of flowing water from the surrounding hills. This made it possible for gardens to be made within the palace, instead of on farmland below its walls. In this respect, it is more like a Persian garden than a Mesopotamian garden. In plan, the Alhambra has similarities with a Roman estate.

Table 3.1   Antecedents and examples of Islamic garden plans

Pre-Islamic gardens	
Pasargadae	Khorsabad
Constantinople	St Gall
Early-Islamic gardens	
Khirbat al-Mafjar	Balkuwara
Madinat al-Zahra	Alhambra

Comparing the four antecedents with the four early examples of Islamic gardens (Table 3.1) leads to the following conclusions, which require further research:

1   The use of water channels as garden features probably originated in Mesopotamia, which relied on irrigation canals. The few examples of canals in Roman gardens (e.g. House of Loreius Tiburtinus, in Pompeii) could have been made by people who had seen Eastern gardens in the course of military expeditions.

2   Peristyle and cloister courts are a possible inspiration for the use of crossing paths in early Islamic gardens.

3   The oldest known examples of Islamic water gardens are in Spain: at Madinat al-Zahra and Granada. The canals at the Alhambra are in a courtyard (the

3.22 Sikandra: Garden historians tend to think that because later Islamic gardens have regular patterns with pools and crossing canals, this must also have been the case with early Islamic gardens.

Court of Lions) but it is rectangular, not square. Since its function was not religious, it is unlikely to have been considered a symbol of paradise and there is no reason to think it influenced later gardens in Persia or India.

4 The plans of Samara and Madinat al-Zahra have central axes, untypical of Roman and Byzantine gardens. This may be a consequence of locating royal palaces inside grid-planned towns. The Romans used grids for provincial and military towns but did not incorporate palaces with their layouts.

5 The heart of a fortified town was the traditional location for a Mesopotamian palace and this is the most probable inspiration for this locational principle at Samara and Madinat al-Zahra.

The caliphs of Islam maintained a strict separation between secular and sacred buildings. Paradise was a place in which one hoped to live after death, not a place to create on earth. The Hadith discourage ostentatious tombs though the prophet said: 'The space that lies between my grave and my minbar belongs to the gardens of paradise.'[18] When Mughal gardens came to be associated with paradise, in the sixteenth century, they were mausoleum gardens, built for deceased emperors assumed to reside in paradise. The Quranic inscription outside Akbar's tomb at Sikandra reads: 'These are the gardens of Eden: enter them to dwell therein eternally.'[19] The construction of a 'paradise' garden for an emperor to enjoy during his lifetime might have been considered presumptuous. The Arabic word for Eden is *Adn*, meaning the everlasting abode of the faithful and *jannat* means gardens. *Jannat Adn* is used in the Quran[20] as the abode of the righteous, not the dwelling place of Adam and Eve.

Timurid gardens

Persia fell to the Seljuk Turks, in 1037, and was invaded by Genghis Khan's Golden Horde in 1219. The Horde followed their leader and acted on his belief that 'The greatest joy is to conquer one's enemies, to pursue them, to seize their property, to see their families in tears, to ride their horses, and to possess their daughters and wives.'[21] When Timur Tamerlane brought a second Mongol army to Persia in 1370, he massacred most of the people but took the designers and craftsmen to his homeland, which is now Uzbekistan. The early Islamic gardens of Persia, which have not survived, are believed to have been enclosed by walls of mud and straw (*pisé*) and were located in towns built of the same material, all of which required regular maintenance.

The Mongol invaders of Persia adopted Islamic culture as wholeheartedly as the Mongol invaders of East Asia adopted Chinese culture (see p. 218). The world's largest empire split apart, with one of Genghis Khan's grandsons (Kublai Khan) ruling China and another grandson (Hulagu Khan) ruling Persia. The western Mongols converted to Islam and Persian became the language of government, with a Turkic

3.23 a, b The gateway to Timur's Palace in Kesh (Shahr-e Sabz) survives with a modern statue of the great Emir placed in the triumphal European style.

language remaining in use by the army. Timur Tamerlane (1336–1405) claimed descent from Genghis Khan and established a Central Asian empire stretching from the Turkish border to the Chinese border. Timur became an enthusiastic builder of palaces, mosques and gardens in a style, influenced by Persia, which is described as Timurid because the alternative names (Sogdian, Transoxanian, Bactrian, etc.) relate to earlier cultures and the modern name (Uzbekistan) relates to a later culture.

Palace gardens

A fragment of the garden palace Timur built in his home town survives. Known to Timur as Kesh, the town is now called Shahr-e Sabz ('the green city') and is 80 km south of Samarkand. It can be entered by what must have been, and may remain, the largest garden-palace entrance in the world. An internal stair leads to a top platform. It has a north view to a reconstructed town wall and a south view to an incongruous Soviet-era park (see p. 301). The Spanish ambassador, Ruy González de Clavijo, who visited in 1404, described the palace garden:

> These palaces had a long entrance, and a very high gateway. On each side there were arches of brick, covered with glazed tiles, and many patterns in various colours. These arches formed small recesses, without doors, and the ground was paved with glazed tiles. They are made for the attendants to sit in, when the lord is here. In front of the first entrance there was another gateway, leading to a great courtyard paved with white stones, and surrounded by doorways of very rich workmanship. In the centre of the court there was a great pool of water, and this court was three hundred paces wide ... Afterwards the ambassadors went to see a chamber, which the lord had set apart for feasting, and for the company of his women, in front of it there was a great garden, in

3.24 a, b A fragment of a tiled pool in Timur's palace garden. It is now dry but the tiled pool in Ben Youssef Madrasah (in Marrakech, Morocco) helps one visualize its former character.

3.25 Carpets were spread on pavements and gardens were used for feasts.

which there were many shady trees, and all kinds of fruit trees, with channels of water flowing amongst them. The garden was so large, that great numbers of people might enjoy themselves there in summer with great delight, near the fountains, and under the shade of the trees. The workmanship of this palace was so rich that it would be impossible to describe it, without gazing and walking over everything, with slow steps.

3.26 The Samarkand oasis, viewed from the citadel of Afrasiyab.

3.27 a, b Use of the Uleg Beg Madrassah as a tourist market hints at the animated character of Samarkand's lost garden palaces. Like Persian garden pavilions, they are likely to have had wooden columns supporting high roofs.

3.28 A painted wood column on a mosque in Samarkand.

3.29 Flood irrigation, with distributor channels, is still used in Khiva.

3.30 Plan of Timurid Samarkand, with the garden locations based on Lisa Golombek and Donald Wilber, *The Timurid Architecture of Iran and Turan.* Princeton, NJ: Princeton University Press, 1988.

Clavijo's memoirs are the best account of the Persian garden style at an important stage in its development. Nothing was being built on such a grand scale in early Renaissance Europe. After resting in Kesh, Clavijo journeyed over the mountain pass to Timur's capital, Samarkand. It is an oasis town, nestling in a ring of hills on the Silk Routes between East and West Asia (see p. 22). These routes were also used by the Golden Horde. For most of the year the Horde rode hard, tended their herds, fought from the saddle and slept rough. Occasionally, they gathered in Samarkand for rest and refreshment. Timur would then provide lavish entertainment in and around his palace gardens. Golombek believes he made a new garden each time he took a new wife.[22] Clavijo describes the scene at his Dilicaya garden:

This house and garden is very beautiful; and on this occasion the lord was very jovial, and he drank wine as well as those who were with him; and the food consisted of horses and sheep, according to their custom. When they had eaten, the lord ordered robes to be given to the ambassadors, and they returned to their lodgings, which were very near at hand. At these feasts such a multitude of people were assembled, that, when they came near to the lord, they could not get on, except by the help of the guards appointed to make way for the ambassadors; and the dust was such that people's faces and clothes were all one colour.

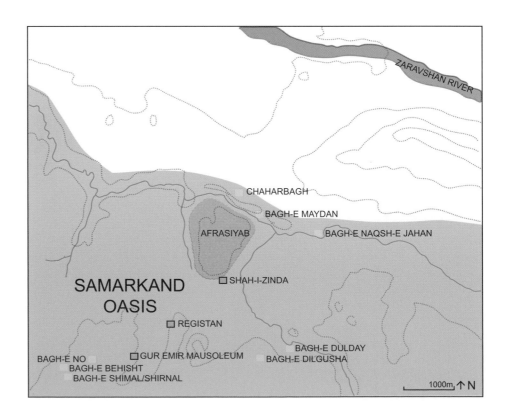

ZARAVSHAN RIVER

CHAHARBAGH

BAGH-E MAYDAN

AFRASIYAB

BAGH-E NAQSH-E JAHAN

SHAH-I-ZINDA

SAMARKAND OASIS

REGISTAN

BAGH-E NO

BAGH-E BEHISHT

BAGH-E SHIMAL/SHIRNAL

GUR EMIR MAUSOLEUM

BAGH-E DULDAY

BAGH-E DILGUSHA

1000m, ↑ N

In front of these gardens there was a vast plain, through which a river flowed, and many smaller streams. On this plain the lord ordered many tents to be pitched for himself and his women; and that all his host, which was scattered in detachments over the land, should be assembled together, each man in his place, and that their tents should be pitched, and that they should come there, with their women, to be present at the festivals and marriages which he wished to celebrate. When the tents of the lord were pitched, each man knew where his own tent should be pitched, and every one, high and low, knew his place, so that the work was done without confusion or noise. After three or four days, twenty thousand men were assembled round the tents of the lord, and a day did not pass without many arriving from all parts.

Encampments and feasting were important garden uses, which may have carried on in Persia since Achaemenid times (see p. 54). They certainly continued when the Persian style of garden making was carried to Uzbekistan and then India (see p. 85).

3.31 The Madrasah Chahar Bagh (or Madar-e Shah) in Isfahan is on the site of an older Persian garden.

Timurid planting
Uzbekistan remains an irrigation-rich country, drawing much of the water used in its farms and gardens from two great rivers, the Amu Darya (Oxus) and the Syr Darya (Jaxartes). The traditional way of distributing this water was with a network of irrigation canals and small channels. Gardens were and are divided into compartments and flooded by turns. Though extravagant in its use of water, this method helps wash salts downward and is well suited to the cultivation of fruit trees and garden plants. Flood irrigation was a dominant factor in the design of Islamic gardens and Timurid gardens are likely to have had walks beside water channels. Flood irrigation makes raised walks a necessity for people wearing fine clothes.

Persian gardens

Persia took the lead in developing Islamic art, architecture and, no doubt, gardens. The qualification is necessary because no gardens survive from the period between 500 BCE (see p. 58) and 1500 CE. This is a tragedy, blamed on the Mongol calamity and other invasions. The next glimpse of Persian gardens inside Persia dates from the Safavid dynasty (1502–1722). The Safavids were of Turkic origin and had an empire which reached into Azerbaijan, Iraq and Afghanistan. Shah Abbas made Isfahan his capital. Many of the city's great buildings can be seen but only remnants of the gardens for which the city was famous survive. There are, however, some European accounts and drawings which yield a good picture of their character.

Sir John Chardin had time to study a Persian garden when waiting three hours for an audience with the Grand Vizir and the Nazir in 1671:

3.32 a, b Bagh Doulatabad in Yazd retains the character of a walled *bustan* (orchard garden).

a

c

d

3.33 Isfahan: **a** a garden pavilion overlooking the Zayandeh River; **b** pavilions overlooking the *chahar bagh*;[24] **c** the Hizar Jarib, drawn by Kaempfer; **d** the site of the Hizar Jarib in a recent photograph.

b

There can be nothing more magnificent than the apartment where he [the Nazir] treated the king. It gives upon a garden that is not very large, but very fine; in the middle thereof is a great basin of water, lined with white transparent marble, the borders whereof are bored for spouts, four fingers distant from the other. Round the basin were spread tapestries of silk and gold, on which were placed cushions of very rich embroidery to sit upon ... On the four sides of the basin, were four perfuming pots of an extraordinary bigness, finely embellished with vermillion gilt, between eight little boxes of ivory, adorned with gold enamelled and full of sweets and perfumes ... At night there were fireworks played off in the middle of the garden. Nobody ever entertains the King of Persia, without giving him the diversion of an artificial firework. The king passed the whole night at the feast in drinking, drawing the bow and in other exertions ... He was carried away about the break of day, not being able to walk or ride.[23]

Engelbert Kaempfer, a German doctor and traveller, visited Isfahan in 1684 and made drawings of its gardens. In essence, they are orchard gardens (*bustans*) enclosed by mud walls and containing water channels, pools, cascades and pavilions. The layouts are rectilinear, with crossing paths, but there is no sign of the Mughal-type perfect squares discussed below. They are *chahar bagh* designs in David Stronach's sense but not in the Mughal sense.

Another European traveller, Cornelis de Bruyn, visited Isfahan's gardens in 1705. He had difficulty gaining access to the shah's gardens but described and drew the Dutch East India Company's garden:

It is surrounded by a high wall of earth, the gate of which is large and lofty ... in the midst of the court of which is a canal which runs on the side of the place, where they receive strangers; behind which is a fine apartment, spread with carpets and full of cushions to sit and rest upon, after the manner of the country ... and a fine fountain with

3.34 a, b, c Most of the extant gardens in Isfahan are comparatively recent but have recognizable similarities with the seventeenth-century illustrations. The flower planting is twentieth century.

3.35 a, b Bagh-e Fin is the best example of what is believed to be a traditional Persian garden. A comparison of the photographs in 2004 and 1919 shows details of the most recent 'restoration'. The paths have been paved, a wall has been removed and the intriguing garden painting in the arch has not been restored.

> *jets of water which, from thence, flows into a canal, and serves to water the garden ... and fruit trees, flowers and plants, as appears by number 108.*[25]

Engraving 108 shows the planting and the curtained pavilion. The pavilion has a tent-like character, supporting O'Kane's argument that 'The rhythms of pastoral nomadism dominated court life in Iran until the twentieth century' with the 'multitude and variety of tents' representing 'the ideal compromise between nomadic and urban life'.[26] Cornelis de Bruyn also drew a pavilion overlooking the Zayandeh river in Isfahan.

3.36 The Bagh-e Babur in Kabul was laid out by the first Mughal Emperor and extensively changed by Shah Jahan a century later. It is closer to the style of traditional Persian gardens than the Mughal gardens of India.

3.37 *Qanats* bring water from distant mountains to fertile oases – and gardens. The four shaft entrances in the photograph give access to an underground tunnel.

3.38 a, b Water is brought by *qanats* from the hills to the Kerman oasis.

Mughal gardens

High Mughal

'Mughal' was the name used by the Timurids and by their descendants, who invaded North India. The 'Great Mughals' are the six emperors who ruled India from 1526 to 1707. They were great builders and garden enthusiasts. Their ascendency came after the Delhi Sultanate, an earlier period of Islamic rule by Afghans. 'Mughal' is an alternative spelling of 'Mongol' and India's first Mughal emperor, Babur, was a descendant of Timur Tamerlane. Babur became a commander at the age of 14, held Samarkand for a short time and then took Afghanistan. In 1526, he defeated the Sultanate army with the first significant use of gunpowder in India. Babur was a well-informed and perceptive man, interested in genealogy, natural history, architecture,

garden design and warfare. His memoirs record the making of an early *chahar bagh* in Kabul and his disappointment that the hot plains of North India lacked the fast and fresh streams necessary for such a garden.

Babur solved the problem of how to make a *chahar bagh* on the plains of India by selecting riverside sites and using ox-powered wells to raise water. It was then distributed in narrow stone-lined channels. This required precise control of levels and falls. Channels were lined because the soil was porous and only limited volumes could be raised by teams of oxen. In Persia, where flowing water was more plentiful, it was distributed in channels by opening and shutting dams. A *qanat* is an underground tunnel bringing water from the mountains, with access from vertical shafts. In India, water was raised from nearby rivers and distributed in gardens by channels set into raised walks. The water was used to flood rectangular planting areas between the

3.39 a, b A well (left) was used to bring water from the Yamuna (right) to the Ram Bagh (Figure 3.40).

3.40 Water channels in the Ram Bagh were used for both ornament and irrigation.

3.41 a, b Carpets were laid on raised walks (painting from Bundi, right, and photograph of a carpet sale in Bukhara, above).

3.42 a, b Stone hoops were used as fixings for canopies (painting from Bundi, right, and channel at the Ram Bagh, above).

walks. Awnings were placed over walkways and carpets were laid on stone platforms, creating delightful sitting areas. One could catch the breeze, sip iced sherbet, watch peacocks and view a living carpet of sweet-scented flowering plants. Their roots were in cool wet soil, deep below the walkway level. The height of garden walks varies and

3.43 a, b Peacocks brought colour and movement to Indian gardens (Tomb of Safdar Jang, left).

is likely to have been decided with regard to the need for a fall and the height of the intended planting. Both flowering and fruiting plants were used.

Babur's garden in Agra is thought to have been on the site of what is now the Ram Bagh. The original layout is unknown but the garden still has an ox-powered well and this must always have been how water was supplied. The present garden has angled and cusped stone cascades which would produce sheets of frothy water if they were working. This feature is known as a *chadar* in Mughal gardens and a *shadirvan* in Persian gardens.[27] The word *chadar* (or *chador*), in Persian, means a sheet of material used as a robe or a tent. It is not used in connection with gardens in either Persian or Hindi.

Another of Babur's gardens, on the Chambal River near Dholpur, was discovered by Elizabeth Moynihan in 1978. Excavation revealed a central terrace, water channels and pools. It was used by Babur as an encampment garden, like Timur's Samarkand gardens, with pools and water features cut into the bedrock. Moynihan wrote:

> *The central terrace dominates the plan with the climax of the design – the progression of lotus pools which gave the garden its name. Carved into the rock, they develop a single floral theme, the 'Life of the Lotus.' The size and treatment of each pool reinforce this theme.*[28]

Babur wrote in his memoirs:

> *Master Shah-Muhammad the stonemason was ordered to design a scalloped octagonal pool on top of the solid rock that had been shaped into a courtyard. The stonecutters got*

3.44 Isa Khan's tomb (1547) is an octagonal building in an octagonal compound, illustrating the manner in which architectural geometry was related to garden geometry.

3.45 Given its position on a mound in the Old Fort (Purana Quila) the Sher Mandal (*c.*1541) is more likely to have been surrounded by beds of flowers than by a *chahar bagh*. The surrounding landform reflects the octagonal footprint of the building.

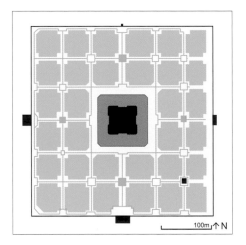

3.46 The plan of Humayun's tomb in Delhi.

to work in earnest. To the north of the spot where the pool of solid rock had been placed were many trees, mangoes, eugenias, and all sorts of trees. In the middle, I had a ten-by-ten well made, and it was nearly finished. The water from the well went into the pool.[29]

Babur's son, Humayun, lived in Delhi's Purana Quila (Old Fort) and is thought to have used the Sher Mandal as a library. It is a pavilion on a hill and as such is unlikely to have had a *chahar bagh*. Humayun was the first Mughal emperor to be buried in a tomb garden, commissioned by his wife. It is a brilliant design which appears to have had a wide influence, both on subsequent designers and on garden historians. Let us take the latter group first. Seeing it as a 'classic', historians have used it to explain the *prior* history of Islamic gardens. Among other points, it is used to argue that: (1) the word *chahar bagh* means a symmetrical quadripartite design; (2) all Islamic gardens symbolize paradise; and (3) the 'classic' Islamic arrangement is to build a pavilion at the crossing point of four canals. For the reasons given in the first half of this chapter, one must doubt whether any of these points has merit. In plan terms, it seems more likely that the layout of tomb gardens resulted from projecting the geometry of the tomb outward, than from drawing the geometry of the garden inward. There are many precedents for symmetrical tombs and the tomb of Sultan Sanjar in Merv had crossing paths.[30] The mausoleum of Ismael Samani in Bukhara is one of the earliest and the mausoleum of Ghiyasuddin Tughlaq is the nearest to Humayun's tomb. An interesting aspect of the water channels in Humayun's tomb garden is that some are at ground level and others are on raised walks. This suggests that flow control was a major consideration in planning Mughal water channels.

3.47 a, b, c Humayun's tomb garden is the oldest symmetrical Mughal garden layout of the type now described as a *chahar bagh*. As with earlier tomb gardens, it seems likely that the symmetry of the garden was a consequence of projecting the geometry of the architecture outwards. The garden has been restored and the *chadars* work.

3.48 The mausoleum of Ismael Samani in Bukhara is an early example of a symmetrical Islamic tomb, seen here with a *hauz* (pool).

3.49 a, b The domestic gardens inside Fatehpur Sikri are not square. They have a long axis.

3.50 Akbar's tomb garden at Sikandra.

3.51 View of the Taj Mahal from Agra Fort.

Akbar, Humayun's son, built a new capital at Fatehpur Sikri, 40 km from Agra. It has two small gardens which have been described as 'the first preserved Mughal palace gardens'.[31] Both are rectangular and both have crossing paths. Neither is square. They were gardens for the living, not for the dead, and they do not look like symbols of paradise. After Akbar's early death, at 56, his wife commissioned a mausoleum in the style of Humayun's tomb garden. The result, at Sikandra outside Agra, has a famous quotation from the Quran over the entrance gate, popular among design historians for its use in arguing that *the* Islamic garden was inspired by a concept of paradise (see p. 72). Akbar's son, Jahangir, left a memoir with many comments about the delicious fruits which grew in his gardens. He was buried in another tomb garden, in Lahore. His son Khurram, whose name means 'Joyful', became Shah Jahan.

Shah Jahan, his father (Shah Jahangir) and their wives made the greatest Mughal gardens. Their work includes the palace gardens in Delhi and Agra, the pleasure gardens in Kashmir and the Taj Mahal tomb garden in Agra. The Red Fort Palace in Delhi has rooms and courtyards connected, like beads on a string, by a water channel on a high terrace running parallel to the River Yamuna. The Kashmir gardens have the site characteristics Babur enjoyed: below mountains and with rushing water. Both gardens are rectangular, terraced and axial. Torrents of fresh water cascade through the gardens, around platforms and through pavilions. They are not calm symmetrical squares. In plan terms, they are more like the old gardens of Isfahan than the Mughal tomb gardens of India.

3.52 a, b The Grape Garden and a screen (*jali*) in Agra Fort.

3.53 a, b The Red Fort in Delhi has a series of pavilions connected by a water channel. One looks forward to the water being restored.

3.54 a, b Nishat Bagh in Kashmir is designed around a canalized stream.

3.55 a, b Shalimar Bagh and Nishat Bagh, on the shore of Lake Dal in Kashmir, were pleasure gardens, neither fortified nor residential. Visitors arrived by boat from the fortress of Hari Parbat on the opposite shore of Lake Dal.

The difference between Mughal residential and tomb gardens is significant. Mumtaz Mahal was buried in the Taj Mahal with Shah Jahan now lying at her side. The tomb stands beside the River Yamuna, as did most of the pavilions in Agra gardens. It has a *chahar bagh* to the south and a Moonlight Garden to the north, across the river. Tomb gardens can symbolize paradise; residential gardens are for pleasure.

3.56 a, b Achabal, Kashmir, is a garden made by a spring at the foot of a mountain.

3.57 Plan of Shalimar Bagh in Kashmir. The original planting is likely to have been very different from its current planting, which is shown on the plan.

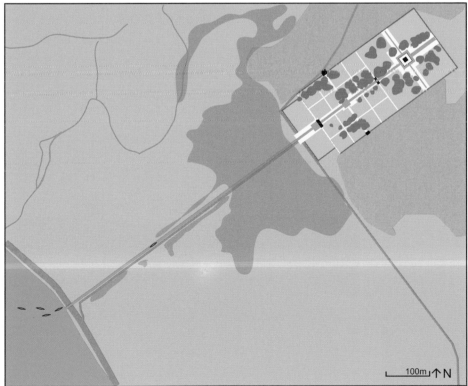

100m ↑ N

3.58 a, b, c The Taj Mahal has a *chahar bagh* between the entrance gate (above) and the mausoleum (right). It did not have European lawns when built.

3.59 a, b The Taj Mahal seen from the Yamuna (left) and from the Moonlight Garden on the far side of the Yamuna (right).

Mughal-influenced and Rajput gardens

The Mughal style of garden design, though introduced by conquerors who spoke Turkic and Persian, has come to be seen as Indian. The famous gardens discussed above were made by an empire which reached its zenith in 1700, and, after a long decline, was ended by the British in 1857. Despite the influence of Islamic and Persian design ideas, Mughal gardens were also the product of Indian skills, knowledge and traditions.

This can be seen in the use of water, in plan forms and in building technology. Perfectly square gardens with crossing canals and central pavilions are not found outside India. Nor is there evidence of lifts being used to raise water in Persian gardens. The Persian and Timurid tradition was to build in brick and apply ceramic tiles as cladding. It was India which had the stoneworkers and the stone. This affected plans, construction details and styles of ornament. As discussed in Part 2 of this book, the first stone buildings in India were Buddhist and based on mandalas.

The Indian-ness of Mughal-influenced gardens is most apparent in Rajasthan and Madhya Pradesh, south of the Indo-Gangetic plain. The Rajputs had varying degrees of independence and developed their own architectural styles. An Indian dimension is also apparent in the gardens made by Muslim princes. This could be a matter of taste or the result of employing Hindu stonemasons familiar with Indian techniques of water management. As will be discussed in the next chapter, India had, in the tank and stepwell (*baoli*), an ancient technique of water conservation suited to a monsoon climate. It had been the central feature of pre-Islamic Indian gardens and had the same function in Sultanate and Mughal gardens. Tanks were the only means of water supply in India's dry season. Let us consider some examples of Mughal-influenced and Rajput gardens south of the North Indian plains.

Mandu

Mandu, the 'City of Joy', is in a wonderful location: a high plateau surrounded by deep valleys and strewn with the remains of palaces, gardens, hills, valleys, woods, farms, stepwells, reservoirs, tombs, a mosque and a madrasah. It was a Hindu settlement before falling to the Sultanate and the Mughals. The Baz Bahadur has an open court with a great flight of steps descending to a pool. The Nil Kanth Palace nestles below the rim of a plateau and has a beautiful pool. The Ship Palace (Jahaz Mahal), stands between two tanks (Munja and Kapur), and has a garden with a rooftop terrace. A pool and a spiral channel are cut into the stonework. The palace was a large harem and the pool was the women's playground. The Champa Baoli has subterranean bathrooms. The architecture is Islamic but the gardens, dominated by *baolis*, are not *chahar baghs*.

Kaliadeh Palace

The sultans of Mandu also built a pleasure palace on an island in the Shipra River, near Ujjain. It overlooks a garden set into the riverbed and, as at Mandu, the garden has a water tank as its central feature. A pavilion stands in the centre of the tank but the garden is not symmetrical. As at Bundi, the prime role of the garden appears to have been pleasure.

Bundi

Bundi was the capital city of a princely state during the Rajput era. The palace has a *chahar bagh*-type garden high above the town. The quadrants are now maintained as

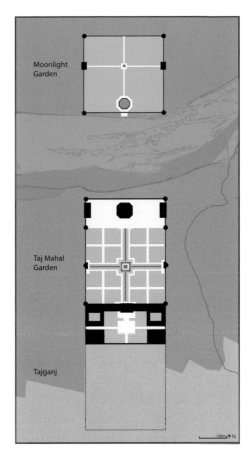

3.60 The Taj Mahal was seen from the Moonlight Garden, reflected in the River Yamuna.

3.61 A stone worker using a hand-held fret saw to repair the tomb of Itmad ud Daula in Agra.

3.62 a, b, c The Ship Palace in Mandu. It would have had orchards and flowers, not lawns or clipped hedges.

3.63 a, b The Kaliadeh Palace, Ujjain, has a garden in the bed of a river.

3.64 A painting in the Palace of Bundi, showing how the planting used to be (see also Figure 1.13).

3.65 a, b, c Deeg Palace garden is within a fortress and surrounded by moats.

lawns but the murals in the adjoining Chitra Shala show lush planting in the sunken areas between the raised walks. Rudyard Kipling lived nearby and wrote:

> *The Palace of Boondi [Bundi], even in broad daylight, is such a Palace as men build for themselves in uneasy dreams, the work of goblins more than the work of men. It is built into and out of the hill side, in gigantic terraces, and dominates the whole of the city.*[32]

The garden must have been designed for pleasure. Gazing on the hot dusty town, its princes and princesses could live in a world of dreams.

Deeg

Deeg was home to the ruler of India's Jat people, who are predominantly Hindu Rajputs. Badan Singh was proclaimed ruler in 1722 and built the Purana Mahal (old palace) at Deeg. Additional palaces were built in and around an extensive water garden, surrounded by moats and water tanks. The gardens have the channels and pools typical of Mughal gardens and are arranged on a crossing axis with a central pool. The fountains are supplied from a roof-top tank, filled by bullock-drawn carts so that the fountains could operate only during festivities. It is a pleasure garden, not a tomb garden.

Islamnagar

Formerly a Rajput town, Islamnagar was taken by an Afghan conqueror in 1715 and became the capital of Bhopal State. It was fortified and a palace with gardens stands within the walls. The Rani Mahal (Queen's Palace) has a rectangular garden and

3.66 a, b Islamnagar: the Chaman Mahal (above) and the Rani Mahal (right) are within a fortified town.

3.67 The Sahelion-Ki-Bari is said to have been made for the 48 girls Sangram Singh received as a dowry.

deep arcades. The Chaman Mahal (Garden Palace) has a *chahar bagh* with pools and fountains. The function is secular but the design appears to draw on the Mughal tomb gardens.

Udaipur, Sahelion-Ki-Bari

The Garden of the Maids of Honour is said to have been made for the 48 girls Maharana Sangram Singh II (1710–1734) received with his dowry. The central feature is a courtyard with a white marble *chhatri* fountain in the centre (a *chhatri* is a domed pavilion). Udaipur resisted Mughal control and the use of a water tank, instead of water channels, gives the garden an Indian identity.

Amber Palace, Jaipur

The Rajput Palace, built in red sandstone and white marble, is within Amber Fort. It has two large rectangular gardens which are Mughal in their plan geometry but richly embroidered in pattern and texture. One of these gardens is in a courtyard. It was a place to walk and to view from an arcade. The other garden, in the lake below the palace, was a decoration to be viewed from the palace, like a European parterre, but also had an elaborate pulley system so that the ladies of the harem could visit the garden by moonlight.

The difference between Mughal gardens and the gardens of non-Mughal princes, described in this section, justifies their classification as 'Indian'.

3.68 a, b The Amber Palace has one garden within the fortress (above) and a second garden in the lake (left). The women of the palace visited the lake garden by moonlight, using chairs operated by a pulley system.

3.69 The Phool Bagh in Orchha was a luxurious *chahar bagh*, made for a concubine. The garden pavilion has become a Hindu shrine.

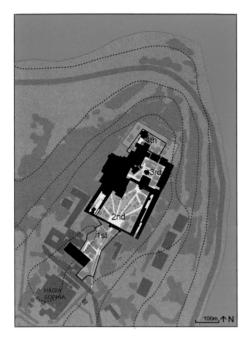

3.70 Topkapi Palace, on the site of a Greek acropolis, is planned with the same sequence of courtyards as a tented encampment.

3.71 Topkapi Palace, seen over the Golden Horn, with the Bosphorus to the left, the Golden Horn to the right and the Sea of Marmara beyond.

Turkish gardens

The Oghuz Turks, like the Aryans, came from North Asia. After the tenth century, they conquered Persia, converted to Islam and established a Persian-influenced Seljuk Empire. Victory over the Byzantines in 1071 let the Seljuk Turks advance into Anatolia – until Genghis Khan, from Mongolia, destroyed their power in the thirteenth century. Osman I won independence for the Turks in 1299 and went on to found the Ottoman Empire in the country which became Turkey. There are some textual and visual records of old Ottoman gardens but even fewer garden survivals than in Persia. A nomadic liking for tents, kiosks, outdoor eating and an encampment lifestyle was characteristic of Turkish gardens. Cooking kebabs out of doors is still popular on Istanbul's shoreline, in Berlin's public parks and elsewhere.

The Ottoman Sultans made palace gardens in Bursa, Edirne and Istanbul. Other gardens were made by the aristocracy. The palaces in Bursa and Edirne were lost in the nineteenth century but Topkapi Palace, in Istanbul, survives. The location of the three palaces in Western Turkey may have influenced their design. The climate is Mediterranean and the pre-Ottoman civilization of the area had been Christian. Summers are hot and dry so that Istanbul, like Rome, had to be supplied with water from aqueducts and cisterns. The city did not have the *qanat* water which gives life

to Persian gardens. In their place, Ottoman gardens had fish ponds, in the manner of Egyptian and Roman gardens. Water channels could have been supplied from ox-powered wells, as in Mughal India, but their construction would have been difficult on rocky sites and there was no real need for them. With better sea views than any other Asian capital, Istanbul had less need for artificial water features. Persian and Mughal gardens looked inward when no views were available but had outward-looking pavilions when, as in Isfahan, Delhi and Agra, they were beside rivers.

Topkapi Palace

Topkapi Palace is the major surviving example of a Turkish garden. It has a wonderful site, formerly the Byzantine acropolis. The hill overlooks the Sea of Marmara, the Bosphorus and the Golden Horn. Topkapi was begun by Mehmet the Conqueror soon after he took the city in 1453. It lies north of the Byzantine Emperors' Palace, and was planned more as a symbol of royal power than a fortress.[33] Like other Turkish palaces, the design was based on the organization of a tented encampment.[34] The early buildings at Topkapi were grouped to make one court for the household and another for receiving guests. Later additions created two additional courts, one more-public and one more-private, so that the palace now has four courtyards. Proceeding from the main entrance, the sequence of courts is from most-public to most-private:

The First Court

The First Court is entered from the Imperial Gate. It has a quotation from the Quran (15: 45–46) above the entrance: 'Verily the God fearing shall be amidst gardens and springs. Enter therein in peace, secure.'[35] This court was used for parades and processions or, on other occasions, to accommodate the horses of visitors or temporary displays of exotic animals. It is also known as the Court of Processions and the Court of the Janissaries, who formed the emperor's bodyguard.

The Second Court

The Second Court is entered by the double-towered Middle Gate. Only the sultan was allowed to proceed on horseback beyond this point. Guests walked the tree-lined path to the entrance to the third court. On important occasions, the route was also lined with courtiers and displays of precious carpets, textiles and other goods, recalling the bazaar at Delhi's Red Fort. The entrance to the Third Court, the Gate of Felicity, was used for occasional appearances by sultans. Beyond is the Chamber of Petitions, used by the sultan for one of his primary jobs: the administration of justice. Those found guilty of serious crimes were executed in the Second Court. The Executioner's Fountain was then used to clean the blood from the swordsman's hands. In essence, the Second Court was an administrative space, flanked by the public treasury, the imperial kitchens, the palace hospital and barracks. It was

> *a completely walled-in rectangular garden, planted with trees and lawns, crisscrossed*
> *by stone paths connecting the major buildings and gates, and lined with tall cypresses.*

3.72 The First Court at Topkapi is thronged with visitors.

3.73 An Ottoman procession in the Second Court at Topkapi (see Figure 3.74).

3.74 The path through the Second Court at Topkapi leads to the Gate of Felicity. Only the sultan was allowed to ride a horse on this path.

3.75 a, b The Third Court at Topkapi was used by the page boys and pupils at the palace school.

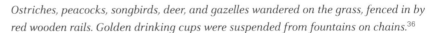

Ostriches, peacocks, songbirds, deer, and gazelles wandered on the grass, fenced in by red wooden rails. Golden drinking cups were suspended from fountains on chains.[36]

The Third Court

The Third Court was used by the royal household and the palace school. It formerly had two sections: 'the first housed the male pages, entrusted to white eunuchs, the second housed the female population, guarded by black eunuchs.'[37] The separation was strictly enforced. The buildings round the Court include dormitories, a page boys' school and rooms for palace officials. Today, it is a lush garden with a European character and some Eastern detailing. The harem is on the east side of the Court.

The Fourth Court

The Fourth Court was the sultan's private garden, to which the harem women were invited on occasion. It was most unusual for other visitors to be admitted but a French visitor left a romanticized description of the scene:

While the concubines played in the garden or swam in its pool, the sultan would retire with his favorite into one of the pavilions, hidden by shutters from the view of outsiders. On these outings the young girls would run about, playing and entertaining the sultan with amusing tricks, such as removing the eunuch's turbans or pushing them into the water, or walking on their stomachs.[37]

3.76 a, b, c The Fourth Court at Topkapi was private to the sultan. It has a cool courtyard and a golden kiosk overlooking the Bosphorus.

The Fourth Court has terraces, pavilions, kiosks, a pool and fountains. Today, the character is less European than that of the other courts, because of the design details and because of the type of space it represents. It has ceramic tiles, spray jets, a golden kiosk and a shady pool. The best adjective to describe their design is 'Turkish'. The pool, the kiosk and the views are characteristic features. It is a courtly space for outdoor living and eating. Topkapi now closes at 5 or 6 in the evening, but one can still imagine the scene on a hot night, with a corpulent sultan, a cool breeze, lithe maidens and lights flickering on ships in the Bosphorus. Encampments would have had equivalent spaces, but without the sea views.

Old drawings represent the planting in Topkapi's four courts. Their style is diagrammatic, with evergreen and deciduous trees shown as cones and globes. They are interspersed and the apparent intention was to symbolize the type of outdoor setting in which tents were erected. The old planting was changed by European gardeners in the nineteenth century so that the Second Court is now planted like a European park. The Third Court, and the terraces below the Fourth Court, are managed as European gardens.

Some information about the lost palace gardens of Istanbul is available. A French visitor saw the Uskudar palace garden in 1576. It was beside the Bosphorus and parties, often a sultan with his concubines, would travel there by boat. The visitor describes three garden compartments. The first was 'like an earthly paradise with its perfumed herbs, flowers and all kinds of trees planted in orderly fashion'. The second was enclosed by a high wall. The third had pavilions spread with 'costly Persian carpets' and 'a quadrangular white-marble pool in which stood a small red-painted boat for the pleasure rides of the royal offspring'. An English visitor reported having seen 'canals of water' but the site was on a rocky shore. There were vegetable gardens, vineyards and orchards.

Necipoglu draws an interesting comparison between Roman and Ottoman gardens. There were Byzantine villas along the waterfront when the Turks arrived and

> It can be argued that with their asymmetrical open designs, bathing facilities, and sacred springs of ancient origin the Ottoman gardens probably came closer to capturing the lyrical spirit of antiquity – as reflected in Pompeian frescoes which depict loosely composed single-story maritime villas with belvedere towers and airy colonnades overlooking the waterfront – than did the rigidly architected formal gardens of renaissance Europe.[39]

Regarded as the point where Europe meets Asia, Istanbul draws on both cultures. But, like Islam itself, the civilization of Turkey can be regarded as more west-facing than east-facing. Doubtless, it would be a different place if South and East Asian religions had spread west. The types of garden which might then have been made are the subject of the next two chapters, on Hindu and Buddhist gardens.

3.77 a–e Something of the historic character of the planting in Islamic gardens can be gleaned from paintings and from re-creations.

Note on Islamic planting

For a garden historian, the most disappointing aspect of surviving Islamic gardens is that their planting has so often been Europeanized. Constance Villiers-Stuart, author of the first book on Indian gardens, wrote:

> Flowering shrubs and some roses still adorn the Taj gardens; but where are the fruit trees? The orange, pomegranate, and lemon? Groves of these should certainly be again planted here, for quite apart from their great decorative value, they formed a special feature of the original design and pious intentions of the founder of this Paradise Orchard. Undoubtedly the different squares of the garden were largely planted with fruit trees.[40]

Her point can be generalized. The mown lawns now so common in Islamic gardens never existed before the nineteenth century. The historic planting was of fruiting trees and shrubs with some flowering plants and with some quadrants used for tulips. The grass which is sometimes mentioned is most likely to have been a cover for bulbs.

Part 2
South Asia

CHAPTER 4

Hindu gardens

4.1 The River Indus flows past Nanga Parbat to irrigate the Indus Valley. The 'Naked Mountain', in Pakistan administered Kashmir, is the world's ninth highest peak.

4.2 Satellite image of the Indus Valley, showing the location of Harappa and Mohenjo Daro.

The Indus Valley

The River Indus flows from the frozen heights of Tibet to the burning shores of the Arabian Sea. As revealed by the satellite photograph (Figure 4.2), the Indus Valley would be a desert without the water of this river. The Indus is 3200 km long, carries twice the volume of the Nile and is one of the Seven Rivers described in the *Vedas*. In ancient times, the chief river was the Sarasvati, described in the *Rig Veda* both as a goddess and as a mighty river nourishing a people.

> *I sing a lofty song, for she is mightiest, most divine of Streams.*
> *Sarasvati will I exalt with hymns and lauds.*[1]

River water allowed permanent settlements to be formed. India's first historical civilization is of a similar age to the other polytheist civilizations discussed in Chapter 2. The name Indus, equivalent to Sindhu in Sanskrit and Sindh in Persian, is the origin of the words Hindu and India. River water supported both the Indus Valley civilization (*c.*3300–1900 BCE) and the Vedic civilization (*c.*1500 BCE–500 CE) which is the main subject of this chapter. As used in the chapter title, 'Hindu' refers to the civilizations which spread south and east from the Indus between *c.*3300 BCE and 500 CE. The development of Indian gardens after 500 is discussed in Chapters 5 and 6 on Buddhist and Islamic gardens.

Historians of Ancient India face the problem that knowledge of the earlier (Indus Valley) civilization comes from archaeology and knowledge of the later (Vedic) civilization comes from texts. There is no overlap and the lack of information is particularly acute

4.3 Orchha is a *tirtha* with chattris, palaces and bathing *ghats*.

for those who study ancient gardens: there are few texts and no physical survivals. This does not diminish the importance of ancient gardens but it forces the historian to rely on geographical, general historical and textual evidence. The first modern historians to investigate the gardens of ancient India were Constance Villiers-Stuart (1877–1966) and Marie-Luise Gothein (1863–1931). Having walked in Gothein's footsteps through the gardens of Europe, I imagined myself back on track when setting off for India. It was with surprise that I read Horst Schumacher's Epilogue to a reprint of *Indian Gardens*. He wrote:

> *Dr. Dieter Gothein, one of her grandsons has kindly advised me by letter of 7 October 1999: 'After the perusal of the copies of her diaries of her journey to East Asia, which are difficult to read, I am able to tell you that she had never entered the Indian sub-continent. She lived with us for over one year in Central Java; after this, she visited Bali and continued to China and Japan. In those days it was customary to refer to the former Dutch India as India. She frequently used this abbreviation in her diaries, which may be the reason for a certain amount of confusion. She must have written her treatise on Indian gardens as well as that on the Malaysian Adat House after her studies of literature.'[2]*

Gothein's *History of Garden Art* has a short section on the influence of Hindu and Buddhist ideas on gardens in India, as part of a chapter on West Asia. Following its publication, she learned Sanskrit and studied the old books, particularly the *Itihasa* group which includes the *Ramayana* and the *Mahabharata*. Not being such a good historian, I have relied on translations. But as with Gothein's *History of Garden Art*, I find myself generally in agreement with her judgements. Since she had not visited India, this continues to be a surprise.

4.4 a, b Temporary buildings (*kachha*) are still built with mud, stiffened with timber and roofed with reeds.

4.5 a, b None of India's ancient gardens survive but texts confirm that palace gardens had lotus pools set among trees.

4.6 a, b North India is dry outside the monsoon season, unless irrigated (Aravelli Mountains).

The picture of Ancient Indian gardens, summarized in the concluding section of this chapter, is remarkably consistent over time. This may be partly because the evidence is thin and partly a consequence of the famous continuity of Indian civilization. Selected textual evidence is quoted below in what is believed to be chronological order. Dates for India's ancient history are speculative and none are available for the Indus Valley civilization, despite its brick architecture. Until 500 BCE, the other peoples of India built in timber and mud, leaving few visual or archaeological remains. Since garden history operates best as a word and image discipline, I have used some photographs of modern India and some speculative diagrams to illustrate the text.

Geography

Glaciers provide a steady supply of water over a long period, with water channels providing both a means of distribution and, as in West Asia, a design feature. Monsoons, in contrast, provide copious water for a short period. Tanks are used to store this water and, as in Indian gardens, to create a different type of design feature. In North East India, almost all the rain falls between June and September. The land is green during and after the rains. But, unless it is watered from rivers, lakes or tanks, the plants are then desiccated, with the tree layer remaining green longer than the herb layer. The wet valley-land used to be covered by thick jungle with a dangerous and unpredictable character. As floods pass through jungles, they are easily diverted by alluvial deposits or uprooted vegetation. Water tends to be dammed and then released, causing new river channels to form. Crocodiles, lions, tigers, elephants and rhinoceros were additional hazards. India's prehistoric settlements were built on

4.7 a, b The monsoon delivers intense water over a short period. Glaciers yield a steady supply of water over a long period. (Bangalore, left, the source of the Ganges, above).

forest margins and tended to be impermanent. These were the safest places to live and provided access to areas for hunting, food gathering and cultivation.

All the peoples of India came from beyond its borders, by land or sea. Most of the migrations are unrecorded, though others are well documented. Each is likely to have brought their own language, ideas and culture. The Dravidians may have come by the coastal route from Mesopotamia, as did the Greeks, Romans and Arabs in later ages. Other substantial migrant groups reached India by land routes from the Himalayan regions: the Aryan, Gujaratis and Rajputs probably came from Central Asia. Afghan and Turkic peoples arrived from North Central Asia and another large group, now described as tribal and Mundaric, were Mongoloid migrants from North and East

4.8 a, b, c Elephants and crocodiles made the riverine jungles of India dangerous for settlers.

Asia. These groups settled in India and rarely attempted to conquer their neighbours. In the first century of the Common Era, travellers wishing to make themselves understood throughout the subcontinent would have required a knowledge of many more languages than European travellers.

The Indus Valley civilization, 3300–1900 BCE

Prehistoric remains of hunter-gatherer camps have been found throughout the Indian subcontinent but yield few artefacts. The oldest cities, including Harappa and Mohenjo-Daro, belong to the Indus Valley civilization. The valley adjoins Iran and the settlement patterns have more similarity with those of West Asia than anything of comparable age on the Indian subcontinent. Some Harappan inscriptions survive but none have been deciphered. One theory is that the people who built the Indus Valley cities were related to the Elamites of South West Iran (see p. 52).

Indus Valley cities traded with Mesopotamian cities and, in a comparable physical environment, also had a civilization which used ceramics, copper and bronze. The Indus cities had a central administrative-religious complex. Houses were built in brick and had flat roofs. Street layouts were regular. From the standpoint of garden history, the most interesting feature of Harappa and Mohenjo-Daro is their town centre water tanks, as they resemble the sacred ponds in Egyptian sanctuaries. Tanks later became characteristic of Indian towns and gardens, with both religious and functional

4.9 The 'great bath' at the centre of Mohenjo Daro may have had both ritual and hygienic roles, as did sacred pools in Ancient Egypt (see p. 49).

roles. The Indus Valley towns did not have unbuilt land which could have been used for residential gardens. The probability, based on the pattern of Mesopotamian cities, is that there were fruit and flower gardens on the low land outside the Indus Valley settlements.

After a long stable period, the civilization of the Indus Valley came to an abrupt end, and there are two main theories concerning why this happened. The older 'invasion theory' is that the cities were destroyed by Aryan invaders from Central Asia; evidence for this theory comes from Vedic texts which describe a nomadic civilization of chariot-born warriors destroying forts and overwhelming local peoples (the *dasyas*). Hymn XX, for example, praises the god Indra (see p. 21) for his part in defeating Vrtra (the demon who caused droughts) and the local Dasa population:

> *Indra the Vrtra-slayer, Fort-destroyer, scattered the Dasya hosts who dwelt in darkness. For men hath he created earth and waters, and ever helped the prayer of him who worships. To him in might the Gods have ever yielded, to Indra in the tumult of the battle. When in his arms they laid the bolt, he slaughtered the Dasyas and cast down their forts of iron.*[3]

A more recent theory, not incompatible with the above, is that the ancient civilization of the Indus Valley was fatally disrupted by a natural calamity. As the meeting point of two tectonic plates, North West India has always been subject to earthquakes. Tectonic shifts could explain the disappearance of the River Saraswati. Its waters, which once flowed west through the Punjab, might now flow east, in the Yamuna, to join the Ganges at Allahabad.

4.10 a, b Fire remains sacred in Hindu culture.

4.11 a, b Cows remain sacred in Hindu culture.

Whichever theory is correct, there were certainly struggles between nomads and settlers. Most readers of this book will be settlers who accept the principle that land can be owned. Our hunter-gatherer and pastoralist ancestors were nomads who collected food where it could be found and had no concept of land ownership. The development of agriculture tends to cause conflict between nomads and settlers, with the settlers taking the best land and defending themselves against human and animal predators. The Vedic people were nomads who chose to settle in Northern India.

South, Central and West India have different climates, languages and peoples. The ethnic groups in ancient India were: tribals (Mundarics), Aryans, Dravidians and Mongoloids. As Pramar observes: 'It has always been a mistake to over-emphasize the Aryan-Sanskritic aspect of Indian culture and to devalue the indigenous tribal-Mongoloid contribution.'[4] In part, the mistake arises because most of the old texts, including those quoted below, were written in the language of the Aryans, even when their authors lived in South India.

The Vedic civilization, 1500 BCE–500 CE

'Vedic' refers to the period in Indian history known from texts (the *Vedas*) passed down by word of mouth for an unknown period of time and inscribed, *c.* 300 BCE, by a priestly caste in North India. The oldest of these texts, the *Rig Veda*, is a collection of poems used on sacrificial occasions. *Rig* means 'praise' and *veda* derives from the verb *vid*, 'to know', so that 'Hymn Knowledge' would be a fair translation. The *Rig Veda* was written in Sanskrit, a refined version of the common language which, as time passed, became a language used only by the upper classes and then only by priests. Most verses in the *Vedas* are hymns but there is some factual information and it has been extensively analysed by linguists, historians, anthropologists, archaeologists, scientists and others. Wherever the Vedic peoples came from, it is evident that they were cattle-herding nomads who became farmers and city builders, always remembering their nomadic past. Tribal memories apparently influenced their religion and a high value was put on significant places in the landscape.

The Sanskrit of the *Vedas* is close to the ancient language of Iran, Avestan, and linguistic analysis has shown that, with a few remarkable exceptions, all the European languages are related to these tongues. This led to the idea of a common linguistic ancestor, called Proto-Indo-European (PIE), and then to the theory that an Aryan people speaking this language, perhaps north of the Caucasus Mountains, had a profound cultural impact on India, Iran and Europe. A rival theory, with little academic support, holds that the Indo-European language developed in Pakistan (*P*unjab, *A*fghanistan, *K*ashmir, *I*ran, *S*indh + *stan*). Garden historians need not take a view on this debate. We can, however, learn something about settlement patterns, and gardens, from India's sacred books: the *Vedas* ('knowledge'), the *Itihasa* ('that which happened'), the *Puranas* ('ancient texts'), *Kavya* ('poetry') and the *Sutras* ('threads'). For garden historians, the *Ramayana* and the *Mahabharata* are the most important texts. The following subsections summarize what can be learned from texts about Hindu gardens.

The *Rig Veda* (*c.*1500 BCE)

The hymns of the *Rig Veda* do not mention gardens but do reveal an ever-present theme in Asian gardens: religious awe of nature, scenery, trees and water:

> *Him, verily, the moons, the mountains followed, the tall trees followed and the plants and herbage.*

> *Yearning with love both Worlds approached, the Waters waited on Indra when he first had being.*[5]

4.12 NASA image (from MISR) looking over the Himalayan mountain wall to the great plains of North India.

The Vedic hymns were composed by priestly families and chanted at tribal gatherings. Their authors roamed a land of barren deserts fringed by snow-capped mountains from which great rivers flowed through wild forests to broad plains. Nazi ideas, about the Aryans as a master race from Atlantis, or North Europe, were racist fiction. The Vedic hymns record the belief system of a Bronze Age society and, to a lesser extent, its history, geography and customs. Fire and sacrifice are central, with the horse sacrifice at the heart of ritual practice.

Though still contested, the predominant opinion among historians is that Aryan culture originated in the western section of Eurasian steppes, the grasslands which

4.13 a, b, c Domestication of the horse enabled the Ayrans, who had been nomadic pastoralists, to migrate from Central Asia into India. Yurts (or *gers*) in Kyrgystan and Xinjiang, and a black tent in Iran.

extend from Hungary to Mongolia.[6] It was a horse-centric culture and it is certain that the horse was domesticated in this region. By 2000 BCE, the steppes had become 'a trans-continental corridor of communication and exchange'.[7] Chariot-borne warriors developed a vibrant pastoral-nomadic culture based on sheep, cattle, horse transport, metallurgy and shared religious ideas. They left no written texts but took great care in passing hymns down the generations.

Horses survived in the dry parts of India and chariot-borne warriors, like those with aircraft in a later age, had military superiority. With experience of cultivating oases in Central Asia, they occupied the drier parts of India with relative ease and then settled on river banks in the lush forests of the Indo-Gangetic plain. They built settlements and engaged in agriculture. Hymns were chanted by *rishis* (sages) at fireside ceremonies, reminding people of their nomadic past. The *Rig Veda* reveals a people proud of their technical and military prowess. Reading the hymns some 4000 years after their composition gives one a sense of being under the stars at a firelight gathering in ancient times. With imagination, one can attend a ceremony on the edge of a forest, see the priests, smell the fire, drink *soma*, enjoy a feast, hear the chanting, delight in the poetry, take pride in a history, share the wonder at nature's power, witness the rituals and glimpse fields in which grains, herbs and flowers grow.

The *Rig Veda* is arranged into ten mandalas (cycles) and is the oldest record of the knowledge and beliefs of any Indo-European people. As Radhakrishnan noted, the poetry 'resembles that of the Homeric Greeks or the Celtic Irish at the beginning of the Christian era'.[8] Iran and Aryan are cognate words. Wherever they came from, the Indo-Europeans had a linguistic, and thus a cultural, ancestor. Genetics are another matter and have not, as yet, provided conclusive evidence. Some of the names of Vedic Gods have similar names in Indo-European languages: Mitra is cognate with the Persian Mithra, Ushas with the Latin Aurora. Agni, the Sanskrit word for fire and the fire god's name, has Latin and Russian equivalents: *ignis* and *ogon*. Hymn 101 from the tenth mandala illustrates the literary style of the *Rig Veda* and provides information about agricultural equipment, boat building and irrigation.

1. Wake with one mind, my friends, and kindle Agni, ye who are many and who dwell together. Agni and Dadhikras and Dawn the Goddess, you, Gods with Indra, I call down to help us.

2. Make pleasant hymns, spin out your songs and praises: build ye a ship equipped with oars for transport. Prepare the implements, make all things ready, and let the sacrifice, my friends, go forward.

3. Lay on the yokes, and fasten well the traces: formed is the furrow, sow the seed within it. Through song may we find bearing fraught with plenty: near to the ripened grain approach the sickle.

4. Wise, through desire of bliss from Gods, the skilful bind the traces fast, And lay the yokes on either side.

5. Arrange the buckets in their place, securely fasten on the straps. We will pour forth the well that hath a copious stream, fair-flowing well that never fails.

6. I pour the water from the well with pails prepared and goodly straps. Unfailing, full, with plenteous stream.[9]

Water from wells and rivers was used to bring dry land into cultivation:

7. When for twelve days the Rbhus joyed reposing as guests of him who never may be hidden, Iley made fair fertile fields, they brought the rivers. Plants spread o'er deserts, waters filled the hollows.[10]

Fields were used for grain and flowering plants:

4.14 Lord Rama's birthplace, the fabled palace city of Ayodhya, still floats above the River Sarayu, and attracts hosts of pilgrims.

7. Thou who hast spread abroad the streams by stablished law, and in the field the plants that blossom and bear seed.[11]

Hymn XCVII from the tenth mandala is in praise of herbs. They are celebrated, like all nature, but particularly for their nutritional and medicinal functions:

3. Be glad and joyful in the Plants, both blossoming and bearing fruit,
Plants that will lead us to success like mares who conquer in the race.[12]
...

15. Let fruitful Plants, and fruitless, those that blossom, and the blossomless,
Urged onward by Brhaspati, release us from our pain and grief.[13]

The gods of the *Rig Veda* personify aspects of nature (Thunder, Fire, Sun, Wind, Dawn) and sacrifices are offered to obtain boons from the gods.

1. I call the lovely Night and Dawn to seat them on the holy grass
At this our solemn sacrifice.[14]

The *Rig Veda* has occasional references to vegetables but the main crops are cereals. From other evidence, it is thought that wheat, barley and millet were grown in the drier northern zone and rice in the wetter eastern zone (Bengal) – knowledge of rice cultivation had developed in East Asia before 4000 BCE. Vedic fields are described as '*ksetra*' (from the *krsi*, to plough). There is little to suggest that fruit or vegetables were cultivated but there are many references to delicious fruits being harvested from forests – as they were harvested in gardens in later periods. The early Vedic peoples ploughed and irrigated enclosed outdoor space but probably did not make pleasure gardens. They accorded high worth to rivers and pools, as their ancestors had always valued the rivers and oases of Central Asia.

The *Ramayana* is acclaimed as the most 'popular, influential, imitated, and successful' book ever written.[15] Sometimes described at 'the Bible of India', it remains influential throughout the subcontinent and South East Asia. In poetic language, the *Ramayana* describes fortified towns with palaces and gardens inside defences. The gardens are groves of flowering and fruiting trees with ponds as central features. In the Fertile Crescent of West Asia, orchards with water channels were the primary garden type. In South Asia, dependent on stepwells (*baolis*) for water in the dry season, the primary garden type was a grove with a tank.

Valmiki put his name to the *Ramayana* but the work is thought to be made up of older tales compiled in their present form c.700 BCE. This makes the *Ramayana* contemporary with another famous epic of travel and war over a beautiful woman: *The Iliad*. Homer's dates are also uncertain. The suggestion that he influenced Valmiki has been rejected but both poets drew on the Indo-European tradition of recited epics. The *Ramayana* is the story of Lord Rama's journey (*ayana*), made after he was exiled from the court of his father. Rama came to be seen as the Ideal Man, brave, generous, even-tempered and ever-faithful to his sweet and virtuous wife, Sita. Their fourteen years of exile, though unjust, were accepted with what Western readers might see as Christian fortitude. Lord Rama is recognized by Hindus as the seventh incarnation of Vishnu. Sita, because she had been found as an infant in a ploughed field, is seen as an incarnation of the earth goddess, Devi. Rama was born in a North Indian town still called Ayodhya. His journey took him through India, where he saw many palaces, to an island (Lanka) identified with Sri Lanka. The quotations below are from Griffith's 1870–74 translation, which has the merit of being in verse, and/or from the 1984–2006 translation by a team led by Robert Goldman, which is more accurate. The first quotation, from Goldman, describes a courtyard palace in Ayodhya:

1. Aboard his chariot in the midst of his delighted supporters, majestic Rama beheld the city crowded with people of every description.

2–3. Rama proceeded down the center of the royal highway. The splendid thoroughfare was fragrant with aloe-wood and adorned with white, cloudlike houses – gleaming and spacious, flanked with all kinds of wares and foodstuffs of every variety.

...

12. On reaching the palace that resembled great Indra's abode, the prince ablaze with royal splendor entered his father's residence.

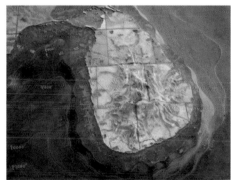

4.15 a, b The *Ramayana* tells of Lord Rama's marriage in Ayodhya and his journey to Sri Lanka. Rama's Bridge (the Ram Setu) is a chain of limestone shoals linking the 'Venerable Island' (Sri Lanka) to India.

4.16 a, b 'Wares and foodstuffs of every variety' are sold on festive days in temple cities.

13. Passing through all the courtyards and turning back all his people, the son of Dasaratha came to the private inner chamber.[16]

The second quotation, from Griffith, describes a similar scene:

Through grove and garden, undismayed,
From house to house the Vanar strayed

4.17 a, b The paintings in Cave 17 at Ajanta (photograph, left and drawing, right) illustrate the relationship between an Indian palace and the garden in which it stood, *c.*500 CE. The subjects of the paintings come the Jataka tales about the previous births (*jati*) of the Buddha.

*And still his wondering glances bent
On terrace, dome, and battlement:
Then with a light and rapid tread
Prahasta's home he visited,
And Kumbhakarna's courtyard where
A cloudy pile rose high in air;
And, wandering o'er the hill, explored
The garden of each Rakshas lord.*[17]

The next two quotations are from the *Aranya Kanda*, with translations by Griffith and Goldman:

*A towering height of solid wall,
Flashing afar, surrounds it all,
Its golden courts enchant the sight,
And gates aglow with lazulite.
Steeds, elephants, and cars are there,
And drums' loud music fills the air,
Fair trees in lovely gardens grow
Whose boughs with varied fruitage glow.*[18]

It is a lovely, dazzling city ringed by a white rampart, with gateways made of gold and towers of cat's-eye beryl.

It is crowded with elephants, horses, and chariots, the sound of pipes resounds there, and its gardens are beautiful, filled with trees bearing any fruit one wants.[19]

These quotations describe the same type of settlement as the oldest illustrations of Indian towns and gardens, executed by Buddhist artists *c*.100 BCE. Since Buddhism developed within the Hindu tradition this is no surprise (see p. 139). The paintings in Cave 17 at Ajanta show a palace with decorated wooden columns supporting a verandah and opening onto a lush tree garden. This design is well suited to India's climate, providing an outdoor living space with sweet fresh air and protection alike from burning sun and crashing monsoon rain. Sculptures on the *toranas* (gates) at Sanchi show one type of town in which palace gardens may have been set. Pramar argues that towns of this type were more likely to have been occupied by merchants than farmers, and to have been more typical of Buddhist than Hindu areas.[20] The town illustrated at Sanchi has wooden fortifications with high towers, so high in fact that we cannot see the internal layout of the town. India has no surviving examples of construction using timber columns but their use by Persian architects, albeit at a much later date, gives an idea of how they might have looked.

Water will always be prized in hot dry climates and bathing has a central place in Hindu rituals. Ponds were and are used for washing, drinking and irrigation. Water cools

4.18 a, b Carvings on the *toranas* (gates) at Sanchi are one of the oldest records of Indian dwellings. Note the protection given to a sacred tree (bottom left).

4.19 a, b Krishna (in blue) stole the *gopis'* clothes while they were bathing.

the air, attracts birds, supports fish, lets the sacred lotus grow and looks beautiful. Kings had pools in their own gardens and provided large tanks of water for public use, variously known as step wells, *baolis*, *baories*, *hauz* or tanks. They are a great Indian invention, a unique contribution to environmental design possessed of beauty and utility. Step wells were also built beside temples, villages and roads. 'One who digs a well has half of his sins absolved when the water has begun to flow forth' (*Vishnudharmottara Purana*).

Kautilya (*c.*300 BCE)

Kautilya's *Arthashastra* is a treatise on statecraft. It includes a section on town planning with a striking resemblance to Chinese advice on the same topic (see p. 195). The *Arthashastra* describes the location of palaces and water tanks within fortified towns. Roads are planned on a grid and lead to gardens and forests beyond town gates. The guidance for planning fortified settlements is as follows:

> *Demarcation of the ground inside the fort shall be made first by opening three royal roads from west to east and three from south to north. The fort shall contain twelve gates, provided with both a land and water-way kept secret. Chariot-roads, royal roads, and roads leading to dronamukha, sthaniya, country parts, and pasture grounds shall each be four dandas (7.3m) in width. Roads leading to sayoniya, military stations (vyuha), burial or cremation grounds, and to villages shall be eight dandas in width. Roads to gardens, groves, and forests shall be four dandas. Roads leading to elephant forests shall be two dandas. Roads for chariots shall be five aratnis (2.3m). Roads for cattle shall measure four aratnis; and roads for minor quadrupeds and men two aratnis. Royal buildings shall be constructed on strong grounds. In the midst of the houses of the*

people of all the four castes and to the north from the centre of the ground inside the fort, the king's palace, facing either the north or the east shall, as described elsewhere, be constructed occupying one-ninth of the whole site inside the fort. Royal teachers, priests, sacrificial place, water-reservoir and ministers shall occupy sites east by north to the palace. Royal kitchen, elephant stables, and the store-house shall be situated on sites east by south. On the eastern side, merchants trading in scents, garlands, grains, and liquids, together with expert artisans and the people of Kshatriya caste shall have their habitations.[21]

The author's name (Kautilya) is believed to be a pen name of Chanakya (*c*.350–283 BCE), who was prime minister to King Chandragupta, founder of the Maurya Empire and the man who first unified India. Chandragupta signed a treaty with the Macedonian founder of the Selucid Empire, opening diplomatic contact between East and West. The palace of Chandragupta's grandson, Ashoka, is described in the next chapter because he became a Buddhist (see p. 151).

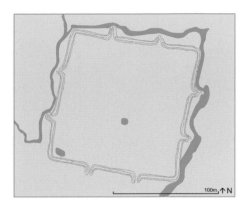

4.20 The town of Sisupalgarh, thought to date from the third century BCE, exemplifies the type of layout described by Kautilya. Roads connected entrance points, as in Chinese towns, and the orientation is north–south (see also Figure 4.28 and 4.35).

The *Mahabharata* (*c*.200 BCE)

The *Mahabharata* is a history of Great India (*Maha*, Great, *Bharata*, India). It is a very long book with few, but invaluable, details of how gardens were used and designed. A stepped tank is the most often-mentioned garden feature and 'The dedication of a tank is more meritorious than that of a hundred wells.'[22] The following passage is part of a wonder tale, explaining how a garden was designed and also touching on the conditional nature of a beautiful girl's surrender, even to a great king:

> *The minister-in-chief caused an artificial forest to be created, consisting of many trees with abundant flowers and fruits, and he caused to be excavated within that forest and towards one of its sides a large tank, placed in a secluded spot and full of water that was sweet as Amrita ... Entering that bower with his dear one, the king beheld a tank full of water that was transparent and bright as nectar, and beholding that tank, the king sat on its bank with her and the king told his adorable wife, 'Cheerfully do thou plunge into this water!' And she, hearing those words plunged into the tank. But having plunged into the water she appeared not above the surface, and as the king searched, he failed to discover any trace of her. And the king ordered the waters of the tank to be baled out, and thereupon he beheld a frog sitting at the mouth of a hole, and the king was enraged at this.*[23]

The integration of tanks and flowering trees in palace gardens is often described:

> *Within that palace Maya placed a peerless tank, and in that tank were lotuses with leaves of dark-coloured gems and stalks of bright jewels, and other flowers also of golden leaves ... Many tall trees of various kinds were planted all around the palace. Of green foliage and cool shade, and ever blossoming, they were charming to behold. Artificial woods were laid around, always emitting a delicious fragrance. And there were many tanks also that were adorned with swans and Karandavas and Chakravakas [Brahminy*

121

4.21 a–d Indian tanks (*baolis*) and steps (*ghats*) continue to have both hygienic and ritual functions.

ducks] in the grounds lying about the mansion. And the breeze bearing the fragrance of lotuses growing in water and (of those growing on land) ministered unto the pleasure and happiness of the Pandavas.[24]

It seems likely that garden 'tanks' were rectangular, because this became the shape of Indian tanks at a later date, but since cut stone was not used for residential or garden construction, one cannot be sure. Later Indian tanks have stone steps, to give convenient access at different water levels. Without steps, or boulders, the banks would have been too muddy to access clean water for washing, bathing and drinking. Gardens belonging to gods are also described. Indra, chief of the gods, lived on Mount Meru and enjoyed the fabled Nandana Garden. The *Mahabharata* has descriptions of both:

And there is that monarch of mountains the golden Meru extending over a space of thirty-three thousand Yojanas. And there, O Mudgala, are the sacred gardens of the

4.22 a–d Hindu culture celebrates rivers and mountains as gods and holy places: **a** Patan; **b, c** Pashtupatinath; **d** Varanasi.

celestials, with Nandana at their head, where sport the persons of meritorious acts. And neither hunger, nor thirst, nor lassitude, nor fear, nor anything that is disgusting or inauspicious is there. And all the odours of that place are delightful, and all the breezes delicious to the touch. And all the sounds there are captivating, O sage, to the ear and the heart. And neither grief, nor decrepitude, nor labour, nor repentance also is there. That world, O Muni, obtained as the fruit of one's own acts, is of this nature. Persons repair thither by virtue of their meritorious deeds. And the persons of those that dwell there look resplendent, and this, O Mudgala, solely by virtue of their own acts, and not owing to the merits of father or mothers.[25]

The 'meritorious acts' mentioned in this passage could include visits to holy sites and rituals. The *Mahabharata* has references to over 300 sacred places.

With regard to the sanctuaries of Ancient Greece, Vincent Scully wrote: 'That place is itself holy and, before the temple was built upon it, embodied the whole of the deity as

4.23 a, b Pilgrimage remains an important aspect of Hinduism. *Tirthas* are often river crossings and bathing places (Orchha–Kanchana Ghat).

a recognized natural force.'[26] Greece and India both revered the Earth Mother and she was worshipped at sacred sites. In Vedic Sanskrit, a *tirtha* could be a ford, steps down into a river, a path to an altar or a place for ritual bathing by a sacred stream. Later, *tirtha* came to mean any sacred site and a pilgrimage is described as a *tirtha-yatra*. Places became holy either through association with a spiritual person or because of their scenic nature: a lake, mountain, forest, cave, river or confluence of rivers. River crossings symbolize spiritual crossings where heaven and earth meet so that prayers can be sent and blessings received. Varanasi, at the meeting of three rivers, is the holiest city in India and the place from which one is most likely to reach heaven after cremation. The *Mahabharata* has much information on sacred landscapes:

> *Dhaumya continued, 'I shall describe to thee those sacred spots capable of producing merit that lie on the west, in the country of the Anarttas, O Bharata, there, flows in a westward course the sacred river Narmada, graced by Priyangu and mango trees, and en-garlanded with thickest of canes. All the tirthas and sacred spots, and rivers and woods and foremost of mountains that are in the three worlds ... always come, O Bharata, to bathe in the sacred waters of the Narmada ... There also is the celebrated tank of the Grandsire, called Pushkara, the favourite abode of the Vaikanasas, and Siddhas and Rishis. Moved by the desire of obtaining its protection, the Creator sang this verse at Pushkara, O chief of the Kurus and foremost of virtuous men! If a person of pure soul purposes a pilgrimage to the Pushkaras in imagination even, he becometh purged from all his sins and rejoiceth in heaven!'[27]*

Indian palaces could have had two types of holy place: shrines for family use and tanks for ritual cleansing. At a later date, shrines and permanent stone temples were

4.24 a, b *Rishis* are honoured, sometimes in gardens (Orchha, left, Lucknow, right). They carry forward Vedic metaphysical traditions.

built outside towns and became places of pilgrimage. In present-day India, there are innumerable shrines and temples inside and outside villages and private houses, and often both indoor and outdoor holy places dedicated to popular gods.

King Shudraka (*c.*100 BCE)

King Shudraka was the author, perhaps honorary, of a play which tells of young man's love for a courtesan in the city of Ujjain. The play is called *The Little Clay Cart* (*Mricchakatika*) and is one of the oldest Sanskrit plays, variously dated from 200 BCE to 400 CE. Much of the action takes place in palace courtyards, gardens and a park outside Ujjain. The detailed descriptions of courtyard use and character are the best from anywhere in Ancient Asia and may throw light on how palace courtyards were used in Egypt, Mesopotamia, Iran and China, as well as in India.

Shudraka's palace was entered through a doorway which had been sprinkled with water and decorated with flowers, so that the 'strings of jasmine garlands that hang down toss about like the trunk of the heavenly elephant'.[28] The portico had bright green mango twigs and jars of water stood between its pillars. The doors were golden and led into a palace with eight courtyards, which are described in Act IV:

1   The *first court* was designed to impress. It had: 'rows of balconies brilliant as the moon, or as sea-shells, or as lotus-stalks; whitened by handfuls of powder strewn over them, gleaming with golden stairways'. Receiving important guests was also a courtyard use in Egypt, Mesopotamia, China and Japan.

4.25 a–l No ancient Indian courtyards survive, but one can use examples of palaces and private houses from later periods to inform the imagination.

2   The *second court* contained bullocks with 'mouthfuls of grass and pulse-stalks which are brought them, right and left, by everybody. Their horns are smeared with oil'. Keeping valuable animals was one of the oldest courtyard uses, in Egypt, China and elsewhere.

3   The *third court* was for recreation and had 'seats, prepared for young gentle-men to sit on. A half-read book is lying on the gaming-table. And the table itself has its own dice, made out of gems. And here, again, are courtesans and old hangers-on at court.' The use of courtyards as living space for women is widely attested in Asia. Less is known about living space for the young men of the palace who enjoyed games and were supplied with female companions from an early age.

4   The *fourth court* was for music: 'the drums that maiden fingers beat are booming like thunder; the cymbals are falling, as the stars fall from heaven when their merit is exhausted' and 'a lute that somebody is holding on his lap like a girl who is excited by jealousy and love'. Music was part of palace life from early times. We now associate music with indoor space but in ancient India the primary use of enclosed rooms was sleeping; other activities took place under roofs supported by open pillars, and in courtyards.

5   The *fifth court* was for preparing food, 'kept hot all the time, and the gusts of steam, laden with all sorts of good smells'. Most cooking was done in court-yards, with the probable use of canopies for protection against rain and sun.

6   The *sixth court* was for craftwork: 'Rubies are being set in gold. Golden orna-ments are being fashioned. Pearls are being strung on a red cord.' The protec-tion of craftsmen, with their valuable tools and materials, was one of the main reasons for fortifying towns and much of their work was done in courtyards. Domestic courts are still used for work in many parts of Asia.

7   The *seventh court* was for caged birds: 'there is a parrot in a cage, chanting like a Brahman with a bellyful of curdled milk and rice. And here, again, is a talking thrush, chattering like a housemaid who spreads herself because somebody noticed her. A cuckoo, her throat still happy from tasting all sorts of fruit-syrups, is cooing like a procuress. Rows of cages are hanging from pegs. Quails are being egged on to fight. Partridges are being made to talk.' Birds were kept for their beauty, for their singing and for fighting, as well as for eggs and meat. Roman courtyards were also used for keeping birds.

8   The *eighth court* was for family use and the visitor noticed the mistress's brother wearing a 'silk cloak' and her mother wearing an 'expansive garment, sitting on the throne'. He remarked her 'greasy feet' and 'what an extensive belly the dirty old witch has got'. Domestic life was, of course, a primary court-yard function. Courts were places for old people to spend their time and for mothers to tend their children.

The courtyard descriptions had to be good, because Indian theatre did not use stage scenery. There is no mention of planting in the eight courts but the palace did have a

4.26 a, b Swings have always been popular in Indian gardens.

4.27 a, b The Ashoka tree (*Saraca indica* is sacred throughout India and valued for its flowers, foliage and medicinal qualities. The name means 'sorrow-less'. White jasmine is used in religious ceremonies, as a hair decoration and to flavour tea. The photograph is of *Jasminum molle*.

tree garden with a lily pond. Rooms must have opened onto interior courts and could also have opened onto tree gardens between the buildings and outer walls. The tree garden is described as follows:

> *Well! What a beautiful orchard! There are any numbers of trees planted here, and they are covered with the most wonderful flowers. Silken swings are hung under the thick-set trees, just big enough for a girl to sit in. The golden jasmine, the shephalika, the white jasmine, the jessamine, the navamallik, the amaranth, the spring creeper, and all the other flowers have fallen of themselves, and really, it makes Indra's heaven look dingy. And the pond here looks like the morning twilight, for the lilies and red lotuses are as splendid as the rising sun. And again: 'The ashoka tree, whose twigs so merry/ And crimson flowers have just appeared/ Seems like a battling mercenary,/With clotting crimson gore besmeared.'* [29]

No ancient Hindu house or courtyard plans survive but the above palace description from *The Little Clay Cart* can be read in conjunction with the first accurate topographic plans of India drawn by Europeans, initially for military use. One such plan shows an Indian town, Madurai, which appears to have been planned on *Vaastu Shastra* lines. As Shokoohy explains: 'It is clear that, as is usual with ancient South Indian towns, Madurai was designed based on the strict rules of Hindu town planning as expressed, for example, in Manasara Silpa.' [30] It is a theoretical square, not a geometrical square, but planned on a north–south axis with a palace near a temple. Tamil texts and some archaeological details suggest that the city is still in the location it was in 2,000 years ago. [31] The palace has courtyards which one can imagine being used in the ways described by King Shudraka.

Kalidasa (*c.*200 CE)

City life has always been hectic and India has an ancient tradition of holy men and women withdrawing to ashrams outside settlements. The word 'ashram' (from the Sanskrit *āsramah*, itself from *a-* + *sramah* 'effort, toil, austerity') is translated into English

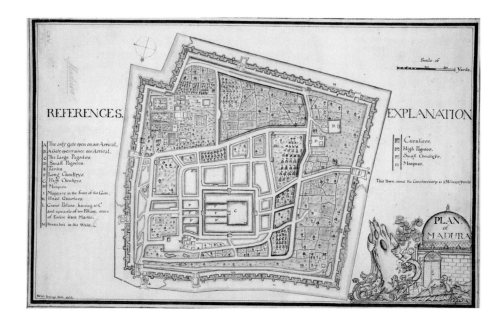

4.28 Plan of Madurai in 1755. The Tirumalai Nayak Palace (top left) survives and still has courtyards, but was rebuilt with the help of an Italian architect.

4.29 Girls carrying water pots in a palace garden (Deeg).

4.30 Flowers are still used as hair decorations.

as 'hermitage' (from the Greek *eremites* 'a person of the desert'). India had hermits centuries before the birth of Christ and the practice of withdrawing from society to live in deserts may have originated in Central Asia. One can imagine that with most people following the herds across the steppes, some individuals would choose a sedentary life of austerity and learning in a desert oasis or a sheltered valley.

Kalidasa is regarded as the foremost Sanskrit poet and dramatist, estimates of when he lived ranging from 100 BCE to 500 CE. He describes woodland ashrams with references to men and women. Ashrams were places to withdraw from towns for a life of prayer and study in natural surroundings. The daughter of a holy man attracted the king's attention.

> *Ah! here are the maidens of the hermitage coming this way to water the shrubs, carrying water-pots proportioned to their strength. How graceful they look! In palaces such charms are rarely ours. The woodland plants outshine the garden flowers.*[32]

Soon, the king announces that:

> *I have no longer any desire to return to the city. I will therefore rejoin my attendants, and make them encamp somewhere in the vicinity of this sacred grove.*[33]

Kalidasa re-tells the *Ramayana* story of a sage who lived in the woods and was tempted by a bathing nymph:

> *Some time since, this sage of regal caste, while performing a most severe penance on the banks of the River Godavarí, excited the jealousy and alarm of the gods; insomuch that they despatched a lovely nymph named Menaka to interrupt his devotions.*[34]

4.31 a, b The *Kama Sutra* advises that a virtuous woman (right, Orchha) should 'surround the house with a garden'. The carving (above, Khajurho) also appears in Figure 4.32 (below).

4.32 The erotic carvings at Khajuraho are often compared with the text of the *Kama Sutra*. It is thought they were made to allow the gods similar pleasures to those enjoyed in palace gardens.

The Godavari River is the second largest river in India, flowing east from Maharashtra to the Bay of Bengal. The inter-linked sweetness of girls, flowers and nature was a theme in Indian literature and flowers were often used as hair decorations.

The *Kama Sutra* (*c.*400)

The *Kama Sutra*, thought to date from *c.*400, is best known for its technical advice on sexual positions, apparently for gymnasts, but it also has useful information on flowers and gardens:

> *A virtuous woman ... should keep the whole house well cleaned, and arrange flowers of various kinds in different parts of it, and make the floor smooth and polished so as to give the whole a neat and becoming appearance. She should surround the house with a garden, and place ready in it all the materials required for the morning, noon and evening sacrifices ... In the garden she should plant beds of green vegetables, bunches of the sugar cane, and clumps of the fig tree, the mustard plant, the parsley plant, the fennel plant, and the xanthochymus pictorius. Clusters of various flowers such as the trapa bispinosa, the jasmine, the jasminum grandiflorum, the yellow amaranth, the wild jasmine, the tabernamontana coronaria, the nadyaworta, the china rose and others, should likewise be planted, together with the fragrant grass andropogon schaenanthus, and the fragrant root of the plant andropogon miricatus. She should also have seats and arbours made in the garden, in the middle of which a well, tank, or pool should be dug.*[35]

The advice for a young man is that he should have a house with a garden containing flowers and a swing:

4.33 a, b The principles of *Vastu Shastra* (building knowledge) and *Vaastu Shastra* (environment knowledge) could be used to plan a temple, a palace or a house. (Avantisvani and Martanda temples in Kashmir).

He should take a house in a city, or large village, or in the vicinity of good men, or in a place which is the resort of many persons. This abode should be situated near some water, and divided into different compartments for different purposes. It should be surrounded by a garden, and also contain two rooms, an outer and an inner one. The inner room should be occupied by the females ... In the garden there should be a whirling swing and a common swing, as also a bower of creepers covered with flowers, in which a raised parterre should be made for sitting.[36]

Viewing a garden can be the prelude to a royal seduction:

During the moonlight festival of the month of Kartika, and the spring festival of Chaitra, the women of cities and towns generally visit the women of the king's harem in the royal palace ... On such occasions a female attendant of the king (previously acquainted with the woman whom the king desires) should loiter about, and accost this woman when she sets out to go home, and induce her to come and see the amusing things in the palace ... Accordingly she should show her the bower of the coral creeper, the garden house with its floor inlaid with precious stones, the bower of grapes, the building on the water, the secret passages in the walls of the palace, the pictures, the sporting animals, the machines, the birds, and the cages of the lions and the tigers. After this, when alone with her, she should tell her about the love of the king for her, and should describe to her the good fortune which would attend upon her union with the king, giving her at the time a strict promise of secrecy.[37]

The scene described in this passage is familiar from Indian paintings of the late-Mughal era. Clearly, the building of gardens with shady bowers, exotic animals, choice fruits

4.36 a, b Ladies bathing and washing in a garden-like setting, in Kerala, and in a garden tank.

square measures'.[42] The 81 squares, on a north–south axis, are each associated with gods. The nine central squares are dedicated to Brahman and generally interpreted as a courtyard.

Water is important to *Vaastu Shastra* because 'deities reside with pleasure in places which abound in water and gardens, whether natural or otherwise'.[43] But 'since tanks and the like do not look charming without shade on their sides, one ought to have gardens laid out on the banks of water'.[44] Water is necessary for ritual washing: 'It may be done also in holy temples, near holy rivers, in gardens, in attractive regions, in a place where the earth slopes down towards the east or the north, or where the water flows from left to right.'[45] Varanasi satisfies these conditions. The site slopes east to the Ganges and if looking north to the Varuna, the water flows from left to right. India has many other holy cities with bathing *ghats* stepping down to holy rivers.

Footpaths are specified for special consideration in the *Brhat Samhita*:

> Outside the house there should be made a foot-path whose breadth must be a third of that of the hall. If the path is in front of the house, the latter is termed 'Sosnisa' – one with a turban; if it is behind the house, it is called 'Sayasraya' – Evening Resort; if it is on the two sides, it is designated as 'Savastambha' – Properly Supported; and if it is laid on all four sides, it is named 'Sushita' – well-placed. All these types are approved by the authorities on architecture.[46]

Interest in *Vaastu Shastra* is reviving but the information needs to be treated with caution. Pramar, following George Michell, believes the *Shastras* were written by priests, not builders, and should be seen as texts on art, not on building construction. Priests are more likely to have been involved in site selection and planning than in construction details.[47]

No cities, palaces or temples survive from the Vedic age but there are many examples of Hindu design from later periods in which echoes of principles found in the Vedic texts can be found, particularly with regard to site selection. Temples are found at *tirthas*, hill-tops, mountain slopes, forests, groves and gardens, near the abodes of the blest or hermitages, in villages, towns and cities or in any other lovely place.[48]

Conclusion

The evidence summarized above makes it possible to draw a few conclusions about the design of Indian gardens between 500 BCE and 500 CE. It is a 1000-year period and, for reasons of climate and culture, there are likely to have been significant geographical variations. More information will surely be uncovered but in the meantime I will risk some general remarks before proceeding to consider the period after 500 CE, and the influence of Buddhism, in the next chapter.

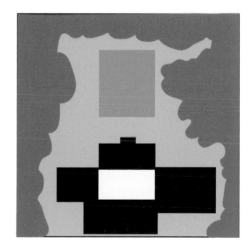

4.37 a, b India has many examples of tanks and pools in palace courts. The pool at Orchha (left) is now dry and the pool in the Lake Palace, Udaipur, (right) is managed as a luxury hotel.

4.38 The only information on gardens in ancient India is textual and relates to palace gardens which had courtyards and lotus ponds.

Vedic dwellings were built in timber and mud. The dwellings of kings, craftsmen and wealthy merchants required defence and were therefore built within fortified towns planned on a grid with a theoretical north–south axis. Palaces had both courtyards and gardens. Courtyards, integral to the design of many but not all dwellings, were primarily for living and working. It should not be assumed that they were square or even rectangular. They were probably mud-paved, swept, occasionally painted and part-furnished with cushions and rugs. Large dwellings could have several types of courtyard. One use was for the men to receive guests. Another was to create protected outdoor space in which women and children could cook, wash, weave and play. Gardens, better described as groves, were the urban equivalent of forest glades, and were probably positioned between courtyard dwellings and protective outer walls. They had flowering trees, stepped water tanks and one or more deep verandahs with thatched roofs supported by painted wood columns. Water was held in 'tanks' which may have been rectangular and may have had wooden steps on at least one side. There were communal village tanks and private palace tanks. Tanks in palace gardens, set amidst flowering and fruiting trees, were used for drinking, bathing, keeping fish and growing the sacred lotus. They were beautiful features with water glistening in the dappled light beneath overhanging trees. Kings would play chess or laze on the verandah while their wives and concubines played in the water or on swings. 'Lotus-eyed' was a popular compliment.

Outside palace compounds, Indian streets bustled with tradesmen and craftsmen, as they still do. Outside the city ramparts, lay small fields and vegetable gardens. By 500 BCE fields were predominantly used for grains and herbs. By 500 CE, they were also used for fruit and vegetables. One might call these horticultural areas 'gardens' but they were not places of pleasure and they were tended by lower castes, not the wealthy Kshatriyas or Brahmins. Confirmation of the distinctions between Indian garden types comes from the following note on origin of the *mali* caste:

4.39 Productive gardens were made outside city fortifications, often with low banks for flood irrigation

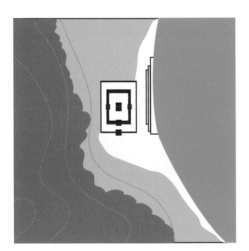

4.40 Riverside sites were used by *rishis* in Vedic times and the creation of temple enclosures began at an unknown date.

The name is derived from mala, a garland, and it would appear that the Mali was first employed to grow flowers for the garlands with which the gods and also their worshippers were adorned at religious ceremonies. Flowers were held sacred and were an essential adjunct to worship in India as in Greece and Rome. The sacred flowers of India are the lotus, the marigold and the champak and from their use in religious worship is derived the custom of adorning the guests with garlands at all social functions, just as in Rome and Greece they wore crowns on their heads. It seems not unlikely that this was the purpose for which cultivated flowers were first grown, at any rate in India. The Mali was thus a kind of assistant in the religious life of the village, and he is still sometimes placed in charge of the village shrines and is employed as temple-servant in Jain temples. He would therefore have been supported by contributions from the cultivators like the other village menials and have ranked below them, though on account of the purity and sanctity of his occupation Brahmans would take water from him. The Mali has now become an ordinary cultivator, but his status is still noticeably below that of the good cultivating castes and this seems to be the explanation.[49]

Constance Villiers-Stuart wrote admiringly of her *mali*'s skill:

I argued at great length against the mali's insistence that the walks should be raised above the garden level, unconsciously clinging, in my own mind, to the opposite English plan of the flat paths with their raised herbaceous borders. The mali won the day, though I was slow, I confess, to see the obvious fact that the walks, in an irrigated garden, must be necessarily raised for the water to pass under them. It was astonishing how quickly and willingly the work was done.[50]

4.41 a, b Stone construction was first used in Buddhist times, but the gardens of ancient India are known to have had pavilions and lotus ponds.

Making water channels was, however, more a lesson in Mughal than Hindu or Buddhist garden design.

Some land outside towns was set aside for sacred places and hunting parks. Shrines were dedicated at significant locations in the landscape: at the junctions of rivers and where hills could be seen. Sacred trees were revered in towns and in the countryside. When stone building began, bathing *ghats* and permanent temples were built on sacred sites but, as in Ancient Greece, the places are likely to have been sacred long before the structures were built. If ascetics or *rishis* were in residence, the place became an *ashram* (hermitage). In early times, animal sacrifices were performed in holy places. In later times, the same sites were used for building shrines and performing acts of worship (*puja*). Jain and Buddhist ideas, discussed in the next chapter, hastened the end of animal sacrifice in mainstream Hindu culture. The essential Hindu garden design concept (a crystal pond in a glade of flowering trees) survived into Buddhist design practice.

4.42 A popular painting of Krishna and Radha captures something of the character of ancient Hindu gardens.

CHAPTER 5

Buddhist gardens

5.1 The eight-spoked Wheel of Dharma symbolizes the Noble Eightfold Path. It leads to *nirvana*, which came to be represented by Buddhist temples in gardens. The Wheel on the Jokhang Temple, beside the Potala in Tibet, is flanked by deer. Buddhism had a profound influence on the design of parks and gardens. Tibetan culture relates to the culture of both India and China.

5.2 The Jokhang Temple represented in a garden setting and the courtyards are in use.

Siddhartha Gautama was born in a classical Hindu garden and raised as a Hindu prince. Meditating under a tree at Bodh Gaya he became enlightened. Gaya was the town's name. *Bodh* means 'knowledge'; *Buddha* means 'the one who has attained all knowledge' and who thus became 'The Enlightened One'. The Lord Buddha's first sermon was delivered seven weeks later in a deer park at Sarnath outside Varanasi. This set the Wheel of Dharma in motion. In the millennium following his death, the historical Buddha came to be treated as a god-like figure and Buddhism came to resemble the devotional religions. But the association with trees, parks and gardens continued, with vast consequences for garden design. Temples, monasteries and princely gardens came to be designed as places for contemplative devotion. This trend began in India and bore rich fruit in Sri Lanka, South East Asia, Tibet, China and Japan. Buddhism became the religious tradition with the most extensive influence on park and garden design. A type of enclosed outdoor space can be associated with each of

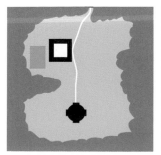 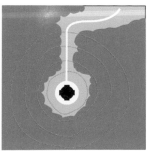 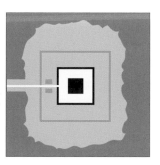

5.3 a Early *stupas* and monasteries were in garden groves; **b** Mahayana *stupas* and temples were often on hills; **c** in South East Asia, temple-mountains were built by god-kings who saw themselves as Bodhisattvas.

5.4 Buddhist monks amongst roses at Bodh Gaya.

the main groups of Buddhist School. Collectively, they are described in this chapter as sanctuaries, meaning sacred spaces. Individually, they can be described as sacred groves, monastic gardens, temple gardens and temple-palace gardens. Different types of sanctuary became characteristic of the various Buddhist sects:

- *Theravada sanctuaries* were often former princely gardens and parks, which were lent to monks for the monsoon season and became permanent monasteries (e.g. Jetavana and Anuradhapura).
- *Mahayana sanctuaries* were often in scenic areas and had *stupas*, monasteries and temples to inspire and inform pilgrims (e.g. Sanchi and Sigiriya).
- *Vajrayana sanctuaries* were symbolic mountains, often on real mountains and built to commemorate the lives of Bodhisattvas, who could be holy men or kings (e.g. Borobudur and Angkor Wat).
- *Sukhavati sanctuaries* were Pure Land Gardens, made under the influence of the three *Pure Land Sutras*. It is not known if any were made in India and those made in China have not survived. Japanese gardens made under the influence of this idea will be discussed in Chapter 7 (e.g. Motsu-ji and Joruri-ji).
- *Zen sanctuaries* were designed for an austere and contemplative form of Buddhism, often using gravel and rocks to make symbolic landscapes (e.g. Ryoan-ji, Saiho-ji).

The distinctions between Buddhist sects are clean in theory but overlap in practice, because the schools formed a community and influenced each other. Coomaraswamy made the following point:

> *The distinction between Hinayana (or Theravada) and Mahayana Buddhism is to a great extent the distinction between rationalism and mysticism. Theravada Buddhism is a doctrine perfectly adapted to the needs of intellectual minds of the aesthetic temperament. It would devote the whole energy of man directly to the attainment of release (Nirvana) from this world of eternal becoming (Samsara). Its genius is essentially monastic.* [1]

Theravada monks sought landscapes and groves with the necessary seclusion for contemplation. At first, they slept under trees and in mountain caves. Later, they welcomed the hospitality in princely gardens and accepted charity from wealthy townsmen. But the first Theravada monks owned no property and made no images. It was Mahayana Buddhism which initiated the art and architecture of Buddhism. Therefore, 'the whole of Buddhist art properly so called … is Mahayana art'. [2] Seeking mystical contact with spiritual truths, Buddhist pilgrims found the experience of physical objects helpful. Mahayana sanctuaries, as places with sacred images, attracted holy men and pilgrims. Design ideas from the Hindu tradition were adapted in gardens and groves. Buddhism, in its turn, influenced Hindu art and architecture.

The further development of Buddhist Gardens, as they are loosely categorized in this chapter's title, continued outside India. Vajrayana Sanctuaries resulted from the idea that certain 'enlightened beings' (Bodhisattvas) remain on earth to help others on the path to enlightenment. When kings realized they too could be Bodhisattvas, elaborate temple compounds like Borobudur and Angkor Wat were made. Pure Land Buddhist Gardens, in Japan, derive from a related theory. Many were founded by retired emperors who became abbots and built paradise gardens on earth, both to help others and to assist their individual preparation for nirvana. Another strand of Buddhism (Zen) drew principles from the older schools: the austerity of Theravada Buddhism, the mysticism of Mahayana Buddhism, and the symbolism of Pure Land Buddhism. The classical Japanese Zen garden, as discussed in Chapter 7, evolved between c.700 and 1700.

Siddhartha Gautama, 563–483 BCE

Siddhartha Gautama, the future Lord Buddha, was born in Kapilavastu, capital of the Sakya kingdom. Kapilavastu is in a part of Nepal now called the Terrai ('moist land') and home to the Tharu people, thought to be part-tribal and part-Mongol.[3] The Terrai is low-lying and marchy, collecting water from the Himalayan foothills. Buddha's father ruled a kingdom which, like his son's faith, drew upon the culture of both the mountains (to the north) and the plains (to the south). His city, Kapilavastu, is on a low hill. Northward, the Bon religion of the Himalayas was animistic and monastic; southward, the religion of the plains was Hindu. Buddha's mother, Queen Maya Devi, gave birth to the young prince in the Lumbini Palace Garden, 26 km east of Kapilavastu. Lumbini became a place of legend and pilgrimage, as recorded by the Chinese pilgrim, Fa-hsien (or Fa Xian), in c.400:

Fifty li east from the city (of Kapilavastu) was a garden, named Lumbini, where the queen entered the pond and bathed. Having come forth from the pond on the northern

5.5 a, b The Terrai ('moist land'), at the foot of the Himalayas, is where Siddhartha Gautama was born.

5.6 a, b Kapilavastu (in Nepal) was the capital of the Sakya kingdom. It is on a low hill in the Terrai. The trees are growing in fragments of the brick city wall. The above photo shows the eastern city gate and the right photo shows lotus growing in a water tank (*baoli*).

5.7 The Buddha's childhood home was Kapilavastu. The Rohini River formerly ran east of the town. 'Beautiful gardens, groves, orchards, tanks and luxurious resorts were abundant in the Sakya Kingdom.'*

Note: *Rijal, B.K., *100 Years of Archaeological Research in Lumbini, Kapilavastu and Devadaha*, Kathmandu: S.K. International, 1996, p. 23.

bank, after walking twenty paces, she lifted up her hand, laid hold of a branch of a tree, and, with her face to the east, gave birth to the heir-apparent. When he fell to the ground, he immediately walked seven paces. Two dragon-kings appeared and washed his body. At the place where they did so, there was immediately formed a well, and from it, as well as from the above pond, where the queen bathed, the monks even now constantly take the water, and drink it.[4]

The garden described in the above passage is unsurprisingly similar to the Hindu gardens described in the preceding chapter and tallies with post-1896 archaeological excavations at Lumbini. The garden's stepwell, now called the Sacred Pond, is surrounded by modern steps which perhaps had wooden predecessors. Siddhartha Gautama married at the age of 16 and lived in the palace at Kapilavastu until, at the age of 29, he decided to become a wandering ascetic. Six years later, having almost starved to death, he accepted buttermilk from a goatherd and sat to meditate under a tree at Bodh Gaya. Enlightenment dawned and the tree was never forgotten. It became world-famous as the Bodhi ('Enlightenment') tree – a Peepal, *Ficus religiosa*. Seven weeks later Siddhartha Gautama delivered the sermon in the hunting park at Sarnath outside Varanasi which set the Wheel in motion:

At Varanasi, in the Deer Park at Isipatana, this unsurpassed Wheel of the Dhamma has been set in motion by the Blessed One, which cannot be stopped by any recluse or brahmin or deva or Mara or Brahma or by anyone in the world.[5]

A community of Buddhist monks was established and its members began to travel throughout North India as mendicants and teachers. Much of their work was done

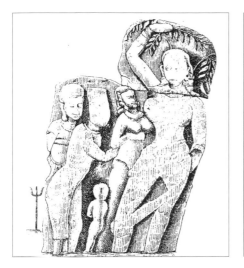

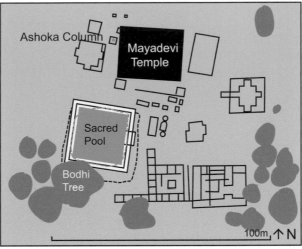

5.8 a, b The carving of Queen Maya Devi and the Buddha child found at Lumbini. The water tank belonged to a palace at the time of his birth and is now a sacred pond in a temple garden.

in rural areas. The Gautama family belonged to the Kshatriya (warrior) caste. The Brahmin (priestly) caste believed Kshatriyas could never be priests. But the new faith was unrestricted. Anyone could become a monk and the path to salvation was open to everyone. Caste-free openness helped the new faith gather support among the non-priestly castes of merchants, warriors and farmers. Pramar, who argues that Buddhism was always a religion of merchants and travellers, traces the monastic architectural tradition to Central Asia.[6] In hot deserts, there was no alternative to travelling by night and sleeping during the day. In cold deserts, the reverse was true; in both, and in much

5.9 The Bodhi Tree at Lumbini marks the Buddha's birthplace. The water tank was part of the garden in his mother's family home. The stone surround is modern.

5.10 The Bodhi Tree at Bodh Gaya is where the Buddha meditated and became enlightened

5.11 a, b, c Footprints and other images came to be worshipped as symbols of the Buddha's presence.

of Central Asia, there was a system of *caravanserais* ('caravan palaces') which had a similar physical form to the early Buddhist monasteries of India. Sleeping cells were grouped round courtyards.

Buddhist symbolism

The Buddha discouraged images of his person. Seeking only to inspire and teach, he had no wish for godlike status. But his disciples felt a need for memorial images of the Blessed One and therefore made symbolic representations of their master: a set of Footprints, an Empty Throne, a Begging Bowl, a Bodhi Tree, an Eight-Spoked Circle. The latter was represented by a chariot wheel (*Dharmachakra*). *Dharma* is a Hindu term for the natural laws on which the world is founded and *chakra* means wheel. A *Chakravartin* is a Universal King who 'sets the wheel in motion'.[7]

In Europe, natural law is seen as a foundation for statute law and civil society. In India, *dharma* is performed by doing one's duty in accordance with natural and divine law. In Hinduism, the nature of life is understood as an endless cycle of rebirth. In Buddhism, the *Dharmachakra*, which can be translated into English as 'Wheel of Law' or 'Wheel of Life', is the great Wheel. It turns as pilgrims advance on life's path. They seek release (*moksha*) from the endless cycle of suffering and rebirth (*samsara*). Buddha set the Wheel in motion. Its Eight Spokes symbolize the Noble Eightfold Path to salvation. The *Dharmachakra* turns once for hearing, once for understanding, and once for learning. Those who follow the path can hope to reach *nirvana*, the condition of peace beyond

5.12 a, b, c The Buddha died in the shade of a Sal Tree (*Shorea robusta*), at Kushinagar, and was cremated at a spot now marked by a brick mound. Below, a statue of the dying Buddha at Kushinagar.

desire. The Buddha attained nirvana when he died, as he had been born, in a verdant grove in the shade of a sal tree (*Shorea robusta*). The Noble Eightfold Path describes the way to escape from suffering. It involves wisdom, ethical conduct and mental development. The eight steps are interdependent: Right View, Right Intention, Right Speech, Right Action, Right Livelihood, Right Effort, Right Mindfulness and Right Concentration. Nature symbols, including trees, have an elevated status in Buddhism.

The first Buddhist Council was held shortly after Siddhartha Gautama's death and measures were taken to continue the master's teaching. Buddhism became the world's first missionary religion, making it essential for the faith's underlying principles to be expressed with simplicity and understood with ease. Buddhism was therefore explained in the people's tongue (*Prakrit*), instead of the priest's tongue (*Sanskrit*), and with what we would call visual aids: painting, sculpture, architecture and landscape. Hindu culture was as old as time. Buddhist culture arose from the teaching of an inspired individual, every detail of whose life therefore had to be remembered for posterity. His sermons were memorized and passed from tongue to ear, as the Vedas had been. Stories about his last incarnation, and all his previous lives, were endlessly retold. Eventually, they were written down and, probably because of its permanence, stone came to be used for architecture and sculpture. Ornamented structures were built in gardens and groves.

Towards the end of his life Buddha suggested that his funerary remains might be placed under a burial mound, which came to be known as a *stupa*. The word derives from the Sanskrit verb *stup*, 'to heap'. Simple earthen burial mounds (*kurgans*) are found across

5.13 a, b The *stupas* at Sanchi are shaped like *kurgans* (see p. 56).

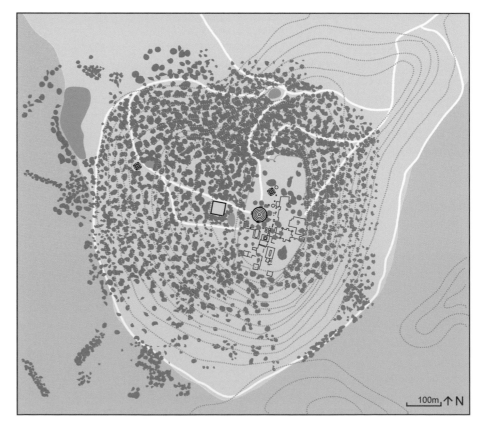

5.14 a, b Sanchi, which has *stupas* and monasteries on a hill, is approached by a pilgrims' ascent-path.

the Eurasian Steppes and North East Europe (see p. 56). Buddhist architecture became increasingly elaborate to attract pilgrims. *Stupas* were built for several reasons: to mark events in the Buddha's life; to contain the ashes of holy men; to commemorate visits by pilgrims to holy sites; to explain and teach Buddhist philosophy. Of the first eight *stupas*, one was at Lumbini and one 'in the garden of Jeta at Sravasti, where the great miracle occurred'.[8] The miracle involved multiple representations of the Buddha. He appeared seated, standing on lotuses and with fire emanating from his body. An intricate symbolic language for the design of *stupas* was established and it became ever more complex as it spread beyond India. The symbolism is not set out in old texts but is interpreted as follows:

- The square base of a *stupa* symbolizes the earth and the four cardinal directions.
- The dome symbolizes the water from which life arose.
- The cone symbolizes fire and the wisdom which destroys ignorance.
- The crescent symbolizes the sky.
- The circular disc symbolizes the wholeness of life.
- The pole above the dome points up to heaven and down to the sacred relics buried in the earth.
- The path symbolizes the journey.

Stupas and temples evolved together. Buddhists continued to employ Brahmin priests for the rituals of birth and death and also followed Vedic practice in relating architecture to landscape. The *Brhat Samhita* (see p. 134) recommends that temple sites should be 'in the vicinity of forests, rivers, mountains and waterfalls' and explains the ritual (mandala) for temple planning: 'the temple site should always be divided into 64 squares. Its central or main gate would be auspicious if situated in one of the four cardinal directions.'[9] No design account of Sanchi exists but the traditional Hindu procedure appears to have been followed. Located on a hill in a forest and south of a range of hills, the Great Stupa at Sanchi has gates facing north, south, east and west. Given the always-close relationship between Hindu and Buddhist architecture, and the fact that stone was worked by men belonging to the same caste (Vaishyas), one can assume that traditional mandala rituals were performed at the inauguration of Sanchi. Nelson Wu wrote:

> As a pilgrim approaches the hill on which the stupa stands, as in the case of the Great Stupa (Stupa I) of Sanchi, the silhouette of the structure against the sky, and particularly the central mast (yasti) will immediately attract his attention. This view at a distance, its strong general statements completely free of details and refinements, may be compared with the religious experience of accepting the fundamental commandments before the rituals and the practice of the vows create issues out of them. It is the primary revelation of truth to be followed by agonizing paths in which one loses sight of it until the time of final salvation.[10]

5.15 a, b The Sanchi Sangharama, as seen by a pilgrim approaching the hill on which the *stupa* stands and, above, pilgrims leaving the Great Stupa enclosure.

It has been suggested[11] that the Sanskrit noun mandala derives from *manda* (meaning 'essence' or 'best part') and *la* (meaning 'container' or 'signpost'), so that a ritual mandala defines 'an essence within a container'. Any kind of cycle, either abstract or concrete, can be a mandala, including the sun, the moon, a circle, a sacred place or a ritual. A square, which defines a circle, can be used to plan a temple. Stella Kramrisch wrote:

> *It is drawn on the ground prior to the building of the temple and on it the temple stands either in fact or symbolically. In principle it is always square and is the record of an architectural rite ... The square is divided into compartments and the diagonals are drawn. The name of the square is Vastupurusamandala. Purusa is the universal Essence, the Principle of all things, the Prime Person whence all originates. Vastu is the site; in it Vastu, bodily existence, abides and from it Vastu derives its name ... The temple building is the substantial, and the 'plan' (mandala) is the ritual, diagrammatic form of the Purusa.*[12]

Pramar criticizes this interpretation, because it derives from art history rather than construction history. He believes the shape of a *stupa* is more likely to come from the shape of a nomad tent and that the central pole was merely a way of inscribing the circle.[13] But Kramrisch's view has much support. Squares and circles are assumed to symbolize heaven and the earth. The central pole is:

> *understood to symbolize the axis mundi in later traditions, but in early monuments is probably a reference to the pre-Buddhist cult of sacred trees. The incorporation of such pillars in stupas demonstrates the process by which sacred trees, such as the Bodhi tree, were replaced by stupas as symbols of enlightenment in Buddhist thought.*[14]

5.16 a, b, c Mandalas are placed on pavements and used to plan *stupas*. Boudhanath (below left) is on an ancient trade route and has one of the largest *stupas* in the world.

5.17 Buddhist monks still produce temple garden mandalas as part of their training.

Sacred trees were common throughout Asia and Europe at that time. Forests were also symbolically significant and sacred groves became important in Buddhism. The sermon which set the Wheel in motion had been delivered in a deer park, which remains a deer park. Though no longer used for hunting, it has a Bodhi Tree planted to mark the spot where the first Buddhists gathered to hear their master.

Once the Wheel had been set in motion, Buddhists began to travel and teach. They slept under trees or in temporary shelters, as Hindu ascetics had always done. When travel became impossible during the monsoon season, they looked for places to rest and meditate. Wealthy merchants donated land for this purpose and monastic communities, called *sangharama*, were founded. The word *sangha* was used for the entire community of Buddhist monks and the word *sangharama* for a specific community (from *sangha*, community and *arama*, garden or grove). A *sangharama* became a visual symbol of Buddhism and the groves became places of pilgrimage.

5.18 a, b The Buddha's first discourse (the Dhamma Chakka Pavattana Katha – 'Setting the Wheel of Dharma in Motion') was delivered under a Bodhi tree in the deer park at Sarnath (Ispatana) (above). The tree in the photograph is in the same location as the original tree. The model in the foreground is of the Buddha delivering his sermon (left).

In Mahayana and Vajrayana schools, the Buddha was worshipped like a god and his image became the central icon for Buddhist art. Sculptors made statues of him; artists painted him; architects made temples to house the artwork. In Tibet, drawing graphic mandalas with coloured sands became part of a monk's training. Like temple gardens elsewhere, mandalas illustrate relationships between an enlightened individual, the creation, the cosmos and the natural world. The relationship between nature and man came to have a great significance for garden design. In India and China, early temples were carved from living rock. In Japan, garden designers made physical representations of paradise (temple gardens) in which to place temples. These artistic and architectural developments took Buddhism on a spiritual and geographical path away from its meditational origin, beneath the shade of a North Indian tree.

Buddhism became a missionary religion, assisted by royal patronage. The faith was adopted by King Ashoka (272–232 BCE), and spread with the Mauryan Empire through North and Central India. It also split into schools, partly because the Buddha had not written a book and partly because he had not defined a procedure for choosing leaders. Current Buddhist schools are divided into three categories (Nikaya, Mahayana, and Vajrayana). Each is associated with a type of sanctuary. Following the Buddha's teaching as closely as possible, the Nikaya schools revered the volumes (*nikaya*) in which his disciples recorded their master's teaching. Theravada Buddhism is the only surviving Nikaya school. *Theravada* means the doctrine (*vada*) of the elder monks (*thera*). Those who follow the doctrines of the elders are the most tradition-conscious Buddhists. 'Southern Buddhism' is sometimes used as an alternative name to 'Theravada Buddhism' but the various Buddhist schools have influenced each other and neither geographical nor doctrinal boundaries are as distinct as their names imply.

Theravada sanctuaries

Buddha spent nineteen monsoon seasons living in the Jetavana ('Jeta Grove') near the ancient city of Sravasti. The site is mentioned in the *Ramayana* and belonged to Prince Jeta when first visited by the Buddha. It was a beautiful garden and the prince said 'No' when a wealthy merchant, Anathapindika ('Feeder of the Poor'), tried to buy the garden for the Buddhist community. Prince Jeta said he would not sell 'even if you could cover the whole place with money' but changed his mind when Anathapindika used gold for this purpose. It is now a garden grove on an eminence rising above the surrounding swamps and paddy fields. During the rainy season it is cool, soft and calm with views over a misty and saturated landscape. The hut where Buddha slept (*Gandhakuti* – 'the fragrant hut') stands near a water tank and is spread with flowers by pilgrims. The Jetavana grew into a famous monastery and a place

5.19 Plan of the Jetavana at Sravasti.

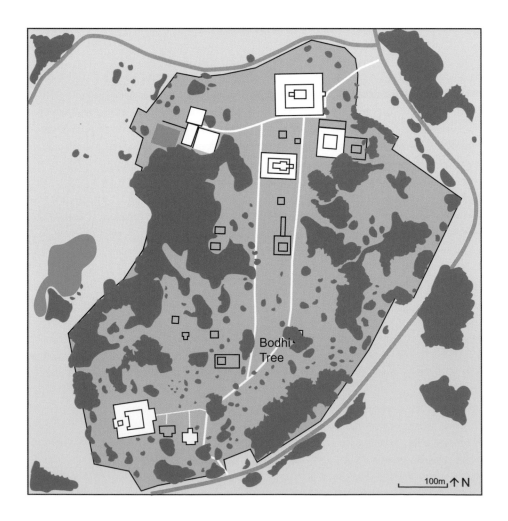

152

5.20 a–d The Jetavana at Sravasti is where the Buddha lived during the monsoon and Jataka Story No. 75 (Maccha-Jataka) records him saying 'Bring me a bathing-dress, Ananda; for I would bathe in the tank of Jetavana.'

of pilgrimage, exerting its influence throughout the Buddhist world. Pilgrims came from China, Sri Lanka and elsewhere and were told about the Buddha and his life. For example:

> *This story the Master told while at Jetavana, about the rain he caused to fall. For in those days, so it is said, there fell no rain in Kosala; the crops withered; and everywhere the ponds, tanks, and lakes dried up. Even the pool of Jetavana by the embattled gateway of Jetavana gave out; and the fish and tortoises buried themselves in the mud. Then came the crows and hawks with their lance-like beaks, and busily picked them out writhing and wriggling, and devoured them. As he marked how the fishes and the tortoises were being destroyed, the Master's heart was moved with compassion, and he exclaimed, 'This day must I cause rain to fall.' So, when the night grew day, after attending to his bodily needs, he waited till it was the proper hour to go the round in quest of alms, and then, girt round by a host of the Brethren, and perfect with the perfection of a Buddha, he went into Savatthi for alms. On his way back to the monastery in the afternoon from his round for alms in Savatthi, he stopped upon the steps leading down to the tank of Jetavana, and thus addressed the Elder Ananda: 'Bring me a bathing-dress, Ananda; for I would bathe in the tank of Jetavana.' 'But surely, sir,' replied the Elder, 'the water is all dried up, and only mud is left.' 'Great is a Buddha's power, Ananda. Go, bring me the bathing-dress,' said the Master.*[15]

Another Jataka story describes a garden made by the Buddha in a previous life: 'The king came to the place, and beheld a garden girt with a fence of eighteen cubits, vermilion tinted, having gates and ponds, beautiful with all manner of trees laden heavy with flowers and fruit!'[16]

153

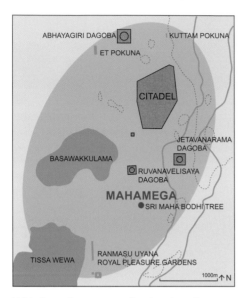

5.21 Anuradhapura was the site of a palace, a town and a *vihara* (monastery). The Mahameghavana (Great Rain-cloud Grove) is drawn as an oval because its boundary is unknown.

5.22 Anuradhapura has bathing tanks surrounded by trees (the Kuttam Pokuna).

Theravada Buddhism remains strong in Sri Lanka and the 'Resplendent Island' has several examples of Theravada groves. The island was settled by Indo-Aryans from North India and became a Hindu country with a caste system. In the third century BCE, King Devanampiya Tissa received a visit from the son of India's King Ashoka. Tissa became a Buddhist and converted his country to the new faith. Sri Lanka remains a centre for Buddhist scholarship with a strong literary tradition and a firm adherence to the 'Way of the Elders' who had created and established the faith in North East India. Possibly for this reason, Sri Lanka took a greater interest in recording its history than its northern neighbour. *The Mahavansa* (Great Chronicle), written in the fifth century CE, tells the history of Sri Lanka and has information on early Theravada groves.

One of the stories in *The Mahavansa* tells of monks who visited King Devanampiya Tissa's capital city at Anuradhapura. In the evening they set off for the hills, to sleep beneath the trees in traditional Buddhist fashion. The King offered them his palace garden as an alternative. He called it a Nandana Garden after Indra's garden on Mount Meru (see p. 12) but the elders (*theras*), declined his offer, explaining that the garden was too near the city and might distract them. King Tissa therefore offered his Mahamegha Garden instead. They accepted and it became a Theravada grove. Here is *The Mahavansa* account:

> So, there in the grove, evening fell. Then the theras set forth saying: 'We will go hence to the mountain.' And they told the king, and the king came with all speed. Approaching the thera he said: 'It is evening-time, and the mountain is far away; but here in the Nandana-garden is a pleasant place to rest.' When they answered: 'It is not fitting for us to be too near the city,' the king said: 'The Mahamegha-park is neither too far nor too near; it is pleasant and water and shade abound there; may it please you to rest there!' ... When the king had bidden them prepare fine beds and chairs in fitting wise, in the pleasant royal dwelling, and had taken leave of the theras, saying: 'Dwell here in comfort,' he returned to the city, surrounded by his ministers; but the theras sojourned there that night. As soon as the morning came, the ruler of the land took flowers and visited the theras, greeting them and offering flowers in homage, and he asked them: 'Was your rest pleasant? Is the garden fitting for you?' 'Pleasant was our rest, O great king, and the garden is fitting for ascetics.'[17]

The name Mahameghavana comes from *Maha* meaning great, *megha* meaning rain-cloud and *vana* meaning grove, garden or park. *The Mahavansa* explains why the garden was named after a 'Great Rain Cloud':

> The king laid out the beautiful Mahameghavana, rich in all the good qualities that its name promises and provided with fruit trees and flowering-trees. At the time that the place was chosen for the garden, a great cloud, gathering at an unwonted season, poured forth rain; therefore they called the garden Mahameghavana.[18]

Anuradhapura, where the Mahameghavana is located, was abandoned in the tenth century and designated a World Heritage Site in the twentieth century. Part of the grove is now the Ranmasu Uyana Royal Pleasure Ground (Gold Fish Park). The description quoted above fits its surviving archaeological features and provides a reasonable picture of the Mahameghavana's former condition. It was a grove of flowering trees and fruit trees with tanks of water for bathing, fish, aquatic plants and irrigation. The Mahavihara ('Great Monastery') which is the centre of Theravada Buddhism in Sri Lanka, was on the site and it contains the oldest chronicled tree in the world – the sacred Sri Maha Bodhi Tree (*Ficus religiosa*) planted in 288 BCE.

The acceptance by Buddhist monks of comfortable accommodation in the gardens of wealthy men led to the development of large brick-built monasteries, often near royal palaces and in association with *stupas*, temples and sanctuaries. These developments were characteristic of Mahayana Buddhism. The new school had a period of popularity in Sri Lanka but by the tenth century the island had returned to its Theravada origins.

Mahayana sanctuaries

Mahayana (Greater Vehicle) Buddhism developed in North West India and after the first century BCE became influential elsewhere. The word is a compound of *maha*, meaning great, and *yana*, meaning vehicle, journey, or path. Mahayana texts sought to bring all Buddhist thought into a single 'great vehicle' to speed pilgrims along the path to nirvana. The ideas might have been influenced by the Bhagavad Gita, the Hindu Song of God. Mahayana Buddhism offers the possibility of salvation from the evils of this world to everyone who worships the Lord Buddha and leads a life of compassion,

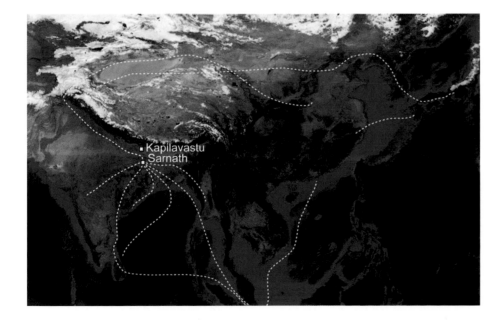

5.23 Buddhism originated in North East India and spread through Asia by land and sea.

5.24 A Kushan carving with the flowing robes characteristic of Graeco-Roman sculpture.

5.25 Painted wood columns, of the kind Ashoka's palace might have had, are still used elsewhere (Samarkand).

charity, self-sacrifice and altruism. Such a person can become a Bodhisattva ('wise being').

Two centuries after the Buddha's death, King Ashoka 'made Buddhism a kind of state religion',[19] as discussed above, and sent Buddhist missionaries to South India, Sri Lanka, Syria and Egypt. He also financed the *stupas* and sanctuaries which led Buddhism towards becoming a devotional religion. Ashoka admired the civilizations of Greece, Iran and Mesopotamia and welcomed visitors from these countries to his capital city in Pataliputra. The following account, attributed to Megasthenes, is thought to describe the palace garden at Pataliputra in the second or third century:

> *In the Indian royal palace where the greatest of all the kings of the country resides, besides much else which is calculated to excite admiration, and which neither Memnonian Susa with all its costly splendour, nor Ecbatana with all its magnificence can vie... there are other wonders besides, which I cannot undertake to describe in this treatise. In the parks tame peacocks are kept, and pheasants which have been domesticated; and among cultivated plants there are some to which the king's servants attend with special care, for there are shady groves and pasture-grounds planted with trees, and branches of trees which the art of the woodsman has deftly interwoven. And these trees, from the unusual benignity of the climate, are ever in bloom, and, untouched by age, never shed their leaves; and while some are native to the soil, others are with circumspect care brought from other parts, and with their beauty enhance the charms of the landscape. The olive is not of the number, this being a tree which is neither indigenous to India, nor thrives when transported thither. Birds and other animals that wander at freedom and have never been tamed resort of themselves to India and there build their nests and form their lairs ... Within the palace grounds there are also ponds of great beauty in which they keep fish of enormous size but quite tame. No one has permission to fish for these except the king's sons while yet in their boyhood. These youngsters amuse themselves without the least risk of being drowned while fishing in the unruffled sheet of water and learning how to sail their boats.*[20]

When the great hall of Ashoka's palace was excavated, 'enough fragments remained to show that the plan of this hall corresponded very closely to the arrangement of the great pillared rooms of state that are among the most striking remains of the Achaemenid palace ruins at Persepolis in Iran.'[21] Combining the archaeological findings with the above account, we can assemble a picture of Ashoka's palace garden. The palace had painted wooden columns supporting a pillared hall. Columns of this type survive elsewhere in Asia. The garden contained tanks of water, lush plantings of fruiting and flowering trees, fish and brightly coloured birds. The details may have resembled an Achaemenid garden but the use of water was different: it was in static tanks, not flowing channels. This was necessary in India because of the long dry season. Irrigation had been practised in India since Vedic times but the channels were used to conduct water from rivers. There were no fast-flowing streams from nearby

mountains, as in Persia. King Ashoka's palace was within the city and his garden is not likely to have had a shrine, because daily acts of worship were not then part of Buddhist practice. But Ashoka's *stupas* were often built in former palace gardens.

The first eight *stupas* were on sites connected to the Buddha's life and teaching: therefore all were in North East India. When the faith spread beyond this region, the Buddha's ashes were distributed between thousands of new *stupas* in places unconnected with the Buddha's life. Many were in monasteries and monastic groves (*sangharama*) evolved from temporary retreats into permanent establishments. Three site selection principles were used for *stupa* sites. The first was to find places where monks had lived and died, including monasteries. The second, drawn from Hindu practice, was to choose sites with scenic and sacred significance, on hills near rivers. The hill could symbolize Mount Meru (see p. 12) and gave the *stupa* prominence. Monks had traditionally slept in caves and a grove on a hill was in the tradition of Buddha spending the monsoon at Jetavana. The formation of permanent monastic communities gave rise to the third site selection principle, drawn from a *Vinaya* story about a man who had found a place for the Buddha to rest:

5.26 a, b Buddhist caves at Ajanta and Udaigiri.

Where now shall I fix the place for the Blessed One to stay in, not too far from the town and not too near, convenient for going and for coming, easily accessible for all who wish to visit him, by day not too crowded, by night not exposed to too much noise and alarm, protected from the wind, hidden from men, well fitted for a retired life?[22]

'Not too near and not too far' became the key principle for locating a *sangharama*. 'Not too near' a town gave the necessary seclusion for meditation. 'Not too far' from a town meant the monks did not have to travel too far to collect the alms on which they lived. The best preserved monastic grove in India is at Sanchi near the River Betwa. It has no association with the Buddha's own life but was used by monks who presumably found it 'not too near and not too far' from the important Buddhist town of Vidisha, at the confluence of the River Betwa and the River Bes. Several *stupas* were built on the hill of Sanchi and a beautiful pilgrim's path winds upward through the dry woods. The grove had residential quarters for monks and several stepwells survive.

Southern Buddhism

Mahayana *stupas* and monasteries were built in South India, many around the rivers Godavari and Kistna (e.g. Amaravati), and also in Sri Lanka. These places had not been visited by the historical Buddha and had no connection with Buddhism before the arrival of missionaries.

5.27 Sigiriya, the best example of a Buddhist garden in the Indian subcontinent, was primarily monastic but may also have been a palace garden for a time.

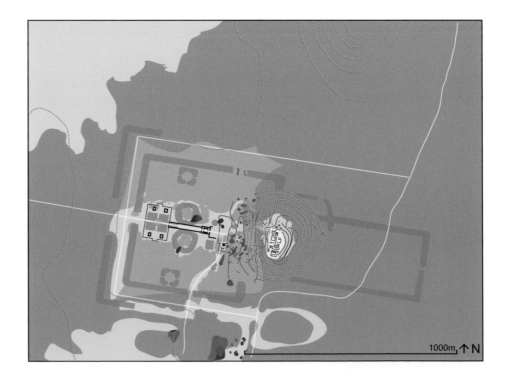

1000m, ↑ N

5.28 a The Lion Gate at Sigiriya, of which only the paws survive, probably symbolized the Lion of the Sakyas (The Buddha); **b** The water garden at Sigiriya.

In addition to Anuradhapura, described above, Sri Lanka has, at Sigiriya, a monastic grove of great interest to garden historians. The history of Sri Lanka (*The Mahavansa*) records that:

> [Sigiriya] *is difficult of ascent for human beings. He cleared (the land) round about, surrounded it with a wall and built a staircase in the form of a lion. He collected treasures and kept them there well protected and for the (riches) kept by him he set guards in different places. Then he built there a fine palace.*[23]

Sigiriya was built on and around a volcanic plug which rises 250 m out of the jungle. A perimeter dyke encloses land around its base, with archaeological remains of buildings at both the high and low levels and a water garden at the low level. The brick-built paws of what was once a lion gate survive. It was perhaps 15m high and behind the paws a staircase has been cut into the rock. In front of the paws, a straight path runs to the perimeter dyke with symmetrical water tanks on both sides. It is often described as palace garden but its former curator has argued that it was built as a Mahayana monastery. He makes the following points: the rock was inhabited by Buddhist monks before King Kasayapa's arrival and again after his death; the king would not have wished to displace the monks or billet soldiers among them; the rock would have been a most inconvenient location for a palace and could not have been re-supplied during a siege; the artwork on the rock resembles the painting at Ajanta; there are comparable Mahayana monasteries in Sri Lanka and India.

The features Sigiriya shares with other Buddhist sanctuaries include cave art, residential accommodation, a woodland setting and water tanks. But the layout of the garden at the foot of the Sigiriya rock is more sophisticated than other Mahayana sanctuaries and one has to wonder why. There are several possibilities. First, it could have been a one-off design by an inspired individual. Second, there could have been similar garden layouts, in Sri Lanka or India, which were not built in stone and have therefore been lost. Third, the plan could derive from other monastic plans. Fourth, the design could have been the work of a craftsman from outside the subcontinent, perhaps from Persia. This latter possibility lacks supporting evidence and, in any case, little is known of Sassanian gardens. The third explanation, that there is a relationship with other monastery plans, is valid but does not upset the first explanation. Sigiriya has another brilliant feature: the massive lion at the foot of the steps. De Silva explains it as a Buddhist lion, signifying the entrance to a monastery. Buddha was known as the Lion of the Sakyas (Sakya Sima).[24] Sigiriya is obviously the work of an active design imagination.

De Silva rejects the theory that there was a palace on top of the rock but there could have been a palace at another location on or near the site, much of which remains unexcavated. There was a close association between palaces and monasteries in Sri Lanka and both institutions used tanks for washing: 'One of the important facets of monastic life, a provision that was ubiquitous, was the use of water for washing the feet of inmates and visitors alike.'[25] Water tanks feature in the Jakata stories, which tell of the previous births (*jati*) of the Buddha and were first written down in Sri Lanka. For example:

> One day the King with a large following went into his pleasaunce, and, after walking about the woods, felt a desire to disport himself in the water. So he went down into the royal tank and sent for his harem. The women of the harem, removing the jewels from their heads and necks and so forth, laid them aside with their upper garments in boxes under the charge of female slaves, and then went down into the water.[26]

Northern Buddhism

King Ashoka promoted the spread of Mahayana Buddhism to the Indus Valley and through the mountain passes of Central Asia. Many of the leading towns in this area owed their prosperity to traffic on the Silk Routes between Europe, China and India. Art, craftsman and religious ideas travelled with the caravans:

> The Silk Road was more than just a conduit along which religions hitched rides east: it constituted a formative and transformative rite of passage. No religion emerges unchanged at the end of that arduous journey. Key formative influences on the early development of the Mahayana and Pure Land movements, which became so much a part of East Asian civilisation, are to be sought in Buddhism's earlier encounters along the Silk Road.[27]

The Kushan tribes were from North China. Using the Silk Routes, they settled in North India *c.*135 and traded with the Roman Empire. European settlers had been

in Central Asia since Alexander the Great reached India in 326 BCE and Kushan coins are remarkably similar to Roman coins. Gandharan sculpture, from the Peshawar valley in today's Pakistan, was commissioned by Kushans but appears to be the work of non-Kushan sculptors. It was the first stone sculpture on the Indian subcontinent and is likely to have been made by craftsmen from the East Mediterranean and Persia. In eastern parts of the Kushan realm, around Mathura, stone carvings of the Buddha show fewer signs of foreign influence.

The Kushans were interested in the religious beliefs of other civilizations with experience of administering multi-national empires. They may have chosen to become Buddhist because the faith was open to people of non-Indian birth. Kushan beliefs are described as Perso-Buddhist or Graeco-Buddhist. They had a stronger philosophical base than traditional Buddhism and made more use of imagery. Indeed, it may have been the Greeks and Kushans who began to worship the Buddha, seeing him as a local equivalent of Apollo. It was normal practice for the Greeks and Romans, 'to identify local deities as corresponding to their own'.[28] The earliest Buddhist statues have the flowing robes which are characteristic of Graeco-Roman sculpture. Buddha images became objects of devotion.

As in West Asia, including Mesopotamia and Egypt, acts of worship were believed to earn boons. In India, 'Once the worship of images came into vogue, temples to enshrine the images could not lie far behind.'[29] Temples were built in monastic sanctuaries which came to be treated as gardens. Later Indian Buddhist temples can be distinguished from Hindu temples only by their imagery. But outside India Buddhist

5.30 a, b 'Om Mane Padme Hum', as written on the stones, is the most famous Buddhist mantra. One of the translations is 'Praise to the jewel in the lotus'.

temples took on new forms and were placed in landscapes and gardens. In South East Asia, these developments were inspired by Vajrayana Buddhism. In China and Japan, they were inspired by Pure Land Buddhism and Ch'an-Zen Buddhism.

Vajrayana sanctuaries

The first Mahayana monuments were *stupas*, as discussed above. Later developments included the building of temples and halls. Temples were carved from living rock, as at Ellora and Ajanta, or built in scenic locations, as at Sanchi and Amaravati, in relation to hills and rivers. But the main development of Mahayana temple building was outside India and often under the influence of Varjrayana ideas. South East Asia has many great structures symbolizing the home of the gods as a hill-top temple-palace in a fabulous landscape. They are among the greatest works of landscape architecture in Asia.

Vajrayana Buddhism

Vajrayana derives from *vajra*, meaning adamantine or indestructible, and *yana*, meaning path, way or journey. Vajrayana is rendered as 'the Diamond Way', because diamonds are indestructible, or as 'the Thunderbolt Way', because Indra's indestructible sceptre (*vajra*) was a thunderbolt. The principles of Buddhism were invoked with magic, chants and rituals to hasten believers on the path to nirvana in a single lifetime. A sophisticated cosmology was developed, partly inspired by Hindu myths. It pictured a Diamond Realm with Five Wisdom Buddhas:

- Vairocana (the central Buddha 'of Endless Light');
- Amitabha (the Buddha of the West);
- Aksobhya (the Buddha of the East);
- Amoghasiddhi (the Buddha of the North);
- Atnasambhava (the Buddha of the South).

The Five Wisdom Buddhas are represented in ritual mandalas and temple plans. They define the geography of the cosmos and the path which believers should take. Buddha, as a god, was the central figure in worship, sitting in calm splendour at the centre of the cosmos.

Kings liked the idea of having divine status. In India itself, the caste system maintained a separation of powers between priests and kings. But the two categories of power were often fused in countries to the east of India. Outside the caste system, Vajrayana Buddhism allowed kings to think of themselves as Bodhisattvas: fully enlightened beings who, instead of a life in nirvana, had chosen to remain on earth and guide their subjects on the great journey. Pilgrims were promised a place in nirvana after following a path on earth which involved learning, rituals, visits to holy places and guidance from priests and kings. Little survives of Vajrayana art or architecture in India. But it flourished elsewhere and influenced the design of Theravada and Mahayana temples. Outside India, temple palaces were built for god-kings (*deva rajas*).

Vajrayana Buddhism spread to South East Asia, Tibet, Nepal, China and Japan. In terms of religious practice, it became characterized by the use of esoteric tantras, mantras and mandalas to attain enlightenment. Tantras are ritual and mystical forms of worship. Mantras are strings of syllables recited to enhance religious concentration. The most famous mantra, *om mani padme hum*, is untranslatable. *Om* and *hum* are terms of praise for the body and for the mind of Buddha. *Padme* means lotus and *mani* means jewel. Buddhism has three jewels. The flower of the lotus symbolizes the aspirant's ascent from muddy waters through purity to enlightenment. One of the many English translations of *Om mani padme hum* is 'Praise to the jewel in the flower of the lotus'. In a Vajrayana context, a mandala is a geometric pattern serving as a microcosm of the universe and as an aid to contemplation. Two-dimensional mandalas include paintings, patterns made with coloured sands and bas reliefs. Three-dimensional mandalas include temples with lotus ponds, palace gardens and *stupas* in a landscape setting. There are many examples in South and East Asia.

Indonesia

India dispatched no military expeditions but became the dominant cultural power in South East Asia. There were numerous artistic, religious and technical exports, including the Devanghiri script. Buddhists followed sea and land routes previously taken by Hindu holy men, traders and settlers. It used to be thought that the founder of the Sailendra dynasty was born in India,[30] sailed to Java and married a princess to become King of the Mountain and Lord of the Isles. This was replaced by a theory of Javanese origin, but this too has been challenged.[31] What is certain is that the Sailendra dynasty was Buddhist and that it ruled Java, Sumatra and Malaya in the seventh, eighth and ninth centuries. At Borobudur, the Sailendra kings made 'the supreme monument of mystic Buddhism in Java, a building which in its style and iconography is one of the great masterpieces of religious art in Asia'.[32] The experience of visiting Borobudur is described by Nelson Wu, interpreting the entire site as a *chaitya* (shrine housing holy relics):

> *The stupa is in a long, fertile valley, again on top of a small hill, nestling against a protective backdrop of mountains. The whole field is thus the nave of the chaitya; the hill the stupa's pedestal; and heaven above its arched ceiling. As the mist rises from the foothills of the valley, this enormous monument reveals its volatile silhouette, light as the rising crest of a wave. It has a comfortable curvature, suggesting a basically simple geometric design, and its crushing weight is distributed effortlessly down its slopes, flowing into the supporting natural hill. Its nine levels symbolize the nine levels of the cosmic mountain, Mt. Meru, complete with a subterranean terrace where the enlightened desire to ascend begins. From this underworld of nightmarish experiences, illustrated by*

5.31 a, b The flower of the lotus: painted at Ajanta and growing in Japan.

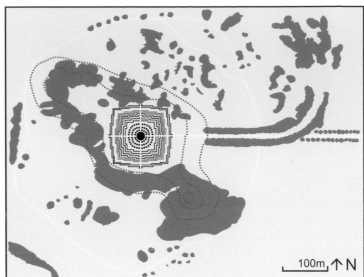

5.32 a, b, c Borobudur is a ninth-century temple *stupa* in Indonesia. It was designed to guide pilgrims through three levels of Buddhist cosmology. They see over a thousand narrative relief panels on the path to the summit.

the bas-reliefs, the entrapped godly nature of man distinguishes the right path from the wrong. Waiting for him above are the square terraces representing this world, and the circular terraces representing the world of God.[33]

Borobudur is both a *stupa* and a temple. The building and its setting informed pilgrims how to reach nirvana and how a king would guide them on the path. As a Bodhisattva, King Sailendra was either a god-king (*deva raja*) or an actual god (*Buddha raja*). Rowland summarized the status of Borobudur as follows:

The whole shrine is then the complete world and its order, the succession of points visited by the sun in its round, the cycle of time materialized in space constituting the Law rendered visible in the geographic, political, and spiritual centre of the realm.[34]

Vajrayana Buddhism offered a route to nirvana at thunderbolt-speed; Borobudur provided a map.

Cambodia

Cambodia was influenced by India, at least from the first century, and its kings alternated between Hinduism and Buddhism. After the seventh century, Khmer kings built temple-mountains symbolizing the home of the gods on Mount Meru. They showed Cambodia, ruled by a god-king, at the centre of the world. This was the theory which led to the building of the great temples at Angkor between the ninth and thirteenth centuries. Each temple-mountain sits at the intersection of avenues leading to gates in the city walls. Angkor Wat has a 4 km moat and Angkor Thom a 9 km moat. Angkor Wat is a microcosm of an Indian cosmology:

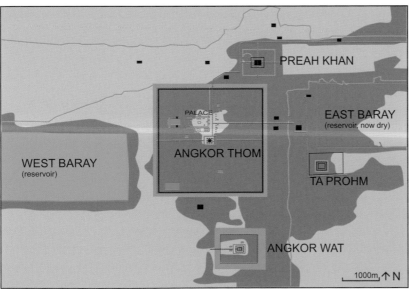

5.33 Angkor Wat is a temple mountain in Cambodia, designed for a god-king.

5.34 Angkor Thom and Angkor Wat were temple enclosures at the centre of a large urban area.

5.35 Wat Tum Sua is a Buddhist temple in southern Thailand.

5.36 The Ananda Temple in Myanmar, built in 1105. It is named after Buddha's disciple and has the form of a temple-mountain. Terracotta tiles illustrate the Jataka stories.

The moat represents the mythical oceans surrounding the earth and the succession of concentric galleries represent the mountain ranges that surround Mount Meru, the home of the gods. The towers represent the mountain's peaks.[35]

Hindus and Buddhists share this cosmology but it was the Buddhist conception of a Bodhisattva which enabled the king to be a god-king (*deva raja*). The Hindu caste system maintained a strict separation between priests and kings. The lands within the moats

were not cities in our, or the Indian, sense of the word as centres of population. The vast enclosure within the encompassing walls and moat was reserved only for temples, and the palaces of the king and nobles, together with buildings for the military and judicial branches of government.[36]

The temples and palaces were supported by an urban area covering an estimated 1000 km². [37] There were two large reservoirs, the West Baray and the East Baray, and a system of canals which has led to the area being characterized as a 'hydraulic city'.[38]

Thailand

Thailand was ruled by the Khmers from the eleventh century and became Buddhist after the thirteenth century. The Wat Chet Yot (Wat Maha Photharam) temple 'is clearly a copy of the Mahabodi temple at Pagan' and thus of 'the original Mahabodhi temple at Bodh Gaya'.[39] Thailand is predominantly a Theravada country and, in addition to building temples on hills, has a tradition of placing giant Buddha statues in the landscape.[40] It was influenced by Mahayana Buddhism and the kings of Thailand were Bodhisattvas.

Myanmar

Myanmar was settled from Central Asia and became a Buddhist country between the ninth and thirteenth centuries. Pagan, the capital, has 5,000 pagodas which are divided between *stupas* and temples. The most famous is the Ananda temple – a stepped pyramid resembling the temples of Cambodia but with characteristically Burmese rounded and pointed spires. It is decorated with sculptures illustrating the Jataka stories. Theravada Buddhism came to be dominant in Myanmar but temple-building continued and most were placed in visually prominent locations.

Nepal

The Buddha was born in Nepal and King Ashoka erected a pillar at Lumbini to commemorate the event. The Kathmandu Valley, according to the *Swayambhu Purana*, was once a vast lake in which a lotus grew. Bodhisattva Manjushri appeared on earth to worship the lotus and it was transformed into the hill on which the Swayambhunath Stupa now stands. He created the Kathmandu valley by cutting a gorge through the mountains to drain the lake. This story elevates a Bodhisattva almost to the status of a creator god. The temple is on a peak and is reached by a flight of 365 steps, known to tourists as 'steps to heaven'. As elsewhere, the stages on the ascent symbolize the journey to nirvana.

5.37 a, b, c Swayambhunath: a sacred tree and the 'steps to Heaven'. The five colours on prayer flags symbolize the five Bodhisattvas, the five elements Blue (sky), White (air), Red (fire), Green (water), Yellow (earth), the five body parts, the five spiritual qualities and other pentads.

Sukhavati sanctuaries

The Buddha of the West, Amitabha (also known as Amida) grew in popularity and his paradise came to be represented in artwork and designs. It was depicted with palace-garden mandalas. They are diagrams showing a palace surrounded by an ideal landscape – the Pure Land of the West, or Western Paradise. Sukhavati is Sanskrit for 'Pure Land'. The land is rich and fertile, planted with fragrant trees and beautiful flowers, especially the sacred lotus (*Nelumbo nucifera*). The rivers are scented and play musical sounds. In Tibetan Buddhism, red is Amitabha's colour and also the colour of love, compassion and emotion. When the sun sets, it too becomes red. Amitabha's emblem is the lotus and he embodies its attributes: gentleness, openness, and purity. The *Pure Land Sutras* have many passages to inspire the design of temple gardens:

> O Ananda, the world called Sukhavati belonging to that Bhagavat Amitabha is prosperous, rich, good to live in, fertile, lovely, and filled with many gods and men ... fragrant with several sweet-smelling scents, rich in manifold flowers and fruits, adorned with gem trees, and frequented by tribes of manifold sweet-voiced birds ... there are lotus flowers there, half a yojana in circumference ... there are no black mountains anywhere in that Buddha country ... there flow different kinds of rivers ... all these rivers are delightful, carrying water of different sweet odor, carrying bunches of flowers adorned with various gems, resounding with sweet voices ... And, O Ananda, the sound which rises from that water is delightful, and the whole Buddha country is aroused by it.[41]

> The Buddha said to Ananda and Vaidehi, 'When the visualization of the trees has been completed, next perceive the bodies of water. The Land of Utmost Bliss has eight bodies of water; the waters of each one of these lakes are made of the seven treasures and are begotten from a wish-fulfilling pearl. The water of each lake flows into fourteen streams, each of which is made of the seven treasures and is wondrous in color. The banks of each channel are golden in color, and the bed is strewn with the sand of variegated diamonds.

> In the Land of Highest Happiness there are waters in eight lakes; the water in every lake consists of seven jewels which are soft and yielding. Deriving its source from the king of jewels that fulfills every wish, the water is divided into fourteen streams; every stream has the color of seven jewels; its channel is built of gold, the bed of which consists of the sand of variegated diamonds.

> In the midst of each lake there are sixty million lotus-flowers, made of seven jewels; all the flowers are perfectly round and exactly equal (in circumference), being twelve yojanas. The water of jewels flows amidst the flowers and rises and falls by the stalks (of the lotus); the sound of the streaming water is melodious and pleasing, and propounds all the perfect virtues ... From the king of jewels that fulfills every wish, stream forth the golden-colored rays excessively beautiful, the radiance of which transforms itself

5.38 a–d Ch'an, or Zen, Buddhism grew from the Buddha's Flower Sermon. It emphasized meditation and spread to China and India. Towards the end of his life, the Buddha took his disciples to a quiet pond. They expected a sermon but he only lifted a lotus flower and held it before them, with the roots dripping, before handing the flower to a disciple and explaining: 'What can be said I have said to you. What cannot be said, I have given to Mahakashyapa.' Mahakashyapa was a disciple.

5.39 The *Pure Land Sutras* describe the land of bliss as a beautiful garden with a lotus pool.

into birds possessing the colors of a hundred jewels, which sing out harmonious notes, sweet and delicious, ever praising the remembrance of Buddha, the remembrance of the Dharma, and the remembrance of the Sangha.[42]

Three *Pure Land Sutras* were written in India, probably in the second century: the *Larger Pure Land Sutra*; the *Smaller Pure Land Sutra*; and the *Contemplation Sutra*. They recount how humans can be reborn in Amitabha's Pure Land: *if* their lives on earth have been pure and *if*, thinking continuously of Amitabha, they praise him, tell of his virtues and chant his name. These ideas became popular in China and Japan. Just as Christianity developed in Palestine, and scarcely survives in that region, so it is with Buddhism in India. It ebbed away, in part because Hinduism adopted many of its principles, shifting its emphasis from sacrifice to devotion, and in part because Muslim conquerors wrecked India's Buddhist monasteries.

China and Japan, the subjects of the next two chapters, became the countries where most Pure Land Buddhist temples were built and where most Buddhist gardens were made. A.L. Basham remarked: 'Even if judged only by his posthumous effects on the world at large [Buddha] was certainly the greatest man to have been born in India.'[43] Among many gifts to mankind, the Buddha had a powerful influence on the gardens of South East and East Asia.

Ch'an and Zen sanctuaries

The South Indian monk Bodhidharma is reported by Chinese sources as having introduced China to the ideas which became Ch'an Buddhism. This was in the seventh century. Later, the ideas spread to Japan and the school became known as 'Zen' Buddhism. Ch'an derives from the Sanskrit *Dhyana*, meaning 'meditation'. The underlying idea is that meditation, as practised by the Buddha, should be the primary route to enlightenment. It is very probable that Ch'an-influenced gardens were made in China but, as discussed in Chapter 6, no evidence concerning their form survives. In Japan, Zen Buddhism was influenced by Pure Land ideas and, as discussed in Chapter 7, what are now called Zen gardens became symbolic representations of sacred landscapes.

Part 3
East Asia

CHAPTER 6

Daoist-Buddhist gardens
in China

6.1 As Sons of Heaven, the emperors of China joined earth to heaven. They admired mountains and water (*shan shui*) and symbolized them in landscape parks and gardens.

6.2 Chinese civilization developed in the Valley of the Yellow River and the first capital was Chang'an (modern Xian).

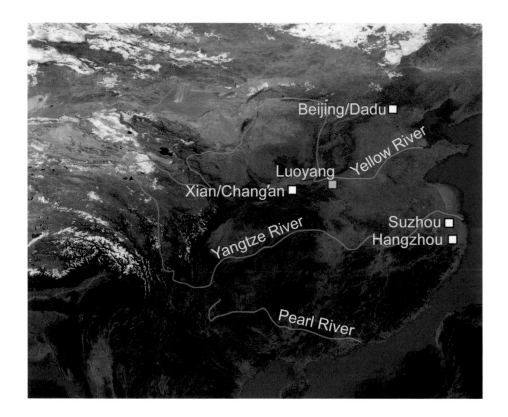

Chinese civilization developed in the most northerly of China's three great river basins. The valley of the Yellow River, in 3000 BCE, was broadleaf forest inhabited by hunter–gatherers and elephants.[1] Agriculture, settlements and culture spread from west to east and north to south, aided by a continuing influx of people, ideas and technology from the steppes, mountains and beyond. Soil erosion, consequent upon forest clearance, could have coloured the water and given the Yellow River its name.[2] The valley has cold dry winters, sweet springs, many floods, burning summers and rich autumns. The harsh and gentle aspects of this climate may have contributed to the belief that Earth had been sundered from Heaven before being ruled by twelve Emperors of Heaven, eleven Emperors of Earth, a series of other divine emperors and the legendary Yellow Emperor from whom China's historical rulers claimed descent. In one creation myth, it was Pangu who separated Heaven from Earth and yin from yang. His body formed the wind, sun, moon, mountains, rivers and forests. His sweat became rain. The ticks on his body became humans. Mankind was thus a relatively insignificant part of nature, inferior to the animistic spirits of Wind, Water, Trees and Mountains which controlled the conditions for agriculture and inspired the work of poets, painters and garden designers. Emperors were Sons of Heaven, they linked Heaven and Earth.

Over the millennia in which it developed, Chinese civilization was characterized by conflicts between nomads and settlers, by high technical skills, by strong governments,

6.3 The Great Wall survives as a symbol of the struggle between nomads and settlers which had such a profound influence on the civilization of China and its gardens.

by the importance of literature and, compared with Europe, by an absence of 'the transcendent truths, the idea of good in itself, the notion of property in the strict sense of the term'.³ China's susceptibilities – to invasions, floods, famines and civil wars – created a need for centralization. Land belonged simultaneously to the emperor and to landowners. It did not belong to farmers. 'Lands were not owned by the cultivators while the owners did not till land themselves'.⁴

6.4 a Wind, Water, Trees and Mountains have a key place in the Chinese love of gardens and the landscapes they represent. **b** The Jade Peak Pagoda (Yufeng Ta).

6.5 Looking north from the Forbidden City.

Emperors lived in fortified palace cities. As Sons of Heaven, they were the only people who could make effective sacrifices at the altars of Heaven, of Earth and of Ancestors. Emperors maintained the harmony of nature and the balance between drought and flood. They could draw assistance from royal ancestors in times of danger. To obtain lesser boons, nobles sacrificed animals to their own ancestors and to nature spirits. As the educated class, they were responsible for administration and generalship. Around *c.*1700 BCE the Shang tribe took control of the Yellow River Valley. Use of horses and chariots, which they are assumed to have learned from Central Asian tribes, gave them military superiority. They built palace cities in which East Asia's first literate culture developed. Their books were strips of bamboo on which characters were scratched. Chinese civilization, and its landscapes, developed in the psychic tension between nature and cities, nomads and settlers, floods and drought, mountains and plains. As in India, a circle came to symbolize Heaven and a square to symbolize the Earth. Symbolically, and often practically, cities were square in plan.

Cities and nature

Cities and Confucius

China's great military theorist, Sun Tzu, wrote in *The Art of War* that 'the worst policy of all is to besiege walled cities'.[5] The unstated corollary of his thesis was that to live in a city was the safest policy. China's ruling families therefore built walled palaces and walled gardens in walled cities with walled compounds for servants, soldiers, administrators, craftsmen and merchants. *Cheng* means both 'city' and 'wall'. The ideal city had a south wall along a riverbank and hills to the north. This layout satisfied geomantic objectives (see p. 188)[6] and facilitated water supply. Cities were begun by excavating moats and tamping earth in layers to build high defensive walls. Fortifications towered above the dwellings they protected. With extra soil placed inside gates, cities also protected against the river floods which plagued China. Sun Tzu lived in the sixth century BCE, near the watery city of Suzhou in the State of Wu.

Imperial cities were built to administer territory. Larger than European cities of equivalent age, most were located in agricultural lowlands to keep them supplied with food and water. Some cities grew organically with periodic extensions of the fortified zone. Others, the administrative centres which have attracted the attention of design historians, were rectangular or square. The size of an administrative city was set by imperial decree, then palace walls were built, then external walls, then internal walls. Unbuilt land within city walls could be used for ponds, food-growing, horse-grazing and gardens. Chinese cities were better suited to horticulture than the dry tells of Mesopotamia and the rocky hill-towns of Southern Europe and the produce helped them withstand sieges. Osvald Siren observed the garden character of old Chinese towns:

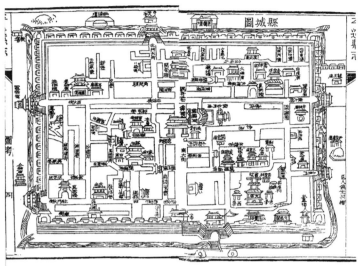

6.6 a, b Pingyao is one of the best examples of an old Chinese city. The present walls date from 1370 and were scheduled for demolition in 1977 – when they once more protected the city from flooding and were therefore retained.*

Note: *Knapp, Ronald G., *China's Walled Cities*, Oxford: Oxford University Press, 2000, p. 89.

6.7 The walls of Qufu, rebuilt under the Ming dynasty, enclosed an area of 10 square kilometres and had eleven gates.* Unlike the walled hill towns of Greece and Italy, Qufu is on flat land with a river (just visible in the photograph) to the south. The old city is unlikely to have had ornamental planting outside its walls.

Note: *Steinhardt, N. (ed.) *Chinese Architecture*, New Haven, CT: Yale University Press, 2002, p. 14.

The majority of the more aristocratic towns in China were to no small extent garden towns whose character derived precisely from the circumstance that large areas were taken up with plantations and pleasure gardens with luxuriant vegetation and a plentiful supply of water, even though they were commonly hidden behind walls.[7]

He explained this partly by climate and partly by 'the uncommonly intimate kinship with Nature that is part of the Chinese temperament'.[8] His observation was based

6.8 Qufu has a hill to the north, used as a walled burial ground by Confucius' family. Mounds are raised over the graves of 100,000 descendants.

6.9 Walls were always important to Chinese cities, houses and gardens. Foliage, sun and shadows made them decorative.

on travels in China after 1918 and his experience in writing about many aspects of Chinese art. Since Siren wrote his book, most cities have changed beyond recognition. The greenery in ancient Chinese cities is most likely to have been trees, planted in courtyards for shade and decoration.

The layout of old Chinese cities is often described as 'Confucian', with scant evidence for The Master having had an opinion on the subject. Confucius (551–479 BCE) lived during the Hundred Schools Era and the *Analects*, which are the primary source for his ideas, were compiled after his death. They contain no recommendations for architecture or city planning and, as the following quotations indicate, Confucius believed technical issues are best left to technical experts:

> *Fan Ch'ih requested to be taught husbandry. The Master said, 'I am not so good for that as an old husbandman.' He requested also to be taught gardening, and was answered, 'I am not so good for that as an old gardener.'*[9]

Confucius' teaching did, however, found a systematic school of thought which, Steinhardt writes, 'proved most influential to China's architecture'.[10] Confucianism guided the layout of cities by stressing orderliness, ritual, propriety and tradition. This resulted in a conservative approach to architectural styles and building types. The emphasis on imperial power and the centrality of the Son of Heaven were symbolized by placing the emperor's palace at the heart of his capital in the midst of his empire.[11] His ritual palace (*ming tang*, 'bright hall') was the centre of the world:

According to Chinese tradition, every capital must possess a Ming t'ang, a ritual palace that is at once imago mundi and calendar. The Ming t'ang is built on a square base (= the Earth) and is covered by a round thatched roof (= Heaven).[12]

Confucianism stressed authority: of an emperor over his subjects, of a father over his children, of a husband over his wife, of a wife over her servants and her husband's concubines. But Confucius' golden rule was exemplary: 'Do not do to others what you would not have them do to you.' Hu sees Confucius' remark that 'the gentleman copies the virtuous' as a primary influence on Chinese aesthetics, and gardens, but does not provide bibliographic support for his argument.[13]

The exigencies of garden ownership in fortified cities were the same in China as in other parts of the world:

6.10 a A typical Chinese house on a north–south axis with halls grouped to form a courtyard. As in Pompeii, covered walks open onto rooms and there are no windows on street frontages. Courtyards were more open in North China and more like light wells in South China. **b** A model of a clan housing.

- When a city wall is first built, there is space for gardens within the walls.
- When the fortified area becomes congested, it is difficult to retain open space for gardens.
- Kings and aristocrats enjoy resort gardens outside city walls.
- Residential courtyards within cities acquire some of the characteristics of gardens but remain functionally distinct.
- Siege warfare destroys gardens.

Distinctions between garden types are important in China, as elsewhere. The statement that 'peonies were popular in the gardens of China' is misleading unless there is a specific reference to historical periods and types of 'garden', which might include:

- large palace courtyards;
- small domestic courtyards;
- scholar gardens;
- monastic gardens;
- hermit gardens;
- horticultural plots, used to supply food and flowers;
- tomb compounds;
- college gardens;
- pleasure parks;
- hunting parks;
- holy mountains.

The evolution of the relationship between Chinese town gardens and landscape parks over three millennia is shown in Figure 6.35. Architecture drew more from Confucianism and gardens more from Daoism. The two belief systems represent poles of Chinese culture which were brought together by Buddhism.

Courtyards

Chinese houses and temples were arranged to form courtyards with the main building on the north side. For a dwelling, this was the master's house. For a temple, it was a hall containing statues of gods: Buddhist, Daoist or Confucian. Daoism (also spelt Taoism) is the oldest of China's three religions but did not have temples or images of gods before the arrival of Buddhism. Apart from their quality and scale, there were few differences between the planning and design of palaces, temples and ordinary dwellings. Residential units in towns were arranged on lanes (*hutong*), to form internal courtyards (*siheyuan*) for family groups. Because a south-facing aspect was the most desirable, the north wing was occupied by the head of the family. Grandparents and elder sons lived in the east wing. Young couples lived in the west wing. Soldiers guarded city gates. Servants guarded house gates and internal courtyard gates. Screen walls (*yingbi*) prevented demons from entering courtyards, because demons fly in straight lines, and also stopped outsiders from prying. Zig-zag bridges also spread confusion among demons.

Courtyard uses were linked to those of adjoining buildings. If frequented by believers, temple courtyards were paved, using gravel and stone paths. If they were places to pass through when visiting statues of gods, in temples or monasteries, courtyards could be planted with trees and grass was allowed to grow, forming sacred groves (see Figure 6.11). Some courtyards in Buddhist monasteries were designed and used as gardens, with pools and garden features. If used by residential monks, courtyards tended to become gardens. There are a number of former Buddhist temples and monasteries in the Western Hills outside Beijing. Graham visited them when still in use by the monks, in the 1920s, and wrote that in the Biyunsi Temple (now part of the Fragrant Hills Park)

> a chain of courtyards has been made with walls of dark rugged rocks. Trees shadow these courts; a thread of a stream moves slowly through their green depths. The pavement is verdant with moss; ferns spring from the moist somber rocks.[14]

Residential courtyards were designed and used according to their owners' means. Poor folk used their yards for outdoor storage, outdoor work, drying clothes and keeping animals, including pigs. They were surfaced with mud, perhaps with stepping stones for wet weather. Rich people paved their yards, put in drains and had servants sweep the paving several times a day. Smaller yards had raised walks round the perimeter, beneath sheltering eaves. There was often a recessed area in the middle of the yard, used for collecting water, as in a Roman *impluvium*, and also for plant pots. Larger yards were bisected by crowned paths so that they could be crossed in wet weather. In the largest residential courtyards central paths were roofed and sometimes passed through areas of trees and grass. Planting trees in courtyards was common, even among poor folk. Rich people used courtyards as ornamental space.

6.11 a–g Agricultural yards had mud walls and mud floors; town yards were paved and drained if the owner could afford it; aristocratic courtyards were decorated with symbols of mountain scenery; ceremonial courtyards were planted with trees.

If a dwelling was large enough to have two yards, then guests were only admitted to the outer yard. Women and children were confined to the inner yard. A large and wealthy clan might have 20 or more dwelling units forming a residential compound in which each unit had a small yard. Confucius' *Analects* contain a comment on the merits of privacy: 'The wall of my Master is several fathoms high. If one does not find the door and enter by it, he cannot see the ancestral temple with its beauties, nor all the officers in their rich array.'[15] Confucius can thus be associated with the high walls and regular layout of Chinese cities. But he was also sensible to the beauty of nature and wrote that: 'The wise find pleasure in water; the virtuous find pleasure in hills'.[16] This remark 'prompted his followers to seek moral discipline and self-improvement amidst the creations of Mother Nature'.[17] According to Wang, Confucius

6.12 a–d The peony and the plum were favourite flowers in Chinese gardens.

metaphorically implied that the wise scholar took pleasure in applying the great wealth of his talent in the administration of world affairs, much like the never-ending flow of water in a river. The kind gentleman, on the other hand, was happy to remain as firm and stable as a mountain while everything was growing luxuriantly in an undisturbed nature.[18]

Many courtyards are now open to the public, embellished with red lanterns and even turf, despite the fact that in old courts there was 'never any clipped turf'.[19] Some flowers were grown in gardens, but in courtyards flowering plants are more likely to have been displayed than grown. Graham observed what may well have been an ancient custom in the 1920s:

The flowers are brought by a pedlar in shallow baskets swinging by ropes from a shoulder yoke. Down the narrow lane he calls his wares; the bargaining at the gate is sharp and swift; soon the court is gay with bloom. Azaleas. Camellia trees in earthen jars. White tiny roses twisted into an intricate trellis. The misty purple blue of China asters, the tawny rust of late chrysanthemums. The flower coolie takes away the used plants so that they may rest until next year. The courtyard, where the life of the family centres, presents a new pattern; it is renewed and enlivened.[20]

It early times, it seems likely that most flowers were grown in horticultural plots and brought to courtyards and gardens as pot plants and cut flowers. In later times, flowers were also grown in gardens, particularly the peony, the lotus and the plum. Between

1982 and 2005 several attempts were made to agree one of these as a National Flower. No agreement was reached because flowers are taken very seriously in China.

Goldfish were also a vital decorative element in Chinese gardens, enlivening the yin element (water) and relieving the severity of the yang elements (rocks and buildings).

> In the garden of the literary man, fish had their decorative place; often they were more in evidence than blossoms. The carp, which the priests called the water-shuttle flower, was first preserved by the Buddhists as an act of merit; then the scholars became interested in their ornamental possibilities.[21]

Freeing animals was a Buddhist tradition and monastery gardens had, and have, special ponds for this purpose.[22] Goldfish were also kept in terracotta jars. Like the courtyards in which they were placed, the beautiful fish reminded their owners of wild nature, far away from the confines of urban life.

Tomb compounds

From early times, mounds were raised above Chinese tombs, like *kurgans* in the steppes. This evolved into the practice of building imperial tombs in walled compounds, placing a temple on a mound and planning a processional path. The route, described as a Spirit Path, was lined with 'lucky animals' – symbolic sculptures believed to bring good fortune. At different times they included camels, elephants and such mythical beasts as the *qilin* and *tianlu*. This could be a ripple of influence from West Asia. Morphologically and mythologically, the arrangement compares with the sphinx-lined avenues to compounds made for Egyptian pyramids. Stylistically, Chinese mortuary sculpture resembles that of West Asia. The Chinese provided deceased emperors with servants, houseware, guardians, concubines, food and drink because they believed the tomb became a home for the occupant's after-life in the spirit world. Wives and servants were buried with their masters in early times and, at a later date, terracotta substitutes were used. The treatment of deceased emperors as though they were still living resembles Egyptian practice and the imperial tombs of Ancient China could be described as tomb gardens. Burial mounds were pyramid-shaped and, as in Egypt, were built in places with landscape significance. Tiger Hill was a burial site (for King He Lu in 496 BCE) on which a monastery and pagoda were built at a later date. The Ming Tombs are in a beautiful valley with mountains to the north and a long spirit path.

Nature and Daoism

Intensive agricultural development may have induced nostalgia for the landscapes which were lost as China developed. Forests were cleared and dangerous beasts exterminated. It is recorded that the Duke of Zhou 'drove the tigers, leopards, rhinoceroses, and elephants far away, and the world was greatly delighted'.[23] In a book entitled *The Retreat of the Elephants: An Environmental History of China*, Elvin explains:

6.13 a, b Goldfish were an important decorative element in Chinese gardens. They were kept in ponds and large pots.

6.14 Model of Qin Shi Huang's tomb showing the grass pyramid and the site where the Terracotta Warriors were unearthed. Their task was to guard his spirit and help rule the spirit world.

6.15 Tiger Hill was a burial site and has become a temple garden.

6.16 A spirit path with auspicious animals, also called 'lucky animals', leads to the Tang Dynasty tombs of Gao Zong (628–638) and Wu Zetian (80 km north of Xian).

6.17 a, b Banpo village dates from *c*.4500 BCE. It had circular and square dwellings, with thatched roofs part set into the ground, surrounded by a defensive ditch.

Overall, though, the picture is one of Han Chinese expansion up to natural limits – coasts, steppes, deserts, mountains, and jungles. It was a multi-millennial transformation of a variety of habitats by some version of the Chinese style of settlement: cutting down most of the trees for clearance, buildings, and fuel, an ever-intensifying garden type of farming and arboriculture, water-control systems both large and small, commercialization, and cities and villages located as near the water's edge as possible.[24]

Similar policies are affecting Africa, South East Asia and South America in our own time.

Peasants' lives were spent on farms they did not own. In summer, they lived in temporary 'nests' among the fields, raised above ground level for protection against wild animals and surface water. In winter, they lived in 'burrows' dug into the warm earth, thatched and grouped into permanent villages. Houses had no windows. A hole in the roof let smoke escape and a hole in the floor let water escape. As with a nomad tent (yurt or *ger*), the door was on the south side to let in as much sun as possible during the frozen winters of North China. When cities became trading centres, in medieval China, the differences between urban and rural architecture disappeared but there were regional variations, including narrower courtyards in the south and group courtyards, sometimes circular, in the Fujian Tulou of South West China. Peasants sacrificed at village altars instead of city altars. Making contact with the spirit world required the help of shamans, known in China as *wu* and *fangshi*. Their successors became Daoist priests.

Shamanism is an 8,000-year-old belief system which appears to have originated in North Central Asia and to have influenced both China through Daoism and India through Hinduism. At its core is the idea that there are two worlds, or rather two aspects of a single world: the material and the spiritual. In India, Brahmins made contact with

6.18 a, b Mountains figure prominently in Chinese beliefs, poetry and painting. Huashan is near the ancient capital Chang'an (Xian) (see p. 199).

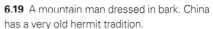

6.19 A mountain man dressed in bark. China has a very old hermit tradition.

anthropomorphic gods. In China, *wu* made contact with impersonal spirits. A *wu* lives in the material world but, using special talents, engages with the spirit world. This involves dances, animals and knowledge of special places in the landscape, which became sacred sites. Most *wu* were female and the pictogram for *wu* indicates 'the complex of dancing, fertility, and pacification'.[25] Ritual nudity was a form of sacrifice to rain gods.[26] Alchemists offered worldly benefits and hopes of immortality. A *fangshi* was a 'man of techniques', with special knowledge of gaining immortality.

Ancient China also had hermits and sages (*shengren*). Typically, they were men who withdrew from society to dwell among mountains, seeking longevity and immortality by living in harmony with nature. The Chinese character for immortal (*xian*) shows a man beside a mountain.[27] To reduce the boundary between the spirit world and the natural world, hermits shunned everything man-made, including fabrics, houses and cultivated food. They dressed in tree bark and lived in caves. Longevity techniques included 'breathing exercises, diet control, gymnastics, sexual hygiene, absorption of solar energies, and meditation'.[28] Special herbs and foods, including the divine grass, aided the quest for longevity. Sages hoped to make contact with the Immortals, who lived in the spirit world but could be contacted in sacred places, including the holy mountains in the west and the blessed isles in the east. Their quest derived from the Yellow Emperor's dream as reported by Liezi. He was a sage who lived in the fourth century BCE and recorded old Chinese myths:

6.20 The yin–yang concept was represented by trigrams in the I Ching and by the Taijitu diagram (above) in the Ming period. Taijitu is translated as 'diagram of the supreme ultimate'.

6.21 Water and stones are yin and yang (Lion Grove Garden).

6.22 Stones became valuable collectors' items. The Zhou Yun Stone, one of the three famous stones south of the Yangtze River, is in the shape of clouds and wrinkles.

On the islands in the eastern seas are immortal beings who live on dewdrops and pine cones. They do not eat grain, they feed on the wind and vapor, and their minds are as clear and still as the mountain lake ... The sun and moon send a gentle light, the seasons are never harsh, the earth is rich, and the inhabitants are kind. The deities bless the land, and the monsters never go near it. This is the land the Yellow Emperor visited in his dream.[29]

The tortoise and the crane, said to live for 10,000 years and 1,000 years respectively, became symbols of longevity. At a later date, Islands of the Blest were made in landscape parks to symbolize and attract these animals, trusting they would extend the lives of their owners. The idea became popular in Japanese gardens (see p. 275) where symbolic turtles supported symbolic islands.

Chinese hermits were often men of letters who withdrew from society, especially in times of social and political upheaval, to retain their moral integrity. Confucius himself taught that 'A gentleman should serve his country when there is truth in the world, but he should withdraw when there is none.'[30] Bo Yi and Shu Qi, princes of the Shang Dynasty, were famous for having withdrawn to the mountains instead of becoming kings. Cheng argues that 'China's private gardens are the artistic expression of an ancient hermit ideology.'[31]

Another aspect of the spirit and material worlds is explained by yin–yang theory. It was developed and recorded in the Hundred Schools Era (770–220 BCE) but characters representing yin and yang are found on oracle bones used for divination in the fourteenth century BCE. Yin and yang are complementary forces created from the 'divine breath' (*qi*). The logogram for *qi* meant 'steam rising from rice as it cooks'. According to an early dictionary of Chinese characters (*c.*100 CE), yin refers to 'a closed door, darkness and the south bank of a river and the north side of a mountain', while yang refers to 'height, brightness and the south side of a mountain'.[32] Everything, including cities, dwellings, gardens and people, has yin and yang aspects. The vertical walls of a city are yang; the river outside the city and the water in its gardens are yin. Vertical stones beside water are yang with yin.

Daoism grew in the context of the traditional beliefs outlined above. It became a philosophical school in the time of Laozi (also spelt Lao Tzu) and then, centuries later, an organized religion. Laozi means 'Old Master' but the master is not thought to have been the sole author of the famous book associated with his name, the *Dao Te Ching*. It is wisdom literature, more like a collection of epigrams than a treatise. The famous first line states that 'The Dao which can be spoken of is not the eternal Dao' (wits render it as 'The Dao which can be spoken is not the real Dao'). The Dao is the way of the universe. It is the spirit of nature. It is the way we should live. Man, as a microcosm, should therefore study nature and act naturally. In the mountains, for instance, a Daoist might observe 'There is nothing in the world more soft and weak than water, and yet

6.23 a, b Collectors' stones and bamboos in the Imperial Garden in the Forbidden City.

for attacking things that are firm and strong there is nothing that can take precedence of it; for there is nothing (so effectual) for which it can be changed.'³³ Water gathers power by following the path of least resistance. Men can do likewise, achieving most by acting in harmony with nature and consequently with the least effort. This came to be viewed as a philosophy of non-action (*wu wei*).

Zhang Daoling lived in the second century and founded a religious community which began the transformation of Daoism into an organized religion with a panoply of gods and ceremonies. He drew on Buddhist practice and on the monastic tradition of India. The Chinese pantheon of immortals included Laozi ('Great Lord on High') and, after his departure from this world, Zhang Daoling ('Celestial Master Zhang'). The ancient ritual of animal sacrifice ceased and later Daoists developed practices to help one attain longevity and join the spirit world. They included breathing exercises, offerings at shrines, sexual purity and the burning of incense. Zhang Daoling spent most of his life in the mountains and, at a later date, Daoists admired the Buddha for having withdrawn from city life to seek immortality. As mentioned in Chapter 8, it is possible that Daoism and Buddhism have a common ancestor in the ancient beliefs of Central Asia.

City dwellers were attracted by the idea of retreat to the mountains and by the longevity, or immortality, which they hoped to achieve through asceticism. Members of the scholar class built thatched huts with small gardens in beautiful landscapes. Emperors made landscape parks as nature retreats. Natural surroundings became places to paint, compose poems, immerse oneself in the totality of the universe and discover the secrets of immortality.³⁴ Siren wrote: 'the gardens best corresponding to the Chinese feeling for Nature were those attached to the huts of recluses or the

6.24 Wang Xizhi (303–361) was a famous calligrapher and poet. He reared geese and his Orchid Pavilion (Lanting, Shaoxing) was the subject of many paintings. Wang wrote:

At the beginning of the third lunar month,
We all gathered at the orchid pavilion in Shanyin County, Guiji Commandery,
For the Spring Purification Festival.
…

This was an area of high mountains and lofty peaks,
With an exuberant growth of trees and bamboos,
Which also had clear rushing water,
Which reflected the sunlight as it flowed past either side of the pavilion.

6.29 A collector's stone in Hangzhou.

6.30 The Cloud Cutting Sword stone on Mt Taishan stands upright, like a sword, chopping the cloud to sow the rain.

haunted stones in wild rugged places, curiously shaped rocks associated with dragons, devils, saints and gods. It was only necessary to transfer a strangely formed stone, or a stone with an attached legend, to an urban garden, to accomplish the innovation in taste. Add to this a sophisticated intuition of the structure of the world and the operations of 'Heaven' subtly suggested by the contours of a picturesque rock, and we have the attitude of the T'ang or Song connoisseur full-fledged.[41]

Lake Tai stones are used in several ways: beside ponds, in trays which symbolize water and beside paths surfaced with water-washed pebbles so that 'the paving is thus a stretch of water, its movement represented by geometric or floral patterns, or images of real or mythical animals (dragon or phoenix), or any other figures suggesting mobility'.[42] Special stones, called scholars' rocks (*gongshi*) were mounted and displayed on scholars' desks. Others, known as dreamstones, were mounted in panels and screens. Sometimes, you 'enter the Gardens of Longevity by the contemplation of dreamstones'.[43] The 'gardens of longevity' are often described in English as 'rock gardens', but 'stone gardens' or 'mountain gardens' or 'landscape gardens' would be more appropriate.

A classical Chinese 'garden' can be regarded either as a large equivalent of a tray garden (*penjing*) or as a small equivalent of an imperial park (*yuan*). Classifying them as 'gardens' can hardly be resisted but 'garden' is a European word and they are more accurately described as 'landscapes' (*shan shui*, 'mountains and water'). Daoists believe there is only one macrocosm: the landscape of nature. But there can be many microcosms: incense burners, inkstones, scholars' stones, tray gardens,

6.31 a
Stones were won with great difficulty from the bed of Lake Tai (*Taihu*).

b
Symbols of heaven (a circle), mountains (*Taihu* stones) and water (swirling pebbles).

c
Taihu stones in the Kong Family Mansion (Qufu). The trays may symbolize water.

d
A dreamstone used to make a *yingbi* in the Forbidden City.

courtyard compositions, holy mountains, sacred landscapes and imperial parks. Each is appreciated with a Daoist enthusiasm for 'mountains and water', reminding their owners of nature and with hopes of attracting the gods to take up residence, as bird tables attract birds.

William Blake gave expression to a Daoist sentiment:

> *To see a World in a Grain of Sand*
> *And a Heaven in a Wild Flower,*
> *Hold Infinity in the palm of your hand*
> *And Eternity in an hour.*[44]

This is the intellectual context in which Chinese 'gardens' evolved. Artists, poets and designers were exploring 'the nature of Nature'[45] – the force which drives the macrocosm; the essential nature of the world: the Dao.

William Blake was, of course, a European and it is worth pausing to review the different circumstances in which Chinese and European gardens were designed. Chief among them is geography. In China, 90 per cent of the population lives on 30 per cent of the land. Beijing has been described as 'one of the world's most uncomfortable capitals, blazing hot in summer, freezing in winter and blanketed in spring by yellow dust blown in from the Gobi Desert'.[46] Central and South China are warm and wet. As shown on Figure 6.32, the valley land on which most Chinese people lived was often flat but near mountains, viewed as the abode of godly spirits. In the absence of public parks and public squares, social life was concentrated on busy streets, private yards and temple courts. Dingle walked across China in 1909 and remarked on the character of its old streets:

> *The contracted quarters in which the Chinese live compel them to do most of their work*
> *in the street, and, even in a city provided with but the narrowest passages, these slender*

6.32 Chinese cities were often walled enclaves on rich agricultural plains near high mountains. The air was foul in cities and sweet in the mountains.

6.38 a, b, c Chengde, still walled and containing deer, is related to the great Zhou imperial parks but was made after 1703.

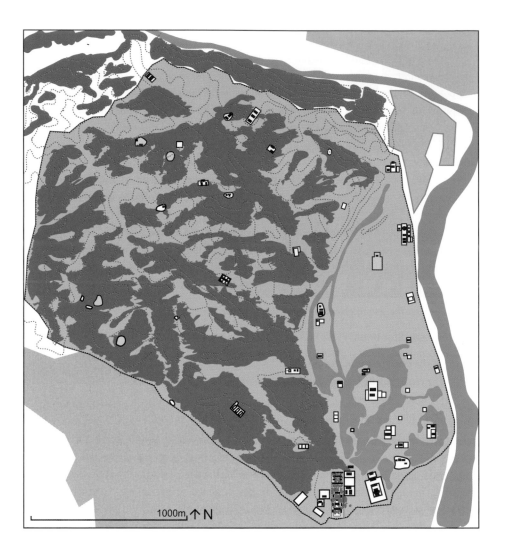

Flowers are associated with mountains, marshes, orchards and girls. They are not mentioned in connection with courtyards.

> *Brilliant are the flowers,*
> *On those level heights and the low grounds.*
> *...*
>
> *The peach tree is young and elegant;*
> *Luxuriant are its leaves.*
> *This young lady is going to her future home,*
> *And will order well her family.*
> *...*

By the shores of that marsh,
There are rushes and lotus flowers.
There is the beautiful lady;
Tall and large, and majestic.

The above quotations do not suggest that Zhou cities had ornamental gardens of the kind we now think of as 'classically' Chinese but it is clear that landscapes around cities were appreciated by emperors, aristocrats and poets. The Chinese word for marsh (*ze*) means 'all the uncultivated lands which have water sources such as lakes, springs, ponds and streams, and which are rich with trees and other vegetation, animals and plants'.[50]

Emperors set aside areas of natural landscape for use when there were no hostile forces in the neighbourhood. The records of the grand historian (*Shi Ji*) (written 109–91 BCE) relate that King Zhou 'gathered rare dogs and horses, and other exotic beasts' and 'once had a great gathering with dancing and music at Shaqiu where wine flowed in pools and meat hung on trees' and 'naked men and women chased one another in the garden'.[51] The latter event could have been a fertility rite or a marriage festival: 'the peasants celebrated every spring with a festival in which the youths and girls of neighbouring villages met in free association, only translated into formal marriage in the autumn if the girls were with child'.[52] Zhou parks were large enclosures with both sacred and recreational roles. Walls kept animals in and peasants out. The enclosed area (*you*) was reserved for noble and sacred purposes, including hunting, feasting and ritual.

6.39 The four cardinal directions were symbolized by an azure dragon, a vermilion bird, a white tiger and a dark warrior. Feng shui experts represent them with a flowing stream to the east, a marsh to the south, a road to the west, and a high mountain to the north.*

Note: *Bialock, D.T., *Eccentric Spaces, Hidden Histories*, Stanford, CA: Stanford University Press, 2007, p. 63.

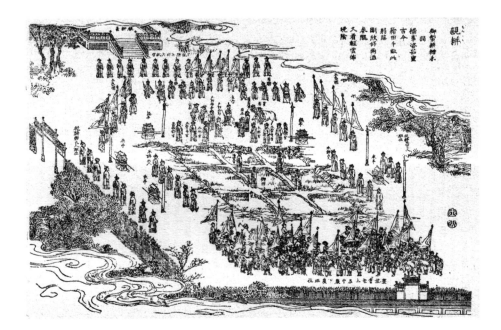

6.40 a, b The Temple of Heaven (above) and the Altar of Grain in Beijing (left). Animals from imperial parks were sacrificed at imperial altars.

The only man-made structure in the you was tai, which was a kind of podium, square or rectangular in shape and rose approximately three to five meters above the ground. The purpose of such podiums was for the emperor 'to look into the four directions', to 'observe the colours of the clouds', and 'to perceive signs of good omen'. In other words, tai was a place for the emperor to come near and pay homage to heaven.[53]

Learning to hunt was a preparation for war. Animals for sacrifice at the Altar of Heaven and the Altar of the Ancestors were caught in the imperial park. It was an earthly 'paradise' belonging to the Son of Heaven and symbolizing his relationship with the spirit world which let him influence the forces of nature.[54] The four cardinal directions were symbolized by the directions in which the auspicious animals look: the green dragon of the east; the vermilion bird of the south; the white tiger of the west; and the dark warrior of the north (an entwined tortoise and snake). The Yellow Emperor himself symbolized the fifth dimension: heaven. Mirrors, and lakes, because they reflected the nature of the world, served as symbolic sources of light for the departed. The backs of mirrors were also decorated with cosmological designs and symbolic maps of the universe. Imperial parks were thus able to represent the world order.

Qin landscapes, 221–206 BCE

A prince from the State of Qin united the country and became the First Emperor in 221 BCE. He ruled as Qin Shi Huang and gave his name to the new state: Qin is pronounced 'Ch'in' and the state became China. Qin Shi Huang made the Terracotta Army and connected a line of northern forts to make the Great Wall, leading to the jest that he also founded China's tourist industry. His capital city, named Xianyang and outside the present walls of Xian, was a rectangular riverside city on a north–south axis. Roofed corridors crossed streets to interconnect palaces.

The result was a city-wide maze of tunnels and closed corridors, linking 277 locations. Each palace was fully furnished for the First Emperor's pleasure, with cooks, girls and guards, none of whom was permitted to leave. This situation allowed the First Emperor to choose his place of rest each night completely at random, turning up at one of the palaces without warning.[55]

Another roofed corridor crossed the city wall to reach a detached palace in Shanglin Park (*Shanglinyuan*), outside the city walls. No visual record of these corridors survives but the idea of joining pavilions with roofed corridors became a feature of Chinese architecture and garden design. Daoists advised Qin Shi Huang that he could further his quest for immortality by keeping his whereabouts secret. He therefore 'flitted from one palace building to another like a celestial being' and lived 'in a fairy land setting of clouds and forests and mysterious mountains'.[56]

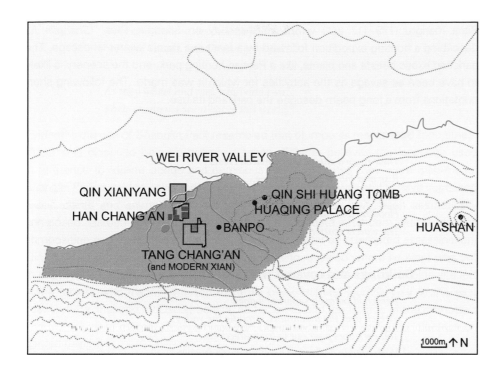

6.41 Plan showing the location of Chang'an under the Qin, Han and Tang dynasties. The drawing also shows the Neolithic village of Banpo, the Huaqing Palace, the tomb of Qin Shi Huang, Mt Huashan and the possible extent of Shanglin Park (in a darker green).

WEI RIVER VALLEY

QIN XIANYANG

QIN SHI HUANG TOMB

HAN CHANG'AN

HUAQING PALACE

BANPO

HUASHAN

TANG CHANG'AN
(and MODERN XIAN)

1000m N

6.42 a–f Roofed corridors became an enduring feature of imperial parks and gardens, though there are no records of their appearance in Qin times.

6.46 Believing it was the home of a god, Huashan (Mount Hua) attracted Daoist pilgrims and seekers of immortality. The Immortal Palm Cliff on the East Peak of Huashan has gelite (opal) veins. They form a palm shape and are viewed as a god's handprint. The clifftop is a famous place for viewing the sunrise.

6.47 An inscription on Huashan.

There is also a record of a Han park, called the Yuan Guanghan, belonging to a wealthy nobleman. It was made outside the walls of Luoyang. Emperor Wu is believed to have climbed Hua Shan. Located 120 km east of Xian, it is still revered as a holy mountain. Chinese documents do not confirm the event, but a mural was found in the Tarim Basin showing Emperor Wu worshipping a Buddhist statue in a temple. Buddhism was predominantly the religion of foreign merchants at this time[64] but it began to influence the transformation of Daoism into an organized religion.

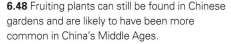

6.48 Fruiting plants can still be found in Chinese gardens and are likely to have been more common in China's Middle Ages.

Johnston analysed the stone maps of Han towns to glean information about urban gardens. They appear to have been places to grow fruit and vegetables.[65] Outside Han city walls, emperors had traditional Chinese landscape parks with lakes, forests and detached palaces. Han cities do not appear to have had small poetic and contemplative gardens, composed like landscape paintings, with miniature hills, lakes, bridges, roofed corridors and moon gates. Nor did the art of landscape painting exist in Han China. What is now known as *the* Chinese garden (i.e. the urban scholar garden) came into being during the millennium after the fall of the Han. Answers to the questions '*When* did it first appear?' and '*Where* did it first appear?' are unlikely to be found but there is a probable answer to the question '*Why* did it emerge?': through the influence of Buddhism. Garden historians overstate the influence of Confucius and under-represent or wholly ignore the influence of Buddhism on Chinese gardens.

Northern Wei landscapes and gardens, 396–534

China endured a long dark age after the collapse of the Han Dynasty, as did Europe after the decline and fall of the Western Roman Empire. The gardens made in these periods have not survived but when light returned to the eastern and western ends of the Eurasian continent garden design had been transformed. China's Dark Age, known as the period of the Six Dynasties, is when Buddhism began to influence the arts. Mountains, trees and other landscape features had appeared in Chinese art before this time but had been emblematic, like the 'lucky animals' and symbolic figures placed in tombs and used to line spirit paths (see Figure 6.15). Artificial mountains had been mere 'heaps of stones'.[66] It was Buddhism which mediated a naturalistic and aesthetic approach to painting, and then to the making of sacred landscapes in gardens. Miranda Shaw summarizes the origins of Chinese landscape painting as follows:[67]

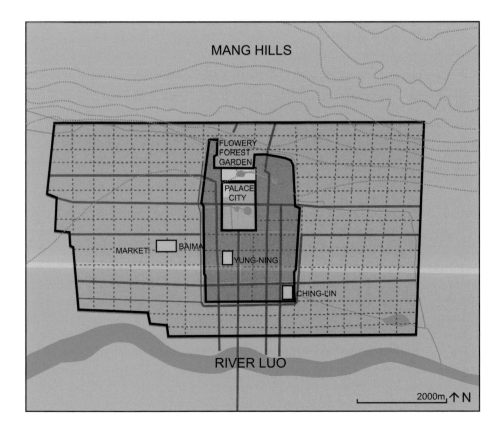

6.49 Luoyang, under the Northern Wei, had three large palace gardens and over 1,000 Buddhist temples and gardens. With mountains to the north and a river to the south, it complied with *Zhou li* and feng shui principles (see Figure 6.37).

6.50 A modern statue of Xuanzang in front of the Big Wild Goose Pagoda (Dayan Ta), which was begun in 652.

- The conviction that the landscape possesses a spiritual force or essence (Dao or *qi*) came from Daoism.
- The idea of retreat into the mountains to pursue self-cultivation was present in alchemy and came to fruition in Neo-Daoism.
- The idea that an image can transmit this essence came from Buddhism.

Two direct Buddhist influences on the use of images as objects of worship can be identified. First, the monk Faxian returned to Xian in 412 CE with detailed accounts of Buddhist temples in India. Second, the Monastery of the Eastern Grove (now Donglin Temple, at the foot of Mount Lushan) was founded by Hui-yuan in 380 CE. Hui-yuan set an image of Buddha in a landscape and when the author of the first Chinese book on landscape painting (Tsung Ping) visited the monastery, he reported that a group of people 'took a vow in front of a statue of Amitabha to be reborn together in his Pure Land'.[68] They believed paintings could serve as substitutes for actual scenes in Nature. Tsung Ping said a painting could take the place of 'a ramble among gloomy and dangerous cliffs'. Siren comments that his view is 'of fundamental importance for the art of gardening as well as for painting'.[69]

Amitabha is the Pure Land Buddha of the Mahayana scriptures (see p. 168). Possessing infinite merit from previous lives, he is able to confer merit upon devotees. Images representing Amitabha in his Pure Land became objects of devotion. Landscape paintings substituted for real landscapes and, over a long period of time, the art of landscape painting became twinned with garden design. Among the Buddhist survivals from the Six Dynasties period are the paintings in the Mogao Caves at Dunhuang and the detailed description of the monasteries and gardens at Luoyang. There were no monasteries in China before the arrival of Buddhism. Afterwards, they were placed 'as we see them in a thousand landscape paintings – high in the hills, their upturned roofs echoing the swoops and hollows of the crags around them; below, the soundless, misty depths of valleys became symbols of the Void'.[70]

Buddhism was patronized by Northern Wei emperors who, not being Chinese, could not claim to be Sons of Heaven. Their capital was the old Chinese city of Luoyang. It was destroyed in 423, rebuilt in 493 and destroyed again in 534. In 2007, the city had a population of 7 m. An official who had known the city as a young man visited the ruins in 547 and wrote a book about the monasteries, palaces and gardens he had once known and loved.[71] Luoyang was then of a similar size to Constantinople and was as important to Buddhism as Constantinople was to Christianity. Luoyang had over 1,000 Buddhist temples and monasteries. The rich believed that gifts of money and property improved their chances of reaching paradise and Mahayana Buddhist monasteries therefore received wealth which was poured into the making of temples, gardens and other artwork. Both Pure Land and Ch'an Buddhism flourished in Luoyang. Some monasteries were in the inner city and others were interspersed with the dwellings of the nobility, beyond the inner walls. Buddhist caves south of Luoyang survive and are

known as the Longmen Grottoes. Another resident of Luoyang, Xuanzang, published an account of his journey to India in 646.

The White Horse Monastery (founded in 68 CE and now called the Baima Temple) is 12 km east of Luoyang. It was named after the white horse on which the Buddhist sutras were carried from North West India to China.[72] The site has an old pagoda, a rebuilt Buddhist temple and a re-created garden (of rather poor quality when photographed in 2007 – see Figure 6.54).

The Eternal Peace (Yang-Ning) Monastery was founded by the Empress Dowager Ling and is described as having a 'nine-storeyed pagoda built with a wooden frame that rose 900 feet (274 metres) high'. This helped monks meditate on 'the precious halls on Mount Sumeru'[73] (see p. 12). The reported height, only 36 m less than the Eiffel Tower, makes one wonder if the author exaggerated.

The Great Orchard (Ching-Lin) Monastery was inside the walls of Luoyang:

6.51 The Longmen Grottoes, 12 km south of Luoyang, have a series of Buddhist caves. They were begun under the Northern Wei and adorned with a floating plastic lotus more recently.

6.52 The Longmen Grottoes have Buddhist caves, statues and pagodas.

205

6.53 A painting from the Dunhuang caves shows the garden paradise of the Amitabha Buddha.

To the west of the monastery was a garden rich with exotic fruit-trees where was unbroken song from the birds in spring and the cicadas in autumn. In the garden was a meditation building containing Jetavana cells which although tiny were exquisitely built. The stillness of the meditation room, the remote calm of the cells, the splendid trees framing the windows and the fragrant azaleas around the steps gave the feeling of being in a mountain valley rather than a city.[74]

Jetavana was the name of the Mahayana grove, outside Sravasti, where the Buddha spent 27 monsoon seasons (see p. 152). Its Chinese cousin, also with cells for monks, was conceived as a sacred grove providing the necessary peace for meditation and 'the feeling of being in a mountain valley'.[75] In the Eternal Peace Monastery 'junipers, cypresses, firs, and fragrant herbs grew around the steps'.[76]

There was a Flowery Forest within the palace compound and the emperor's Forest (Hua-lin) Park was north of Luoyang's palace.[77] It had a Pool of the Heavenly Deep surviving from Han times. The Wei emperor 'had a P'eng-lai Mountain constructed in the lake with an Immortals Lodge on it'. The buildings in the park 'were connected by "flying passages" that climbed the mountains and strode across the valleys'. The park was used to keep 'a white elephant presented by the King of Gandhara' and to stage an encounter between a tiger, a lion, a leopard and a bear. On coming to the throne in 531, Kuang-ling decided that 'To hold birds and beasts in captivity is to go against their nature. They should be sent back to the hills and forests'.[78] This was a classic Buddhist sentiment. The poor lion died on its return journey to Persia but the White Horse Monastery has a pond for freeing animals.

In Luoyang, wealthy officials also had gardens. The Minister of Agriculture's garden was east of the city and outside its walls. It is described with poetic licence, as are scenes in surviving Chinese gardens – possibly because they were inspired by the home of gods:

None of the princes could rival the beauty of his gardens with their trees, hills and ponds. He had a Ching-yang Mountain constructed that looked quite natural; there was range upon range of towering crags, while deep chasms and cavernous gullies led into each other. Tall forests of giant trees blotted out the sun and moon; mists drifted in the wind through the hanging creepers and dangling vines. Rough stone paths would seem to be impassable and yet allow a way through; the beds of torrents would twist around and then run straight.[79]

No trace of Luoyang's gardens survives but written accounts make it clear that Buddhism was the driving force behind their creation, as it was in Heian Japan (see p. 243). Even commentators who see Buddhism as an 'outlandish cult' which 'invaded' China agree that its 'influence and its transformation of the Chinese outlook on life and nature' were profound.[80] Buddhism is the world faith most connected with gardens. Siddhartha Gautama, who became the Buddha, was born in a garden and raised in a

6.54 The Qiyun Pagoda at the White Horse Monastery dates from 1175. The garden is a modern re-creation of the fifth-century garden rockwork. The first Buddhist temple in China was established here in 68 CE.

garden. After becoming enlightened, he spent the monsoon seasons living in gardens and the dry seasons preaching in gardens and parks. The Amitabha Buddha lives forever in a garden. Buddhist monks in India and China followed his example by making gardens (*sangharama*, see p. 150) for their communities. I think the Buddha had more influence on Chinese gardens than Confucius.

A twelfth-century Chinese philosopher (Chu His or Zhu Xi) wrote: 'Buddhism stole the best features of Daoism; Daoism stole the worst features of Buddhism.'[81] Daoists often resented the popularity of Buddhism, but in gardens the two faiths came together: there was full agreement about the importance of meditation and retreat; Buddhism brought a love of images, temples and gardens; Daoism stressed the significance of water, islands and forests. It is difficult to distinguish Chinese Buddhist and Daoist architecture. In gardens, disentangling the two faiths is impossible. Take the example of mountains: Daoist hermits retreated to mountains; Amitabha lived among mountains; temples were built on mountains as symbols of Mount Sumeru – including the Hall of Supreme Harmony in the Forbidden City. The coming together of the two faiths led to the scenic composition of mountains, lakes and temples in what can be described as Daoist-Buddhist gardens. They are unlike Buddhist-influenced gardens in the Indian subcontinent.

The *Pure Land Sutras* form the strongest link between Buddhism and gardens. They contain a vivid description of the Amitabha Buddha in his Pure Land paradise (see p. 168). Images were produced, known as palace mandalas, which show the Buddha

6.55 The Dunhuang Caves.

sitting in a temple-palace on a hill in an ideal garden. Though most of China's early Buddhist paintings were destroyed, an eighth-century silk painting called 'The Paradise of Amitabha' was found in a cave at Dunhuang (see Figure 6.53). Pure Land Buddhism merged easily with Daoism. As we have seen, it was traditional for Daoist hermits to retreat to mountains and for emperors to retreat to detached palaces in landscape parks:

> *In sculpture and painting, Buddhist iconography was adopted and adapted to fit native systems of belief, while the Buddhist temple became the model for all Chinese temples, Daoist and Confucian. Scrolls of silk and paper became the format for written and pictorial records, replacing the bamboo slip 'book' records of the Han. The handscroll was quickly joined by the hanging scroll as the favourite format for painting. In all these ways, and in many others, Buddhism left a large imprint on Chinese art.*[82]

In gardens, Buddhist influence led to the aesthetic composition of contemplative landscapes. They had artificial mountains with trees, rocks, ponds and small pagoda-like temples. The word 'pagoda' derives from the Pali word, *dagoba*, equivalent to the Sanskrit word *stupa*. Landscape scrolls were unrolled to show progression through scenes with temples. Garden walks were planned on similar lines.

The period of the Northern Wei and the Southern Dynasties was followed by the Sui Dynasty (581–619), in which Buddhism spread through the Chinese empire, and by the Tang Dynasty, which became the golden age of Chinese Buddhism. It parallels the growth of Christianity in Carolingian Europe (*c.*580–840).

Tang landscapes and gardens, 618–906

The Tang Dynasty was the period in which garden design, landscape painting and poetry became sister arts – with Daoism and Buddhism as their parents. Both faiths were concerned about immortality and celebrated the life of a hermit in natural surroundings. Daoism brought a reverence for nature to the family. Mahayana Buddhism brought a devotional attitude and the practice of making offerings to statues in temples. The collection of scholars' rocks (*gongshi*) began in the Tang dynasty[83] and, like real mountains, they appealed to both Buddhists and Daoists.

Wang Wei (701–761), the great Tang poet and landscape painter, loved mountain scenery and was also famous for the design of his own garden:

My Villa in Mount Zhongnan

> *Since my middle-age years,*
> *I enjoy practicing Buddhism.*
> *Now I am old,*

6.56 The Wangchuan Villa belonged to Wang Wei. He was a Tang Dynasty poet, musician, painter and statesman who studied Ch'an Buddhism and established a monastery on his estate.

I live by Mount Zhongnan.
When I am in the mood,
I go out wandering alone.[84]

Fields and Gardens by the River Qi

I dwell apart by the River Qi,
Where the Eastern wilds stretch far without hills.
The sun darkens beyond the mulberry trees;
The river glistens through the villages.
Shepherd boys depart, gazing back to their hamlets;
Hunting dogs return following their men.
When a man's at peace, what business does he have?
I shut fast my rustic door throughout the day.[85]

Wang Wei's poetry survives but his garden, like the great Tang landscape paintings, has been lost. Sullivan comments, in a history of Chinese landscape painting, that: 'This new attitude to what man can do with nature also helped to bring about the birth of garden designing as a fine art'.[86] He identifies Wang Wei as 'one of the truly great figures in Chinese intellectual and artistic history'.[87] From the Tang Dynasty onwards, and under the influence of Buddhism, garden designers were either painters themselves or invited help from famous painters when planning gardens.

Landscape painting and garden design are 'word and image' arts. The use of a brush for both calligraphy and painting formed an 'indissoluble bond' between poetry and

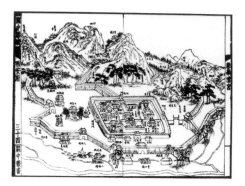

6.57 a, b The Imperial Resort Palace, known as the Huaqing Palace, is 35 km east of Xian. The buildings are new but the hot springs at the foot of Mount Lushan have been the setting for palaces and gardens since the Qin Dynasty. At one time, the palace had protective walls and roofed corridors climbing into the mountains, as shown in the drawing.

painting.[88] As literary arts, they became joint contributors to garden design. Poems were incorporated into paintings. Poetic inscriptions were placed beside garden scenes and in natural landscapes. Famous landscapes were 'quoted' in garden designs, visually and with text. If the quill pen had been used for writing instead of the brush, as in Europe, the link between word and image might have been less strong and Chinese gardens might have evolved in a different direction.

Wang Wei's country retreat was located on the Wang River some 40 km south of Chang'an (Xian). He began 'the tradition of describing the beauty of a garden in poems'[89] and his villa became what 'every Chinese scholar since would like to recreate around him'.[90] Copies of what is thought to be paintings of this estate survive as engravings. Paintings and design ideas were copied over and over again, much as musical compositions are replayed with a performer's individual interpretations. The painting thought to be Wang Wei's garden shows his villa nestling between a river and the hills (Figure 6.56).

Bai Juyi, another famous Tang poet-gardener, classified himself as a 'middle hermit' because, unlike 'petty hermits' who live in the mountains, he could enjoy a life in which 'you are spared hunger and cold' with the comforts of a city and the seclusion of a garden.[91] After governing Hangzhou and Suzhou, he returned to Luoyang to make his own garden and enjoy the life of a 'middle-class hermit'. It had a music pavilion, a reading pavilion, a lake and three islands connected by bridges. He transported Lake Tai stones, white lotus plants and pleasure boats to his own lake.[92]

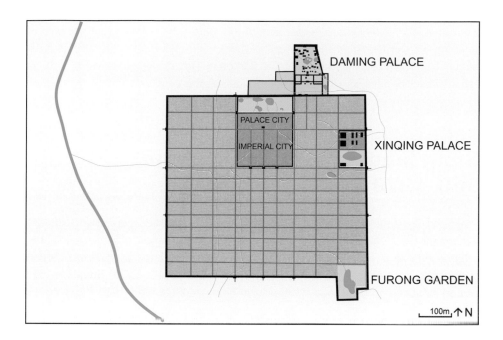

6.58 The Tang capital of Chang'an, on the site of modern Xian, had gardens within the walled compound and large parks, not shown, beyond its walls.

6.59 Trees and water were highly valued in Ch'an monasteries.

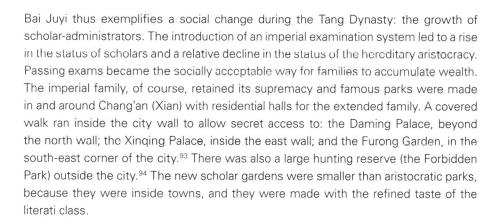

Bai Juyi thus exemplifies a social change during the Tang Dynasty: the growth of scholar-administrators. The introduction of an imperial examination system led to a rise in the status of scholars and a relative decline in the status of the hereditary aristocracy. Passing exams became the socially acceptable way for families to accumulate wealth. The imperial family, of course, retained its supremacy and famous parks were made in and around Chang'an (Xian) with residential halls for the extended family. A covered walk ran inside the city wall to allow secret access to: the Daming Palace, beyond the north wall; the Xinqing Palace, inside the east wall; and the Furong Garden, in the south-east corner of the city.[93] There was also a large hunting reserve (the Forbidden Park) outside the city.[94] The new scholar gardens were smaller than aristocratic parks, because they were inside towns, and they were made with the refined taste of the literati class.

The literati were gentleman-artist-scholar-administrators, some of them sufficiently wealthy to endow monasteries. Buddhist establishments became rich so that 'the normal expenditures of monasteries apparently required only one-fourth to one-third of their income'.[95] Wealth led to envy and Emperor Wu-tsung pillaged the monasteries, as did Henry VIII of England to solve a financial crisis in the sixteenth century. Wu-tsung ordered the destruction of Buddhist monasteries in 845 and promoted Daoism. Though subsequently reversed, his order began a long decline in the status of Chinese Buddhism. The Buddhist lands of Central Asia were lost from Chinese control. A rebellion in 884 led to the destruction of Chang'an and Luoyang. Then, in 907 the Tang Dynasty itself fell and most Tang art was destroyed in the ensuing civil war. Ch'an

(Zen) Buddhism survived the persecution of 845 better than other sects because of its emphasis on meditation and because its monks were willing to undertake physical labour. Like Carthusian endowments in Europe, Ch'an monasteries were built 'in beautiful secluded places where the only sound was the wind in the trees and the rain falling on the stones of the temple courtyard'.[96]

Song landscapes and gardens, 960–1279

The Song Dynasty established a new order. It is sometimes compared to Italy's Renaissance but was four centuries earlier. China had a period of peace under the enlightened rule of civilized and art-loving emperors. Landscape painting and garden design enjoyed a golden age, in harmony with nature poetry. Ch'an Buddhism had a deep influence on landscape art. Sensitive brushwork showed trees and rivers as symbols of the flux which permeates the world. Just enough material survives to form a picture of Song Dynasty gardens. The evidence includes Marco Polo's description of Hangzhou, Li Gefei's description of Luoyang, the stone map of Suzhou, incidents in landscape paintings, a few garden fragments in China and some Song-influenced gardens in Japan (see p. 256), about which Siren wrote: 'Nothing is more likely than that parks of similar kind existed at the Zen (or Ch'an) monasteries in the environs of Hangzhou.'[97]

Li Gefei wrote 'A Record of the Celebrated Gardens of Luoyang' c.1095. It is a useful sequel to the description of Luoyang in 574 (see p. 206). As before, only aristocratic gardens were described. The most spectacular garden belonged to Duke Fu of Zheng. 'The pavilions and terraces, flowers and plants were all carefully designed and cultivated by himself. Therefore, whether it is the zigzagging or the straightforward paths, whether it is open spaces or dense woods, everything reveals his profound deliberation.' Peonies were displayed in all the gardens. The Flower Garden of the Temple of Celestial Kings was devoted entirely to peony cultivation. It had 'no pools or pavilions' and during the flowering season

> those in the city whose livelihood depends on the peony flowers all dwell here ... they put up tents and set up shops, with the accompaniment of pipes and strings ... When the season is over, the place turns back into one of debris, with nothing but broken walls and abandoned stoves facing each other.[98]

A description of Song parks by a European observer also exists. Marco Polo saw Hangzhou shortly after it fell to the Mongols, in 1276, and considered the city was 'beyond dispute the finest and the noblest in the world'. Hangzhou still advertises itself as 'the most beautiful city in China'. In Marco Polo's time it was inhabited by wealthy families and craftsmen so that:

6.60 A Song Dynasty painting showing pot-grown peonies, *penjing* and a peacock.

6.61 a, b, c Hangzhou's West Lake is still surrounded by beautiful scenery and is still used by pleasure boats.

All along the main street ... running from end to end of the city, both sides are lined with houses and great palaces and the gardens pertaining to them, whilst in the intervals are the houses of tradesmen engaged in their different crafts.[99]

He was enchanted by the West Lake:

A trip on this Lake is a much more charming recreation than can be enjoyed on land. For on the one side lies the city in its entire length, so that the spectators in the barges, from the distance at which they stand, take in the whole prospect in its full beauty and grandeur, with its numberless palaces, temples, monasteries, and gardens, full of lofty trees, sloping to the shore. And the Lake is never without a number of other such boats, laden with pleasure parties; for it is the great delight of the citizens here, after they have disposed of the day's business, to pass the afternoon in enjoyment with the ladies of their families, or perhaps with others less reputable.[100]

Hangzhou's West Lake resembled an imperial park but was for aristocratic use. It survives, still popular for boating, still ringed with pavilions and gardens. More can be learned about the use of this type of space from contemporary accounts of Japanese gardens (see p. 248).

Marco Polo also visited Suzhou, 200 km north of Hangzhou. He thought it 'a very great and noble city' but did not describe the gardens for which Suzhou is now famous. A stone map of the city in 1229 shows a town layout which is similar to modern Suzhou, including some of the spaces which are now famous gardens. The Blue Waves Pavilion Garden (Cang Lang Ting Yuan) is named after a garden building which existed at the time Marco Polo was in Suzhou. Then beside a pond, it was moved to the top of a small hill when the garden was re-designed. A 1696 drawing of the re-designed garden shows it with a more open character than today. Much of the space was probably used to grow fruit and vegetables.

The most dramatic visual information about everyday life at the time Marco Polo was in China comes from the Qingming Scroll. It is 10 m long and is thought to represent the Northern Song capital of Dongjing, now buried in silt beneath the modern city of Kaifeng. The original scroll was painted in black ink and is in the Beijing Palace Museum. Many later copies were made, some in colour, and the Scroll was also used, far too loosely, to build the Millennium City Park within the walls of modern Kaifeng.

The original Qingming Scroll begins in the countryside and takes the viewer along the river, through the city walls and down the main street, past courtyards and gardens. The city may well have had north–south and east–west streets but it is higgledy-piggledy and needs to be compared with Marco Polo's hometown (Venice) to fit his account of it being 'like a chess board'. There is a brilliant eighteenth-century coloured version of the Scroll in the Taiwan Palace Museum. The artist may have had a better idea than we do of how Dongjing's gardens looked in the twelfth century. His imagination

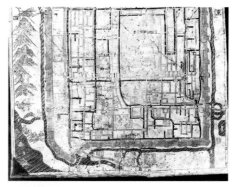

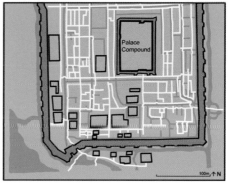

6.62 a, b The southern half of the Stone Map of Suzhou, also shown as a tracing, is recognizably the same as the modern city and some of the unbuilt land is still used for gardens. The central palace compound does not survive.

6.63 a–e Visual information about the character of China's old cities can be obtained from the Qingming Scroll, a street in Pingyao and a re-created bridge and palace in Kaifeng.

extends beyond the city wall into an imperial park with lakeside palaces, pavilions, walkways, bridges, deer, flowering trees, grottos and ladies taking the air. Compared to the countryside and the town, there are few people in the park and it would have had sufficient privacy for the frolics Marco Polo reported. Marco Polo's description of a Hangzhou palace in the late thirteenth century, below, can be read in conjunction with the eighteenth-century version of the Qingming Scroll ('Facfur' is Polo's spelling of *Tianzi*, meaning Son of Heaven).

On certain days, sacred to his gods, the King Facfur used to hold a great court and give a feast to his chief lords, dignitaries, and rich manufacturers of the city of Kinsay. On such occasions those pavilions used to give ample accommodation for 10,000 persons sitting at tables ... On entering [the palace] you found another great edifice in the form of a cloister surrounded by a portico with columns, from which opened a variety of apartments for the King and the Queen, adorned like the outer walls with such elaborate work as we have mentioned. From the cloister again you passed into a covered corridor, six paces in width, of great length, and extending to the margin of the lake. On either side of this corridor were ten courts, in the form of oblong cloisters surrounded by colonnades; and in each cloister or court were fifty chambers with gardens to each. In these chambers were quartered one thousand young ladies in the service of the King. The King would sometimes go with the Queen and some of these maidens to take his diversion on the Lake, or to visit the Idol-temples, in boats all canopied with silk. The other two parts of the enclosure were distributed in groves, and lakes, and charming gardens planted with fruit-trees, and preserves for all sorts of animals, such as roe,

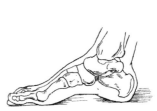

6.64 The palace section of the Taiwan version of the Qingming Scroll.

6.65 a–d Foot-binding (far left and above) caused ulcers and deformities which made walking difficult for girls with long dresses and bound feet. Roofed corridors eased the problem. The costumes are in the style of the Qing Dynasty.

red-deer, fallow-deer, hares, and rabbits. Here the King used to take his pleasure in company with those damsels of his; some in carriages, some on horseback, whilst no man was permitted to enter. Sometimes the King would set the girls a-coursing after the game with dogs, and when they were tired they would hie to the groves that overhung the lakes, and leaving their clothes there they would come forth naked and enter the water and swim about hither and thither, whilst it was the King's delight to watch them; and then all would return home. Sometimes the King would have his dinner carried to those groves, which were dense with lofty trees, and there would be waited on by those young ladies.[101]

The town section of the extended Qingming Scroll in Taiwan shows several gardens. Some look like monastery gardens and others look like the gardens of scholar-administrators. As in the description of Luoyang quoted above (see p. 206), they have ponds, mountains and rocks. But they are not filled with plants, making one wonder if the 'hares and rabbits' seen by Marco Polo helped manage the vegetation. There are roofed corridors, which Polo calls 'cloisters', round the garden courts but they are more rectangular than the corridors in extant Suzhou gardens. These corridors must have been useful for the ladies with bound feet who were the predominant users of palaces and their gardens. Foot binding is known to have been widespread in Song dynasty China. Ladies with long gowns and embroidered silk shoes walked with difficulty on feet deformed into the shape of a 'golden lotus'.[102] In Suzhou, 'Summer is long, hot, humid, and frequently wet. Winter is short and mild.'[103] Roofed corridors are climatically excellent garden features.

6.66 a, b The Jade Islet in Beihai Park was the site of Kublai Khan's palace. It now has a white *stupa* on the summit and the Floating Gallery on the lakeshore.

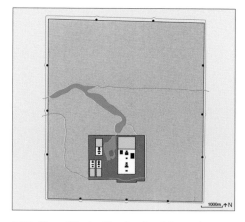

6.67 Plan of Dadu. The details of the park area, in green, and the city area, in grey, are not known.

Yuan landscapes and gardens, 1271–1368

The Yuan Dynasty replaced the Song Dynasty and built a new capital called Dadu on the site of what is now Beijing. Kublai Khan was a Mongol and a grandson of Ghenghis Khan, but he employed Chinese advisers and they designed Dadu on traditional Chinese lines. Marco Polo was there between 1266 and 1291 and gave the following description:

> As regards the size of this city you must know that it has a compass of 24 miles, for each side of it hath a length of 6 miles, and it is four-square. And it is all walled round with walls of earth which have a thickness of full ten paces at bottom, and a height of more than 10 paces but they are not so thick at top ... The streets are so straight and wide that you can see right along them from end to end and from one gate to the other. And up and down the city there are beautiful palaces, and many great and fine hostelries, and fine houses in great numbers. All the plots of ground on which the houses of the city are built are four-square, and laid out with straight lines; all the plots being occupied by great and spacious palaces, with courts and gardens of proportionate size. All these plots were assigned to different heads of families. Each square plot is encompassed by handsome streets for traffic; and thus the whole city is arranged in squares just like a chess-board.[104]

It should be noted that Dadu's spacious palaces had *both* 'courts' and 'gardens' but the character of the gardens is unknown. Since the whole city was planned 'just like a chess-board' with the houses built 'four-square', it does not seem probable that they had irregularly shaped water gardens like those which survive in Suzhou. They are more likely to have been rectangular courts with symbolic compositions of stones and plants, like the present Imperial Garden in the Forbidden City.

Kublai Khan's palaces in Dadu were arranged round lakes and hills, in the traditional way of imperial Chinese parks. Marco Polo described the walled palace city as follows:

> You must know that it is the greatest Palace that ever was. The roof is very lofty, and the walls of the Palace are all covered with gold and silver. They are also adorned with representations of dragons [sculptured and gilt], beasts and birds, knights and idols, and sundry other subjects ... Between the two walls of the enclosure which I have described, there are fine parks and beautiful trees bearing a variety of fruits. There are beasts also of sundry kinds, such as white stags and fallow deer, gazelles and roebucks, and fine squirrels of various sorts, with numbers also of the animal that gives the musk, and all manner of other beautiful creatures ... A river enters this lake and issues from it, but there is a grating of iron or brass put up so that the fish cannot escape in that way. Moreover on the north side of the Palace, about a bow-shot off, there is a hill which has been made by art [from the earth dug out of the lake]; it is a good hundred paces in height and a mile in compass. This hill is entirely covered with trees that never lose their

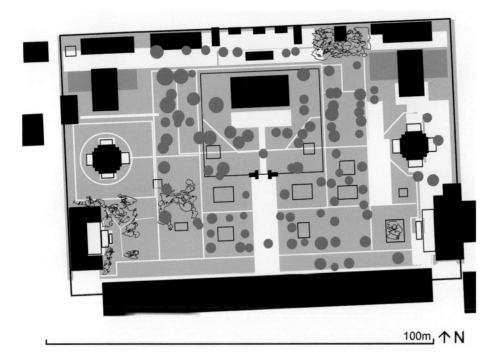

6.68 a, b The Imperial Garden in the Forbidden City.

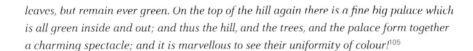

leaves, but remain ever green. On the top of the hill again there is a fine big palace which is all green inside and out; and thus the hill, and the trees, and the palace form together a charming spectacle; and it is marvellous to see their uniformity of colour![105]

The area described above is Dadu's palace city. An outer wall enclosed the urban area. Inner walls enclosed the three palaces and their courtyards. Even the imperial park was inside the walled city. It was a landscape of lakes, hills and palaces. The artificial lake was so large that it was described as a sea (*hai*). Earlier landscape parks, though also enclosed, had been outside the city walls. The Mongols, coming from a cold dry plateau, had both a love of water and a fear of being attacked by the people they held in thrall. Kublai Khan's Dadu was destroyed when the Yuan Dynasty fell but the area of artificial lakes and hills was retained. It is now called Beihai (Northern Sea) Park, west of the Forbidden City in Beijing.

Kublai Khan also had a summer palace at Shangdu, which Marco Polo spelt Xuanadu. It is in dry grassland 275 km north of Beijing. The outline of the city survives and it is difficult to see how it can ever have had the qualities imagined by Coleridge, who called it Xanadu, making one wonder if Coleridge confused reports of Shangdu with those of Dadu:

> *In Xanadu did Kubla Khan*
> *A stately pleasure-dome decree:*

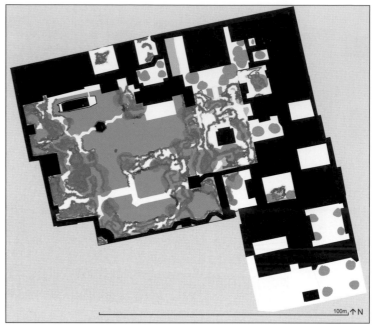

6.69 a, b The Lion Grove Garden (Shi Zi lin) began as a Buddhist monastery and became a scholar garden. Though much re-worked, the stone garden is one of the oldest to have survived.

Where Alph, the sacred river, ran
Through caverns measureless to man
Down to a sunless sea.
So twice five miles of fertile ground
With walls and towers were girdled round:
And there were gardens bright with sinuous rills,
Where blossomed many an incense-bearing tree;
And here were forests ancient as the hills,
Enfolding sunny spots of greenery.[106]

With the Chinese population heavily taxed to support the Mongol elite, private gardens did not flourish under the Yuan Dynasty. Buddhist monasteries, however, were treated favourably and continued to have gardens. The Shi Zi lin (Lion Grove Garden) in Suzhou was founded by the Zen Buddhist monk Tianru Weize and begun in 1342. The garden was at the rear of the 'Lion Forest Temple of the True Bodhi Master'. It was named in memory of his teacher, Monk Zhongfeng who taught at the Lion Cliff (Shizi Yan) in the Tianmu Mountains. 'Lion' was a reminder of Buddha, the 'Lion of the Sakyas', and of the lion-shaped rocks used to build the garden. It was normal for Buddhists to teach in mountains, forests and gardens. Literati visited the garden but it is unlikely to have been a place for frivolity. Most of the garden was destroyed and has been rebuilt (see p. 232). The central stone mountain survives and, though changed, 'is the only one of this antiquity to exist today.'[107] There is a fourteenth-century painting of the garden, by Ni Zan, showing it more open than today with a rocky hill behind a group of buildings but no lake.[108] Clunas comments that its present appearance is 'no guide to its arrangements in the Ming and the intriguing possibility of a central role for Buddhist symbolism in the popularization of garden rocks must remain no more than a speculation'.[109] The safest assumption is that the popularity of garden rocks had Daoist and Buddhist origins in a shared Central Asian heritage.

Ming landscapes and gardens, 1368–1644

The overthrow of the Yuan Dynasty and the establishment of the Ming Dynasty, in 1368, were accompanied by a pride in having ended a period of foreign rule. Though they had adopted many aspects of Chinese culture, it could never be forgotten that the Yuan emperors and their soldiers were descendants of Genghis Khan. Having seen them off, Ming dynasty emperors re-appraised Chinese history to lay the basis for a secure future. Many aspects of society were re-organized. As in Renaissance Europe, the aim was to distil what was best in the social, artistic and philosophical traditions of the preceding two millennia. This resulted in a new urban synthesis and what is now regarded as the classical Chinese garden.

The synthesis is described as Neo-Confucian because the Confucian approach was revived, modernized and integrated with Buddhism and Daoism. Originating in the Song Dynasty, this became the philosophical framework for Ming rule, visually represented by drawings of Confucius, Laozi and Buddha drinking vinegar from the same jar and agreeing that 'the three teachings are one'. Together, they provided a way of organizing society (Confucian), a way of worshipping the gods (Mahayana Buddhist), and a way of learning from nature (Daoist). A revised examination system was introduced to ensure that all bureaucrats had the necessary ability to run the state in accordance with Neo-Confucian principles. This re-established the literati class of garden makers.

Dadu was rebuilt after the Ming victory and the name of the city was changed first to Beiping ('northern peace') and then to Beijing ('northern capital'). Three city walls (outer, middle and inner) were built to protect the inhabitants. The Ming outer wall was in a similar position to the Yuan outer wall but enclosed 40 per cent less land. The Yuan landscape park inside the middle walls was retained with the water level raised to extend the area of the water surface. The innermost wall, which survives, enclosed the palace now called the Forbidden City. Material excavated from the moat was used to form a hill in Jingshan Park (Coal Hill). It is at the north of the Forbidden City and therefore confers feng shui benefits on the palaces to the south. There are seventeen palaces within the Forbidden City, most with their own courtyards. The City bestrides

6.70 Only the innermost wall of the Forbidden City survives.

6.71 Plan of Beijing showing the Forbidden City, Jingshan Park and the three Seas: Beihai, Zhonghai and Nanhai. The Central and Southern Seas (Zhongnanhai) are an exclusive compound for the Chinese Communist Party, which governs China.

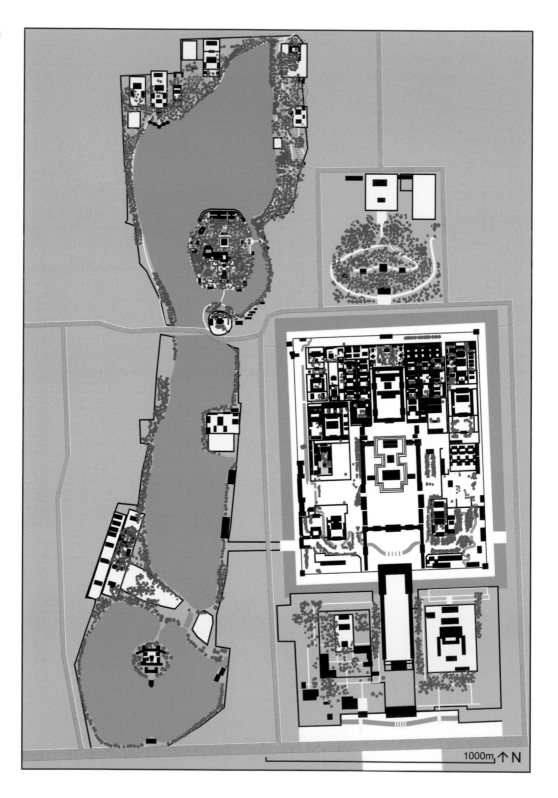

1000m ↑ N

an 8 km north–south axis, passing through numerous walls and gates so that there is no end-to-end view, as on a European avenue, and no public access to the central section of the route which passes through the Forbidden City. This urban form has come to symbolize and summarize the long Chinese tradition of city, park and garden design:

> *The Beijing which thus emerged in 1420, with extensions in 1553 ... is a centric and symmetrical layout. It symbolically represents Confucian ideas of a sacred emperor, the Son of Heaven, residing at the centre of the universe, coordinating the ways of 'heaven' with that of humans on earth.*[110]

Beihai Park, as it is now known, was reserved for the imperial family. This was an old tradition but in Beijing the park within the city walls came to be used more like a garden. It became a place for elegant boat trips and summer feasts, similar to the Mughal court's use of the gardens around Lake Dal in Kashmir. Mughals, Manchus, Han Chinese and Ottoman Turks remembered their nomadic histories and enjoyed outdoor life in luxurious surroundings. Today, the North Sea (Beihai) is open to the public for boating while the Middle Sea (Zhonghai) and the South Sea (Nanhai) remain exclusive pleasure grounds for the ruling elite. The government compound is called the Zhongnanhai. It is the headquarters of the Communist Party of China and the government of the People's Republic of China. Within the Forbidden City itself there are four substantial gardens: the Imperial Garden and the gardens of three palaces: for the Establishment of Happiness, for Compassion and Tranquility, and for Tranquil Longevity. They are more like courtyards than Suzhou-type gardens.

The character of private gardens changed during the Ming dynasty, paralleling the evolution of the imperial enclave from a hunting park to a civilized landscape park. In a book entitled *Fruitful Sites*, Clunas outlines a three-stage model for the development of Ming gardens:

- a focus on the morally good life of self-sufficiency;
- a concern for rare and splendid plants;
- a focus on matters of aesthetic taste.

He views these changes as a process of aestheticization, with the functional role of gardens giving way to a more luxurious role:

> *Groves of fruit trees gradually became less prominent in the garden landscape, to be replaced by rare flowering shrubs of no possible economic value, including types imported from south-east Asia.*[111]

The changes are exemplified by the gardens of the Wen family. Wen Zhengming (1470–1559) was a leading Ming dynasty scholar, painter, author, poet, calligrapher and garden virtuoso. He was a contemporary of Michelangelo and a comparable figure in the art of China.[112] Wen's own garden was comparatively modest but later

6.72 a The Forbidden City seen from Jingshan. **b** Beihai Park, looking towards the Forbidden City.

6.73 Plum trees are grown for their blossom and their fruit. The Meihua (Plum Blossom) Mountain outside Nanjing is associated with Xu Wei, a Ming dynasty painter and poet.

gardens belonging to his family were 'splendid' and 'extravagant'.[113] He helped design the Garden of the Humble Administrator (also called the Garden of the Unsuccessful Politician) which was built *c*.1510 on the site of the Dahong Temple in Suzhou and is far from humble. In 1533, Wen Zhengming produced a record of the garden with prose, poems and illustrations. Though there is still a garden on the site (see p. 232), the boundaries have changed and the original structures and plantings have gone. Wen Zhengming's paintings show the old garden to have been much more open than it is today, with grass and trees with fenced walks, bridges and enclosures with pavilions (see Figure 6.74a).

Design advice for scholar gardens was published in *The Craft of Gardens* (*Yuan Ye*) by Ji Cheng. The author lived *c*.1582–1642 and explains how he came to be a garden designer:

> In my youth I had a deep interest in woodlands, and evaded fame among the hills and valleys. For a long time I made a living from landscape gardening. I felt as though I was cut off from the things of this world, and only heard distantly of the turmoil of current events. I had a deep desire to become a hermit but unfortunately I did not have the power to purchase a mountain of my own.[114]

His book therefore contains an account of how to 'borrow' a mountain to enhance a garden scene. 'To borrow from the scenery means that although the interior of a garden is distinct from what lies outside it, as long as there is a good view you need not

6.74 a, b The Humble Administrator's Garden (Zhou Zheng Yuan) is more richly planted now than in Wen Zhengming's time.

6.75 The Garden of the Humble Administrator uses borrowed scenery (*jie jing*). The Beisi Pagoda (Beisi Ta) is 1 km outside the garden boundary.

be concerned whether this is close by or far away'.[115] He restates the ancient basis of Chinese garden design as follows: 'If you build your hut by a mountain torrent, it seems you are sure to find peace and quiet. But if you bring the mountains to your home, what need is there to search for remote places?'[116] Shapes, sounds, colours and scents can also be borrowed.[117] Ji Cheng was attracted by the traditional hermit's life but also by the money he could earn as a designer. He is known to have worked in Yangzhou, a city which had grown rich on its monopoly of the salt trade, and he designed a Garden of Reflections for the nobleman (Zheng Yuanxun) who wrote the Foreword to his book on garden design. This garden had a 'vegetable garden and flower plantation' and also an area of 'pavilions divided by rivulets and ponds and connected by winding covered walkways and bridges'.[118]

The Ming court became too comfortable: while the imperial family enjoyed its palaces and gardens, eunuchs ruled the empire and took every decision on the basis of who offered the largest bribe. Gardens became status symbols. A new class of professional garden designers began to emerge and 'among the materials used for the enjoyment of a garden, wine appears to have been indispensable.'[119]

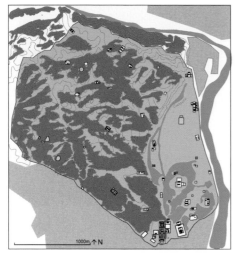

6.76 a, b The Imperial Mountain Resort for Escaping Summer Heat (Chengde) is enclosed by a wall, as were all imperial parks.

Qing landscapes and gardens, 1644–1911

Imperial parks and gardens

Manchu invaders forced the seaward end of the Great Wall in 1644. They captured Beijing, founded the Qing Dynasty and gave China yet another period of rule by mounted warriors from the north. The conquest of South China was slower but by 1682 10 million Manchus ruled 350 million Chinese. Never forgetting the relatively small size of their population, the Manchus thought it best to adopt Chinese traditions and the country became deeply conservative. While Europe embarked on a period of rapid growth and change, China scrutinized its past. The arts, including garden design, stagnated. It is probably this factor which has led commentators to write about '*the* Chinese Classical Garden', as though it was a single thing which existed in the Bronze Age (Zhou Dynasty) and never changed. The new rulers felt more secure in North China and most secure in palatial enclaves, funded by taxing the Han Chinese. Beijing's Forbidden City, built under the Ming, remained the ceremonial capital and three great summer palaces were made: the Yuanming Yuan and the Yihe Yuan, both outside Beijing, and Chengde in the hills to the north. The Beijing pair were known to Westerners as the Old Summer Palace and the New Summer Palace.

Work on Chengde, the Imperial Mountain Resort for Escaping Summer Heat began in 1681. It is beyond the Great Wall, 255 km north-east of Beijing and 145 km south of the Mulan Hunting Ground. Chengde is enclosed by a 10 km wall and Mulan by a 650 km wall. Lord Macartney was given a tour of Chengde, which he knew as Jehol, in 1793. His guide to the eastern garden was the Qianlong Emperor himself. Then 83 years old, he was a great military leader, the author of 42,000 poems and a lavish patron of the arts. Chengde put Macartney in mind of 'the magnificence of Stowe, the soft beauties of Woburn or the fairy-land of Painshill'.[120] He was a perceptive critic: the English landscape designers who worked at this time were also concerned with 'the nature of Nature' and also used scenic quotations from an ancient world. But Chengde was on a grander scale:

> As we moved onward an extensive lake appeared before us, the extremities of which seemed to lose themselves in distance and obscurity. Here was a large, magnificent yacht ready to receive us, and a number of smaller ones for the attendants, elegantly fitted up and adorned with numberless vanes, pennants, and streamers.[121]

Two days later, Macartney had a tour of the western garden, ending with a visit to a viewing pavilion:

> It is one of the finest forest scenes in the world, wild, woody, mountainous and rocky, abounding with stags and deer of different species, and most of the other beasts of chase not dangerous to man ... These woods often clamber over the loftiest pinnacles

6.77 a, b Boating on the lake and the pagoda at Chengde.

of the stony hills, or gathering on the skirts of them descend with a rapid sweep, and bury themselves in the deepest valleys. There, at proper distances you find palaces, banqueting houses and monasteries.[122]

I saw everything before me as on an illuminated map, palaces, pagodas, towns, villages, farm houses, plains and valleys watered by innumerable streams, hills waving with woods and meadows covered with cattle of the most beautiful marks and colours.[123]

Imperial use of the Mulan hunting ground reminds one of the Shanglin Park Rhapsody (see p. 200). Each year, the Qianlong emperor took 10,000 men on a hunting expedition to Mulan. They operated a ring hunt, with animals contained by a wall of nets. For the remainder of the year the emperor lived with a great retinue of ladies and eunuchs. Chengde was designed as a symbol of 'the Manchu ambition to dominate the cultural, physical, and metaphysical geographies of Eastern and Central Asia'.[124] It proclaimed the Manchu's supposedly ancestral right to rule Manchuria, Tibet and China – together with their religious status as the linchpin of Daoism, Confucianism and Buddhism.

In Beijing, the Manchus occupied the ceremonial Ming palace now called the Forbidden City. It was a fortified palace and, though adjoining a landscape park, the Manchus did not particularly like it. As an alternative, they made the Yuanming Yuan beyond the walls of Beijing. It was of great extent, but designed as a pleasure park and garden, rather than a hunting park. Work on the estate began in 1707 and at the time of its destruction, by the British and French in 1860, it was five times the size of the Forbidden City. In 1775, the Qianlong emperor spent 168 days in the Yuanming Yuan,

6.78 a The Yuanming Yuan, right, was a landscape park but with so many detached palaces that it took on a garden character.
b A reconstructed pavilion in the Yuanming Yuan gives an idea of the garden's former character – and of why it was used as a summer palace.

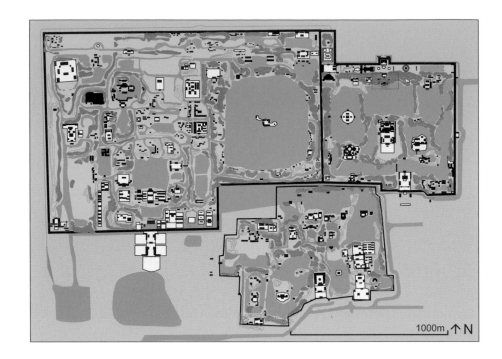

1000m ↑ N

105 days in the Forbidden City and 66 days in Chengde. In 1752, he returned from Chengde and wrote a poem on the Yuanming Yuan:[125]

> *Now I admire the picturesque hills,*
> *Now I enjoy boating on lakes,*
> *Maple trees are still in red,*
> *They inspire me to write poems.*

Wong describes a typical day, on which the emperor returned from the New Year celebrations in the Forbidden City. He travelled to the Yuanming Yuan in a heated palanquin borne by eight bearers:

> *Upon arrival, Qianlong and his entourage went through the Inner Palace Gate and stopped at the Honoring Three Selflessnesses Court to pray briefly. Then he proceeded to his living quarters on the Nine Continents for a short rest. The next activity of the day was to take a boat ride to pay homage in the Buddhist temple at the Gentle Clouds Cover All to worship at the Anyou Palace of the Ancestral Shrine. On the way back, he stopped at the Eternal Spring Fairy Hall to see his mother. He returned to the Nine Continents for resting before having dinner at the All-Happy Garden, situated south of the Wall of Sravasti.*[126]

Though outside the walls of Beijing, the Yuanming Yuan was protected by its own wall – and by 3,456 Manchu soldiers. The estate was maintained by 986 garden staff

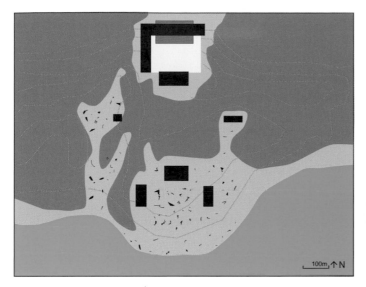

6.79 a, b Plan of Hall of the Gathering Orchid, in the north-east sector of the Yuanming Yuan, and a photograph of its site.

and 502 eunuchs. Boats were the preferred method of travel within the garden, which Westerners might compare to Worlitz in Germany, the Cypress Gardens in South Carolina or the Norfolk Broads in England. There was less use of covered walkways than in private gardens, possibly because the Manchu women did not bind their feet. The Yuanming Yuan contained hundreds of halls, pavilions, temples and monasteries. Many were on islands, planned on traditional courtyard lines but amidst flowering trees and shrubs. The Yuanming Yuan was not a Suzhou-type garden. It was a landscape park but with so many detached palaces that it took on a garden character. In terms of design philosophy, the Yuangming Yuan has one characteristic in common with gardens made in Europe during the same period: it was eclectic. The Qianlong emperor looked back to Chinese history. If he found a historical idea or a garden he admired, he ordered a copy for the Yuanming Yuan. When the French sent an embassy to China he asked them to make a European-style section for the Yuanming Yuan. Since they built in stone, this section was not entirely destroyed in the fire of 1860. The ruins can still be seen and led some observers to the mistaken belief that the predominant style of garden architecture was European. An accurate drawing of the Yuanming Yuan survives, in Paris, and is being used to guide some restoration work.

Scholar gardens

Most of the extant private gardens in China date from the Qing dynasty and the few which are older were re-made during this time. Today, the largest group is in the Suzhou area, but there are other private gardens throughout China. Suzhou has a better climate for gardens than Beijing. It is warmer and wetter. Marco Polo visited the city in the late thirteenth century and found it 'a very great and noble city', noting 'some 6,000 bridges, all of stone'. He did not comment on the gardens for which

6.80 Suzhou still has some canals and arched bridges, which are now being conserved and gentrified.

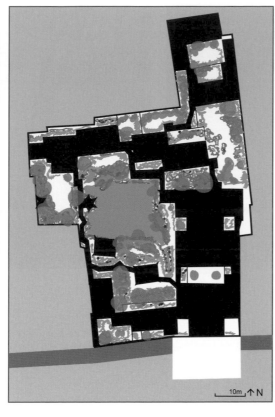

6.82 Recessed areas in courtyards were used for collecting water and growing pot plants, as well as for washing, drying, preparing food and other domestic activities.

6.81 a, b, c The Master of the Nets Garden in Suzhou (Wangshi Yuan) is highly regarded but occupies only 0.6 hectares. It was begun in 1140 and took its present form in the Qing Dynasty.

10m ↑ N

Suzhou is now famous, though some are on land which was used for gardens in the thirteenth century. Let us consider four famous examples. They have different origins, as temples, productive gardens and scholar gardens, but their features are comparable:

- They are closed off from the town by high walls, providing privacy and security.
- The gardens adjoin areas of courtyard housing, formerly owned and used by an extended family.
- The gardens can be viewed from a network of walks, corridors (*lang*) and pavilions, but their circulation systems are separate from those of the courtyard housing, so that the gardens could be used and visited without traversing the courtyards.
- The gardens display an elegant and light-hearted use of colour and pattern.

The Lion Grove Garden (see p. 220) was separated from its temple and became a private garden owned by the Zhang family (*c.*1650). There were several changes of ownership and after a period of neglect the garden was reclaimed in the nineteenth

6.83 a, b, c The Surging Waves Pavilion (Cang Lang Ting Yuan) seen from across the river which now forms a boundary but was once part of the garden.

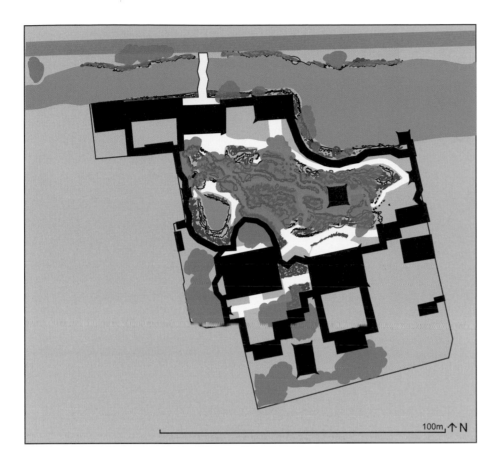

100m, ↑ N

century. Having evolved from a solemn monastic garden into a luxurious scholar garden, it is less open and has more pavilions. A roofed corridor runs along the south and west boundaries. The Huxin Ting Pavilion, reached by zigzag bridges, stands in the middle of a pond which has a Stone Boat in its north-west corner. Other pavilions allow one to look down on the water. It is a beautiful garden, but much changed from the period when it was a Buddhist retreat. Large tour groups being addressed through loudhailers further erode its contemplative seclusion.

The Surging Waves Pavilion (Cang Lang Ting, also called the Blue Wave Pavilion) has given its name to a famous garden, started by Su Shunqin (1008–1048). He was a government official, a scholar and a poet,[127] who purchased the site after retiring from his job. Before that it had been used to grow flowers for the palace, then at the heart of Suzhou. Su Shunqin may have used the land, like the Humble Administrator discussed below, to grow flowers and vegetables. He built the Surging Waves Pavilion in a waterside position, probably for use as a study. It was moved to a rocky mound in 1696 and is now separated from the water by a roofed corridor. The property became a temple in the fourteenth century and later reverted to being a private dwelling. From

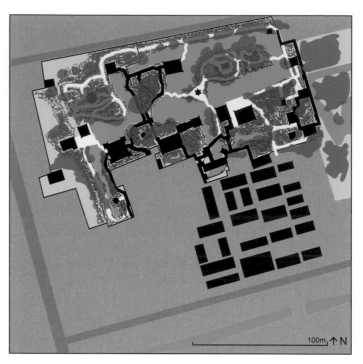

100m ↑ N

6.84 a, b, c The Humble Administrator's Garden (Zhou Zheng Yuan) is on the site of a former monastery.

the 1696 drawing of the garden, it appears that the lake which now forms its northern boundary lay wholly within the property. The building of a public road on land which was once part of the garden could explain both the construction of the roofed corridor and why the pavilion was moved onto a mound: to retain the view. An inscription on one of the columns states that 'Both near and afar/Rivulets and hills/Capture our affection'. South of the Surging Waves Pavilion is a small pond, ringed by another roofed corridor. It connects the residential quarters to the garden. A stone engraving of the garden was made in 1883 and shows the layout much as it is today.

The Humble Administrator's Garden (Zhou Zheng Yuan) was made on the site of the Dahong monastery, which had left it strewn with ponds. The Humble Administrator was Jing Pu, also known as Wang Xianchen. He purchased the land in 1533, used it to grow fruit and vegetables and built rustic pavilions.[128] Sometimes called the Unsuccessful Politician, because he withdrew from the court after being demoted, he wrote:

> I have not visited distant places, gone to parties, celebrations or even funerals, but have stayed inside my garden for thirty years, working in the heat of summer and the cold and wet of winter; not even for a single day have I left the garden.[129]

Wen Zhengming's drawings of the garden, discussed above (p. 224), show the garden before its re-design, in 1679 and again in 1742. Its character now belongs to the

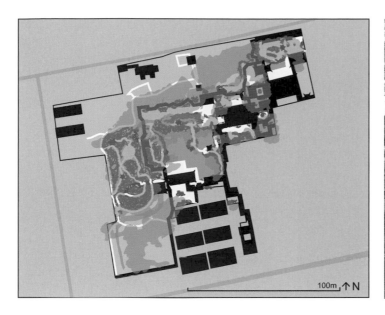

6.85 Plan of the Lingering Garden (Liu Yuan).

6.86 a, b The Lingering Garden (Liu Yuan) was described by Dorothy Graham as 'the most beautiful garden in the Ming tradition'.*

Note: *Graham, D., *Chinese Gardens*, New York: Dodd, Mead & Co., 1938, p. 92.

Qing dynasty. The garden has evolved from a horticultural retreat into a grand garden attached to a large residential compound (to the south and not open to the public as part of the garden). Though larger than Suzhou's other famous gardens, the Garden of the Humble Administrator is planned in a similar manner. Roofed corridors and zig-zag bridges link the residential courtyards to a romantic domain of woods, water and pavilions.

The Lingering Garden (Liu Yuan) was 'founded in AD 1522 by Xu Shitai, a civil servant in charge of the emperor's horses and carriages'.[130] In 1876, it was purchased and greatly enlarged by the Sheng family, which opened it to the public during the Spring Festival (Qingming Festival). This required a separate entrance. Graham judged that in 1938 it was 'The most beautiful garden in the Ming tradition' and, 'a place of poignant loveliness'.[131] Cheng sees it as an application of the principle of essay writing to garden design. It has 'the prelude, the development of the theme, an argument from different angles, and the conclusion'.[132] The 50 m corridor is the prelude, with glimpses of the main garden; then the wider garden view opens, then there are two routes – the argument stage; then one gets a final view – the conclusion. There is also a 'quotation' from China's garden history: a Penglai Island in the pond.

A detailed picture of how private gardens, like those in Suzhou, were designed and used can be found in China's greatest novel. *The Story of the Stone* is also known as

6.87 The Grand View Garden (Daguanyuan) in Beijing was made for a China TV film of *The Story of the Stone*.

6.88 The stones and grotto in Prince Gong's Garden can be associated with the Imperial Concubine's visit in *The Story of the Stone*.

the *Dream of the Red Chamber*.[133] It is believed to be based on the life of its author Cao Xueqin (*c*.1715–1764), who lived in Beijing. Prince Gong's garden in Beijing is sometimes identified as the model for this garden but has only a few features which can be associated with the story. *The Story of the Stone* tells of a young man (Jia Baoyu) who reaches manhood and, by the end of the tale, finds a wife. It has Daoist and Buddhist themes. The stone in the title is a piece of Jade incarnated as Baoyu. The dream in the alternative title is an erotic dream, re-enacted with a maid who knew she was destined to be Baoyu's concubine when he reached manhood. The story is about a path to enlightenment, both religious and sexual.

The use of courtyards and gardens is as separate in the novel as was their physical design. Courtyards were service areas for adjoining rooms. Gardens were for scholarship, entertainment and society. Roofed corridors led to garden pavilions and protected ladies with fine clothes and bound feet from water and mud. Some of the maids 'hardly set foot outside their own courtyards from one year's end to the next'. On one wet day 'the maids amused themselves by blocking up the gutters and letting the water collect in the courtyard' so that ducks could swim there. A scholar has a room overlooking the garden, with books and paint brushes. A pavilion is set with tables for food and wine. Junior maids stand by 'with spittoons, fly-whisks and napkins in their hands behind the chairs'. A garden entertainment is organized with 'not only the customary plays, but also juggling, acrobatics, story-telling by blind ballad-singers'. A lady gets drunk at her birthday party and while returning to her apartment finds one of her maids near 'the passage-way which led from Grandmother Jia's rear courtyard'.

Because the maid refused to explain why she was there, the lady threatened to have her mouth torn, or scorched with a red-hot iron, but chose instead to call for 'two men with a rope and whips to flog her to a jelly'. The maid therefore confessed to being on watch. The lady tiptoed across the courtyard to find that, bored with his maids and concubines, her husband had bribed a clan wife into his bed. The gardens and courts of the red mansions are a microcosm of aristocratic Chinese life, not so different from the palace intrigues of Versailles. As an exercise in regal geometry, Paris is in fact the closest Western counterpart to Beijing, and, but for such geographical obstacles as the Alps, the Pyrenees, the Channel and Russia, might well have become the 'Northern Capital' of a European superstate.

The *Dream of the Red Chamber* contains a famous description of a garden made for the Imperial Concubine's visit. It was also used for a flawed re-creation of the fictional garden in Beijing – the Grand View Garden (*Daguanyuan*). In the novel,

> the digging of pools, the raising of hills, the siting and erection of lodges and pavilions, the planting of bamboos and flowers – in a word, all matters pertaining to the landscaping and layout of the gardens, were planned and supervised by Horticultural Hu.

When the work was complete, they considered asking the Imperial Concubine to suggest inscriptions but decided it would be better to present her with alternatives written on lanterns because

> if we wait until she has already visited the garden before asking her, half the pleasure of the visit will be lost. All those prospects and pavilions – even the rocks and trees and flowers will seem somehow incomplete without that touch of poetry which only the written word can lend a scene.[134]

6.89 Prince Gong's Garden has a 'small retreat almost hidden among the hundreds and hundreds of green bamboos'.

6.90 Scholars liked to have studies overlooking gardens (drawing from a seventeenth-century scroll).

The stern father, his artistic son and two 'literary gentlemen' then go to inspect the newly completed garden:

> They now left the pavilion and crossed to the other side of the pool. For a while they walked on, stopping from time to time to admire the various rocks and flowers and trees which they passed on their way, until suddenly they found themselves at the foot of a range of whitewashed walls enclosing a small retreat almost hidden among the hundreds and hundreds of green bamboos which grew in a dense thicket behind them. With cries of admiration they went inside. A cloister-like covered walk ran round the walls from the entrance to the back of the forecourt and a cobbled pathway led up to the steps of the terrace. The house was a tiny three-frame one, two parts latticed, the third part windowless. The tables, chairs and couches which furnished it seemed to have been specially made to fit the interior.[135]

Possible inscriptions were inspired by famous poems, remembering that 'to recall an old thing is better than to invent a new one'. The son suggests 'The Hopeful Sign', drawn from the lines: 'Above the flowering apricot/A hopeful inn-sign hangs.'[136] The

6.91 a, b The La-Mei (*Chimonanthus praecox* 'wax plum') and the Chinese plum (*Prunus mune*) are highly valued because of their early flowering times. Ji Cheng wrote that 'the plum flower is like a lovely woman coming through moonlit woods'.*

Note: *Cheng, J. (trans. A. Hardie) *The Craft of Gardens*, New Haven: Yale University Press, 1988, p.121.

literary gentlemen are delighted. The father accuses his son of being a show-off. The book gives a brilliant picture of Qing society before the twentieth century.

The development of Chinese gardens was checked by the fall of the Qing dynasty in 1911 and brought to a standstill by the establishment of the People's Republic of China in 1949. It began to revive with China's returning prosperity towards the end of the twentieth century. In 2006, a friend was asked to design a private garden in Beijing 'for a new house of breathtaking bad taste, the garden was to be like a courtyard of the imperial palace with a barbecue area, the main axis centring on the carport for the armoured stretch Rolls Royce'.[137] Recent trends in China are discussed in the Afterword.

CHAPTER 7

Shinto-Buddhist gardens
in Japan

7.1 Japanese gardens became more Buddhist and more abstract than Chinese gardens, with rocks and gravel used to symbolize mountains and water (Kongobu-ji Temple).

7.2 For climatic and religious reasons, the gardens of Japan were more places to be viewed, than places for walking or physical exercise.

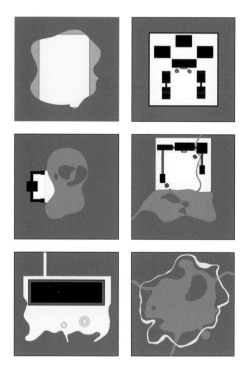

7.3 a–f Diagrams showing the evolution of Japanese gardens: Shinto *niwa*, Heian palace, Pure Land temple, *shinden-zukuri*, Zen garden, stroll garden.

The islands of Japan were settled from continental Asia, setting the pattern for a unique civilization which learned from the mainland but always set its own course. This became true of Japan's language, script, religion, architecture and gardens. By 10,000 BCE, migrants had established a hunter–gatherer civilization. It is called the Jomon Culture, from a pattern used on ceramics, or the Tree Culture, because it used trees for building construction, ornaments, canoes, bows, buckets, combs and bark clothing. The Jomon Culture had gods, sacrificial rituals, pit dwellings and the skill to make the world's oldest surviving pottery. But the society was not literate and the earliest written information about Japan comes from a Chinese text of 57 CE.

Something of the Jomon Culture survives among the Ainu people of Northern Japan but it was largely overwhelmed by a new wave of migrants from Continental Asia. This led to the Yayoi period (*c.*300 BCE–250 CE), which saw the introduction of a new language, rice cultivation, shamanism, iron-making and bronze-making. The religion of the Yayoi Period merged with older Japanese beliefs and with Confucianism and Daoism from the continent. Buddhism was brought to Japan in 552 CE and by 627 the country had 46 Buddhist temples. From this point onwards Buddhism became a key influence on the development of Japanese gardens. Even today, most of Japan's famous gardens are temple gardens. The others are palace gardens designed in the style of temple gardens. No other country has so many surviving temple gardens and they provide some indication of how Buddhist gardens may have looked in ancient China.

Shinto *niwa*

Shinto is the pre-Buddhist religion of Japan. The name derives from *shin*, meaning gods or spirits, and *tao*, which, as in Taoism (or Daoism), means 'way' or 'path'. Shinto is translated as 'the Way of the Gods' or 'the Way of the Spirits'. Objects in nature (e.g. the sun) and gods who lived in forests, rocks, seas, rivers and mountains were worshipped. Ceremonies and festivals were held but statues and temples were not made before the arrival of Buddhism. One of the oldest surviving temples is the great shrine of Ise (690) dedicated to the sun goddess Amaterasu Omikami. Offerings were made to obtain boons, as when:

> *His Lordship sent a prayer to the Great Shrine of Ise. Drafted by the master clerk and lay priest Miyoshi Yasunobu, its purpose was to ask for peace and tranquillity in the country and for the wealth and prosperity of the people.*[1]

The shrine at Ise comprises a sanctuary and buildings. It is a place of worship and a god's home. Sacred spaces (*niwa*), surfaced with gravel, were made in Japan before the arrival of Buddhism. The word *niwa* derives from *ni*, clay, and *ha*, place. In the *Chronicle of Japan* (*Nihon Shoki*) a *niwa* was 'a place purified for worship of the gods'.[2]

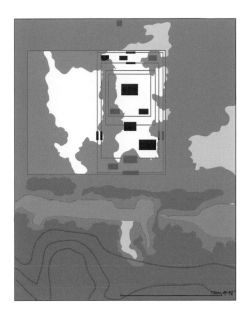

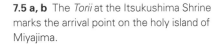

7.4 a, b Ise Jingu has a sacred expanse of gravel (*niwa*). There are two adjoining sites which are used in turn to rebuild a shrine on a 20-year rotation. The westerly niwa, in the photograph, will be the site of the shrine from 2013–2033.

7.5 a, b The *Torii* at the Itsukushima Shrine marks the arrival point on the holy island of Miyajima.

7.6 Meoto-Iwa, near Is, is a famous example of the Shinto regard for the rocks and their spirits.

In modern Japanese, *niwa* is used to mean garden or courtyard. In old Japanese, a *niwa* was a sacred space and not a garden. Stones were spread to enhance the purity of the space.

Shinto sanctuaries have ceremonial gates (*torii*) which may have developed independently in Japan or may have arrived with Buddhism. They mark entry points to a sacred space and are reminiscent of the *toranas* at Sanchi (see p. 146). The degree to which the idea of sacred space derives from Shinto or Daoism cannot be determined. The *Encyclopedia of Shinto* puts the point as follows:

> Rather than saying that agricultural rituals or ancestor veneration practices (sosen sūhai) were influenced by foreign cultures, it is better to say that they represent a general note of similarity throughout the East Asian cultural sphere.[3]

But one of the most characteristic features of Japanese gardens is the reverential care with which they are maintained. The classical Japanese garden is cared for by priests as a sacred place.

Asuka gardens, 538–710

The idea of making temple gardens reached Japan from China during the Asuka period. In 607, the Empress Suiko had sent an envoy (Ono no Imoko) to the Chinese capital, Chang'an, and a trained garden designer (Michiko no Takumi) sailed from Korea to Japan soon afterwards. He designed a Buddhist garden with a representation of Mount Sumeru, additional Buddhist imagery and a bridge.[4] No visual records of Asuka gardens survive but there are textual accounts of China's Buddhist gardens under the Northern Wei (see p. 205) and Sui dynasties.

Nara gardens, 710–784

Nara was Japan's capital from 710 to 784 and the city's name is used for a period which has great importance in the history of Japanese art and also helps illuminate a gap in the history of Chinese art. Nara is, for example, the best place to see the character of wooden buildings and silk landscape paintings which were made during China's Tang Dynasty (see p. 208). Nara was planned on the model of Chang'an (see p. 211) which was then China's capital. In Japanese history, Nara represents an approach to religion, town planning, art, architecture and gardens which was as new as the first Roman town in Britain or the first British town in America. Nara's grid layout survives and projects into what is now a deer park. At the point where the old grid meets the park, the Todai-ji (Great Eastern Temple, 743, rebuilt 1709) and the Nandaimon (South Gate, 1199) provide an authentic glimpse of the character of an early Japanese town.

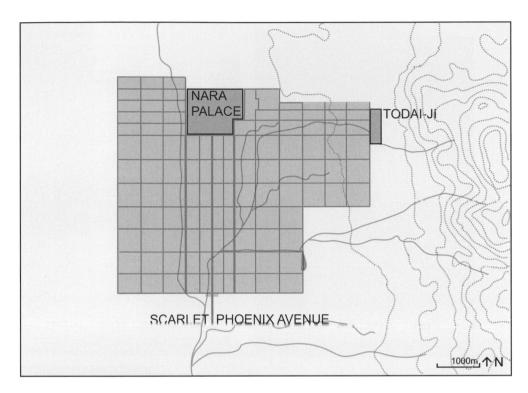

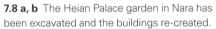

7.7 The plan of Nara was modelled on the Chinese capital, Chang'an (see p. 211). The palace compound occupied 1.3 km² and had several gardens. Todai-ji survives and garden remains have been excavated in the palace compound.

7.8 a, b The Heian Palace garden in Nara has been excavated and the buildings re-created.

7.9 a, b The deer park at Nara and, right, Todai-ji
Temple.

7.10 A re-created *niwa* and palace (called the
Heian Shrine, in Kyoto).

Nara was planned on a north–south axis. The city was unwalled but buildings and
roofed corridors were used to enclose a ceremonial *niwa* courtyard. The probable
character of the space can be seen at the re-created palace (called the Heian Shrine)
in Kyoto. The original palace in Nara has not survived but the Shosoin, a treasure store
built in 756, survives in excellent condition. It housed treasures for use by the Emperor
Shomu in the next world. One of them was a tray garden in which 'pieces of wood
with rough natural surfaces are set up to create a fantastic landscape with towering

pinnacles and craggy cliffs'.[5] This suggests a Daoist approach (see p. 183) to gardens in the Nara period and it is likely that the place described in the following poem was outside the city and was designed like a small version of a Chinese imperial park:

> *Clear and deep-brimming is the pond,*
> *Fresh is the garden with opening flowers,*
> *Frolicking birds skim the waves, then scatter –*
> *Pleasure boats wander among the isles.*[6]

Heian gardens, 794–1185

The name Heian is used for the period (794–1185) in which Heiankyo, now Kyoto, became Japan's capital. It remained so until 1868 and is therefore the Japanese city which has the most historic gardens. Like Chang'an and Nara, Kyoto was planned on a north–south grid but the similarity between the cities of China and Japan should not be overstated. As Soper remarks: 'Neither Nara nor Kyoto was walled in the Chinese sense, and neither was completed by the sort of vast imperial park and hunting preserve that sprawled beyond the northern limits of Chang'an.'[7] Kyoto's social, political and geographical circumstances were different from those of China. Power lay with the aristocrats, not with the emperor, and the city was defended by an army

7.11 The *niwa*, fenced trees and main hall (Shishinden) of Kyoto Imperial Palace. The tree protection can be compared with the carving at Sanchi (Figure 4.18).

7.12 Only the pond survives at the Shinsen-en and it is still used for pleasure boats.

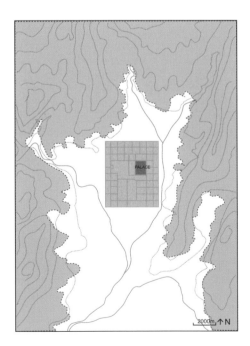

7.13 Plan of Heianko, which became Kyoto, showing how it is protected by wooded mountains.

and mountains, not by city walls. The proximity of well-wooded hills made hunting parks superfluous, as in Ancient Greece. Temperatures are less extreme than in North China and rain falls throughout the year. A poet wrote that in Kyoto 'a natural medley of willows and cherry blossoms weave themselves into a brocade'.[8]

Kyoto's palace compound was on the north fringe of the city. Since it contained an official residence and government offices, the open space was 'as bare as a parade-ground, except for a few fenced-in clumps of green'.[9] The 'clumps' were fenced compartments for trees, as can still be seen in Kyoto's imperial palaces. Emperors also made detached palaces with gardens. What little power they had was passed to their children so that they could enjoy a life free of court ceremonial. As 'cloistered emperors' (*Daijo Hoo*), they lived in garden palaces which can be compared to 'detached' imperial palaces outside the walls of Chang'an and Luoyang (see p. 193). But they also drew upon the character of Pure Land Buddhist monasteries. The reason for their hybrid character, which explains much of the uniqueness of subsequent Japanese gardens, is that retired Japanese emperors frequently became abbots, hoping to achieve Buddhahood after death. The combination of temporal with religious status resulted in landscapes with formal, symbolic and hedonistic qualities. As in China, one could make a case for speaking of Japanese 'landscapes' instead of 'gardens'.

A fragment of an old imperial garden, which survives as a public park, was originally 'a large lake-and-island park in the imperial Chinese manner'. It was called the Divine

Spring Garden (*Shinsen-en*) and, as in the Nara period, the divinities celebrated were of varied origin. A god living in a spring was a Shinto idea. Making a 'lake-and-island garden', to represent the Islands of the Immortals, was a Daoist idea. Placing statues of gods in temples and gardens was a Buddhist idea. Shinto, Daoism and Buddhism came together to produce Heian gardens and Heian architecture:

> In such great houses, then, there met and mingled what survived of three once partially independent architectural traditions: the pomp of the Chinese palace, the intimacy of the Japanese home, the other-worldliness of the Buddhist temple. From this association, as we shall see, Heian Buddhist architecture as a whole derived a tendency toward secularization. From it, even more directly, Heian architecture as a whole – the way of building favoured by the gentry, that is to say the court nobles, Kuge, and their imitators – derived an ideal type: the kind of mansion described in modern histories by the term shinden-zukuri.[10]

The *shinden* style (*shinden-zukuri*) influenced both temple gardens and palace gardens.

7.14 The Taima Mandara shows the Amida Buddha in his Pure Land with a temple garden.

Temple gardens

Pure Land Buddhism flourished among Japan's aristocracy during the Heian period. It was believed that honouring the Amida Buddha and reciting his name would improve one's chance of joining him in paradise at a later date. Mandalas, known in Japan as *mandaras*, were drawn on silk and used to inspire temple and garden layouts. As

7.15 The Sacred Lotus being admired by Japanese ladies.

7.16 A lotus pond in front of the Five Storey Pagoda at Horyu-ji. The Pagoda is one of the oldest wood buildings in the world.

7.17 Buddhism encouraged contemplation in natural settings.

discussed in Chapter 4, the word mandala can mean the performance of a sacred ritual, a prayer used at the ritual or an image of the ritual. The type of mandala which influenced Japanese garden design derives from the *Lotus Sutra* and shows the Buddha sitting in a temple/pagoda in a paradise garden.

The *Lotus Sutra* is believed to have been written in Kashmir *c.*100, to have been translated into Chinese *c.*290, to have been brought to Japan by the monk Saicho *c.*804, and to have had a profound influence on Japanese gardens. The *Sutra* promotes the idea that we live 'in the mud of blind passions'[11] but like another product of muddy waters, the sacred lotus, we can 'put forth the blossoms of the Buddha's perfect enlightenment'.[12] Bodhisattvas, are 'enlightened beings' who live 'in immeasurable numbers like Ganges sands'.[13] In the Western Paradise they have 'jeweled dwellings made of sandalwood' and 'immaculate gardens and groves where flowers and fruit abound, flowing springs and bathing pools'.[14] Therefore, wrote Shinran, a Japanese Buddhist monk who lived from 1173–1262, 'let us … aspire to go to the Pure Land!'[15] The *Lotus Sutra* advised aspirants that

> *wherever the sutra rolls are preserved, whether in a garden, a forest, beneath a tree, in monks quarters, in the lodgings of white-robed laymen, in palaces, or in mountain valleys or the wide wilderness, in all these places one should erect towers and offer alms.*[16]

Further, one should engage in:

- contemplation of the sun;
- contemplation of the water;
- contemplation of the land;
- contemplation of the treasure trees;
- contemplation of the treasure ponds;
- contemplation of the treasure pavilions;
- contemplation of the lotus throne;
- contemplation of the Buddha-image;
- contemplation of the true body of Amida.[17]

This led to one of the happiest ideas in the entire history of garden design: the perfect place for contemplation is a Pure Land garden. The idea can be explained as follows:

- Life on earth is beset with suffering.
- The cause of suffering is the desire for worldly possessions.
- Through meditation and contemplation, we should renounce desire.
- Those who follow this noble path will be happy on earth and will be reborn in the Pure Land.
- Images of the Buddha in his Pure Land assist meditation (images can be painted or they can be built, as palace gardens).

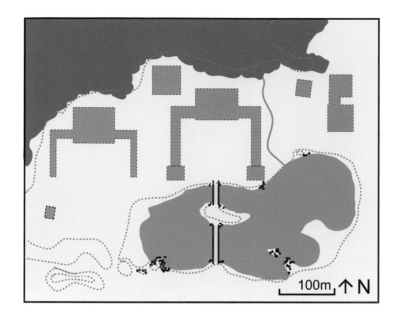
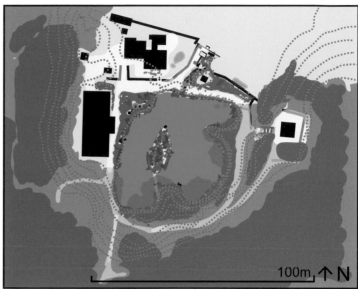

7.18 a, b Motsu-ji and Joruri-ji are two of the best examples of Pure Land Buddhist temple gardens. The buildings at Motsu-ji are shown as they once were and the vegetation is shown as it now is. Joruri-ji is shown as it now is, after a restoration project (see Figure 7.20).

● Living in a Pure Land garden is a preparation for living in the Pure Land itself (the Western Paradise).

Temples and villas were therefore designed with treasure ponds and treasure pavilions in Pure Land Gardens. The Three Treasures of Buddhism are: (1) Buddha himself (the 'Thus Gone One' – *Tathagata* in Sanskrit); (2) the Buddha's teaching (*dharma* in Sanskrit); and (3) the community of Buddhists (*sangha* in Sanskrit). In temple gardens, pagodas and halls containing images of the Buddha and the Bodhisattvas were placed on hills and beside lakes. East–west was the preferred orientation for gardens, because Amida's paradise lies in the west.[18] Most of the Heian Pure Land gardens have gone but there are survivals at Motsu-ji and Joruri-ji.

Motsu-ji, in Hiraizumi, 450 km north of Tokyo, is an example of a Pure Land temple garden. Once the focus of a temple complex, it was destroyed. But in 1976 the garden was researched and restored so that it now provides 'an informed glimpse of how the temple garden might have appeared centuries ago'.[19] The layout is that of a *shinden* estate. It has a north–south axis passing over bridges and an island to reach what was once a three-sided courtyard. The courtyard was enclosed by roofed corridors and had a Buddha hall in place of the sleeping hall which occupied this position in palace gardens. As homes for aristocratic abbots, temple gardens were used 'to entertain guests in the same way as palaces'.[20] Ceremonial festivities were held in the courtyard and boating parties enjoyed the lake.

7.19 The Motsu-ji garden was carefully excavated and re-created.

7.20 a, b The Amida Hall, lantern and pagoda at
Joruri-ji.

Joruri-ji, in the Tono Hills outside Nara, survives in better condition but is not in the *shinden* style. The temple and pond were made in 1157 and represent the Western Paradise of the Amida Buddha. As on a Taima Mandala, there is one image for each level of paradise, with only the highest-born able to attain the highest level. There is also a pagoda on the hillside, representing the Eastern Paradise of the Healing Buddha (Yakushi Nyorai). It has a Buddha statue on the first floor, forever looking out at the paradise of Lapis Lazuli (*Joruri*). The Healing Buddha holds a medicine bottle to cure the sick. Virtuous pilgrims hoped for rebirth on a lotus flower near the Buddha's feet. The sun rises in the Paradise of Yakushi and sets in the Paradise of Amida.

The lake in the Pure Land garden at Saiho-ji Temple was made in the eighth century and survives. But since the original buildings have gone and the planting has changed, it is discussed in the section on Kamakura gardens (see p. 254). There are also Amida Halls at Byodo-in and Hokai-ji south of Kyoto.

Palace gardens
No Heian palace gardens survive but a good deal is known about their character. The information comes from paintings, from a design manual (the *Sakuteiki*) and from one of the world's oldest novels, *The Tale of Genji*. The *Tale*'s authoress belonged to

7.21 Plan of Byōdō-in. The garden formerly extended to the Uji River.

7.22 Red lacquered bridges (restored) leading to the Amida Hall (Phoenix Hall) at Byodo-in. The Hall, completed in 1053, contains a statue of the Amida Buddha.

the Fujiwara clan and had learned Chinese. This was normal for aristocratic boys but uncommon for their sisters. Her husband died when she was young, in 1001, and the novel was begun soon after. It is twice the length of *War and Peace* and tells of a world in which it was stipulated that the only men a girl should ever meet were her father and her husband. The authoress lived with women and wrote for women. They dreamed of romance – and did not always obey the rules.

The first half of the novel is about the life and loves of Prince Genji. Rich, handsome and kind, he builds a palatial home for his wives and concubines but gets into trouble over too many illicit affairs. His favourite lady, Murasaki, after whom the book's authoress is named, dies childless. On her deathbed, thinking that 'Amitabha's paradise could not be far away'; she 'had scriveners at work on the thousand copies of the *Lotus Sutra* that were to be her final offering to the Blessed One'.[21] Genji liked to spend the night in a lady's apartment and exchange poems with her the morning after. Girls with skill in poetry and calligraphy were his favourites. Days were spent sojourning in boats and listening to music. Gardens were scenery, to be viewed from a boat or, in the silence of the moon, from the bed of a beautiful and accomplished lady. Gardens were not places for walking or working. The following quotations from *The Tale of Genji* describe how a Heian garden was designed and used.

7.23 a, b *Genji*-type festivities took place on Isawa pond, now the location of Daikaku-ji Temple.

The wishes of the ladies themselves were consulted in designing the new gardens, a most pleasant arrangement of lakes and hills. The hills were high in the southeast quarter, where spring-blossoming trees and bushes were planted in large numbers. The lake was most ingeniously designed. Among the plantings in the forward parts of the garden were cinquefoil pines, maples, cherries, wisteria, yamabuki, and rock azalea, most of them trees and shrubs whose season was spring. Touches of autumn too were scattered through the groves ... In the northeast quarter there was a cool natural spring and the plans had the summer sun in mind. In the forward parts of the garden the wind through thickets of Chinese bamboo would be cool in the summer, and the trees were deep and mysterious as mountain groves. There was a hedge of mayflower, and there were oranges to remind the lady of days long gone. There were wild carnations and roses and gentians and a few spring and autumn flowers as well. A part of the quarter was fenced off for equestrian grounds. Since the Fifth Month would be its liveliest time, there were irises along the lake.[22]

Music and other exciting sounds came from the boat as it was poled up and down the river. The young women went to the bank for a closer look. They could not make out the figure of the prince himself, but the boat, roofed with scarlet leaves, was like a gorgeous brocade, and the music, as members of the party joined their flutes in this impromptu offering and the next one, came in upon the wind so clearly that it was almost startling. The princesses looked out and made note of the fact that even on what had been announced as a quiet, unobtrusive expedition Niou was the cynosure of numerous eyes; and they told themselves that he was a man a lady would happily await if he deigned to come once a year. Knowing that there would be Chinese poems, Niou had brought learned scholars with him. As evening came on, the boat pulled up at the far bank, and the music and the poetry gathered momentum. Maple branches in their caps, some only tinged with autumn red and some quite saturated, several of Niou's men played 'The Wise Man of the Sea'.[23]

Ninth-century Japan is described as 'a miniature model'[24] of China and the garden activities described above are not unlike those in Marco Polo's account of Chinese gardens (see p. 212). The scale of Kyoto gardens is smaller because Japan is smaller and its rulers were less wealthy than their Chinese counterparts. No complete Heian garden survives, but there is more information about them than about Chinese gardens of the period. This includes some illustrative material, some descriptive text and a few surviving features. The components of a *shinden*-style garden, arranged on a north–south axis in the Chinese manner, were:

- a main hall with side pavilions;
- a three-sided courtyard, south of the sleeping hall;
- a pond garden with islands and trees;
- a protective outer wall.

The hall was unpartitioned. It was a sleeping space at night and a living space by day. The courtyard had a lake to the south, buildings to the north and garden corridors enclosing its east and west sides. It was gravel-surfaced, like a *niwa*, and used for ceremonial events and festivities. There may have been trees on the fringe of the courtyard but an extent of gravel was required for the ceremonies which 'originated in the perennial rites of the early emperors when ruling was still a matter of magic and gods rather than politics'.[25] Buildings were raised on columns and connected by decks. One or more streams with vegetated banks ran beneath the floors and through the courtyard. As in China, winding stream banquets were held with cups floating in the stream and each guest expected to drink the wine and compose a poem. The stream ran from east to west before turning south for feng shui reasons. Important guests viewed ceremonies from within sleeping halls. Less-important guests stood in the courtyard. Ceremonies were Shinto, Daoist, Confucian and Buddhist.[26] Pond gardens had dragon boats and the islands, linked by vermilion-painted bridges, had platforms for musicians. Using islands to represent the Islands of the Immortals was a Daoist idea.

Advice on the layout of a *shinden-zukuri* estate is given in a famous design manual, the *Sakuteiki*. Probably written by Tachibana Toshitsuna (1028–94), it is a short practical essay on 'the act of setting stones upright' to create the type of space we now call a Japanese garden. The *Sakuteiki* explains how to plan ponds, islands, waterfalls, streams and southern courtyards. Principles for the arrangement of these elements

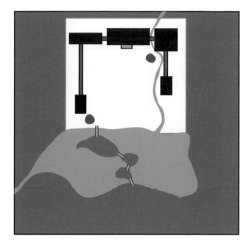

7.24 The *shinden-zukuri* style was less symmetrical than its Chinese predecessors.

7.25 Model of a *shinden-zukuri* estate.

7.26 Osawa Pond is the oldest surviving fragment of a *shinden-zukuri* garden.

are drawn from Buddhism, from yin–yang theory, from feng shui and from 'nature' itself. The Japanese phrase *'shotoku no senzui'*, translated into English as 'nature', has the literal meaning: 'the natural condition of mountains and water'.[27] *Senzui* (or *sansui*) derives from the Chinese word *shan shui* (*shan*, mountain, and *shui*, water). In connection with painting, *sansui* is translated as 'landscape' painting. Inaji believes there is a correspondence between the garden design principles in the Sakuteiki and Xie He's *Six Laws of Painting*.[28] The arts of garden design and landscape painting were twins as much in Japan as in China.

Shinden-zukuri estates had strong outer walls and were planned on a north–south axis, distinct from the east–west axis of temple gardens. The outer wall provided security against intruders and wooden halls with strong columns and thin walls were, as Ashihara explains, less likely to crush their occupants during an earthquake than were heavy stone buildings. The importance of gardens for earthquake safety was confirmed by the great Tokyo earthquake of 1923:

> *Tens of thousands of people took refuge in large gardens throughout the city and saved their lives. In some instances, all the trees in the garden were burned to the ground, but many lives were saved through the ponds. In no few instances did the gardens check the havoc of the sweeping conflagration and hundreds of houses behind them escaped destruction. These facts are bound to influence our gardens in future.*[29]

The southern courtyard of a *shinden-zukuri* estate was surfaced with sand or gravel and used for both ceremonial and social events. The fourth side of the courtyard opened onto the lake and water garden. In accord with the *Sakuteiki*, the lake had islands and stages for musicians. Gardens were no more used for walking than for barbecues or outdoor games. The oldest extant fragment of a *shinden-zukuri* estate is the Osawa Pond (Saga-no-in) now part of the Daikaku-ji Buddhist Temple. There are islands in the lake and its bottom is surfaced with small stones packed into the clay. Another glimpse of a *shinden-zukuri* estate is provided by the Heian Shrine in Kyoto (Figure 7.10). It was built in 1895 as a re-creation of a hall of state in the time of Kyoto's founder, the Emperor Kammu (737–806). The white gravel courtyard (*niwa*) is probably as near as one can get to the appearance of a Heian *niwa* but the garden is not to the south of the courtyard and has been designed in the style of the Meiji Period (see p. 276).

Books on Japanese architecture state that the origin of the *shinden*-style 'was certainly Chinese'[30] but the differences should be noted. First, the planning of Chinese palaces was symmetrical, while *shinden*-style estates were asymmetrically planned. Second, the courtyards of Chinese palaces were enclosed by buildings and walls on four sides. *Shinden*-style courtyards open onto pond gardens. Third, the courtyards of detached palaces in Chinese parks were enclosed by roofed corridors on the garden front, as shown on eighteenth-century versions of the Qingming Scroll (see p. 216). It would therefore be more accurate to state that Japanese gardens began to diverge from Chinese models in Heian times.

Towards the end of the Heian Period, Japan was subject to a second wave of Chinese influence, this time from the Southern Song Dynasty (1127–1279). Japanese ships made their way up the Qiantang River to Hangzhou (see p. 214) and returned with numerous artefacts and with information about Ch'an (Zen) Buddhism and landscape painting. Kuitert suggests the influence of Song landscape paintings on Japanese gardens came through the import of artwork and art criticism.[31] The Ch'an temples around Hangzhou had garden courts but no details of their layout are available.

7.27 a, b Zen gardens in Enkaku-ji Temple, Kamakura. The Pond of Sacred Fragrance (Myokochi) was designed by Muso, though its character has changed. Muso lived in the grounds of the Obai-in sub-temple (right) though it too has been re-designed since his time.

Kamakura gardens, 1185–1333

The Kamakura period takes its name from a coastal town 50 km south of Tokyo and 460 km north-east of Kyoto which still has a number of Zen temples with gardens. Kamakura became a seat of power in the first half of Japan's medieval period when, lacking unity, the country was ruled by a warrior hierarchy of shoguns, *daimyos* and *samurai*. It was the time when Buddhism, previously limited to the upper class, became a popular religion. As often before, strife led people to seek spiritual solace on earth and paradise thereafter. The military class turned to Zen Buddhism and, as in Christian Europe, gardens lost their high society role. They became places for meditation. There is a parallel between Japan and England in the Middle Ages. Feudal isolation allowed the faiths of both countries to develop separate identities from their continental neighbours. England was strongly influenced by continental culture after the invasion of 1066 but soon became proud of its independence. Japan resisted Mongol-led Chinese invasions in 1272 and 1281, but was strongly influenced by the continental culture of China's Song and Yuan dynasties.

Buddhism was discouraged in medieval China (see p. 211) but not in medieval Japan. Quite the reverse: in a period of civil strife, Pure Land Buddhism and Zen Buddhism became dominant influences. Zen is a Japanese version of the Chinese word Ch'an, meaning meditation. Zen Buddhists believe that escape from the endless cycle of desire and suffering should be obtained by meditation and discipline, not by worshipping gods, reciting mantras or making gifts to monasteries. Dogen, a monk who had visited Ch'an monasteries in China, emphasized the role of 'sitting in meditation' (*zazen*). He wrote: 'To study the Way (Dao) is to study the self. To study the self is to forget the self. To forget the self is to be enlightened by all things of the universe.' Furthermore:

7.28 Zen gardens are contemplative (Ginkaku-ji).

7.29 Kongobu-ji Temple on Mt Koya has the largest 'Zen garden' in Japan but is the centre of Vajra (Shingon) Buddhism. The design is said to represent a pair of dragons emerging from a sea of clouds.

For zazen, one should have a quiet place. Spread a thick sitting mat. Do not let in drafts or vapors; do not admit rain or dew ... The place where you sit should be bright; it should not be dark either day or night. The technique is to keep it warm in winter and cool in summer.[32]

This required special halls in precisely designed settings. As applied to medieval Japan, Paul Varley argues that the term 'Zen Culture' describes a set of aesthetic tastes 'such as simplicity, restraint, and a liking for the weathered, imperfect and austere (*sabi* and *wabi*) which, although not exclusively Zen in origin, certainly came to be associated with the Zen attitude'.[33] Kuitert argues that since there is no mention of 'Zen gardens' in the literature of Japan before the 1930s, the idea probably results from a government initiative to portray Japanese culture as more harmonious than Western culture.[34] But monastic halls and gardens were certainly designed for the type of meditation described by Dogen and it is useful to have a name for this approach to gardens. Religious institutions survive far longer than individual families and came to own most of the old gardens in Japan. Their austere courtyard compositions of gravel and rocks appear to have their closest relatives in the incense burners, tray gardens and contemplative courtyards of China (see p. 189).

Palace gardens

Palace gardens were influenced by Zen Buddhism in the Kamakura period. With ceremonies held in halls, instead of in gardens, estate owners no longer needed large courtyards or boating lakes. Wealth became distributed among a larger number of families so that estates and gardens became smaller. This trend continued into the Muromachi period. But the reduced size of gardens and dwellings did not stop courtyards and lakes from being *conceived* as intrinsic elements of an ideal garden.

They simply took on new forms. In large gardens, boating lakes were replaced by aesthetically composed ponds. In small gardens, real lakes were replaced by symbolic areas of raked gravel. One could say that gravel was used to 'paint' a lake in a garden scene. Aesthetic principles drawn from landscape painting were translated into garden design principles.

A parallel architectural change in the Kamakura period was that general-purpose halls (*shinden*) were superseded by halls with specialized rooms. The new style of estate layout was called the *shoin-zukuri*, meaning desk-style. The desk (*shoin*) gave its name to the study itself, to an architectural style and to a style of estate layout. The study was a place to think and to display works of art while offering tea to cultivated guests. This began the evolution of the *shinden-zukuri* into the *shoin-zukuri* and planted the seed from which tea gardens evolved. The first stage was to partition sleeping halls (*shinden*) with movable screens. This created a need for a second garden which could be viewed from the north-facing side of the partition. In its developed form, the *shoin-zukuri* had northern and southern gardens with specialized roles.

Temple gardens

Two famous temple gardens survive from the Kamakura period, though both have been changed. Saiho-ji and Tenryu-ji began as palace gardens and evolved into temple gardens. They show the influence of Song Dynasty ideas on garden design and indeed are better places to study these ideas than China itself (see p. 212). Muso Soseki (also known as Muso Kokushi, 1275–1351) is associated with both gardens but he was a busy man and it is likely that he was more an advisor than a designer. Hayakawa sees him as a 'great priest' and a man who 'truly revolutionized Japanese garden design in the medieval age'.

Saiho-ji was begun in the Heian period and re-designed in 1339. It has a small dry garden on the side of the hill and a pond garden in the valley below. The dry garden, which is the earliest surviving example of a *kare sansui*, was reserved for 'special spiritual discipline from which the laity was excluded'. It was designed as an aid to contemplation and, though few can see it, represents 'a huge tortoise, floating in the mossy sea, head back, flippers at rest'.[35] The pond garden in the valley represents the Western Paradise of the Amida Buddha and is of particular interest for its Song-influenced rock work with groups of boulders symbolizing the Three Treasures of Buddhism. 'The place seems a forest, deeply shadowed, with dark water gleaming in its depths. There is no carefully organized landscape picture here.'[36] However, the feature for which Saiho-ji is best known today is the profusion of its moss. It is called the Moss Temple (Kokedera) but the moss developed at a later date. There is a circuit path, as in later stroll gardens, but not the sequence of artfully composed representations of famous views. Kuck, who has been quoted in this paragraph, gives the following summary of the garden's significance: 'Saiho-ji, therefore, marks

7.30 a–d Saiho-ji, a Zen Buddhist temple, began as a Pure Land garden. It has the earliest *kare-sansui* garden (bottom right). (See Figure 7.31.)

a definite change in garden development, with the disappearance of the old, gay, open Heian pleasure park, while it foreshadows the new subjective feeling in gardens of the coming [Muromachi] age.'[37]

Tenryu-ji was begun in the Heian period and re-designed in 1344. Like Saiho-ji, it is seen by Kuck as transitional between 'the old shinden lake garden' and 'the coming popularity of the stroll style'.[38] But the particular interest of Tenryu-ji to garden historians is that 'In its composition the rock arrangement shows the same principles found in Song landscape painting.'[39] The idea of using upright stones in gardens came from China but the surviving Chinese examples are later. As discussed in Chapter 5, the reasons for using stone in this way were partly Daoist and partly Buddhist. The stones forming the waterfalls and waterside compositions at Tenryu-ji are more

7.31 Saiho-ji, famous as the Moss Temple, is at the foot of a hill in a damp valley. (See Figure 7.30).

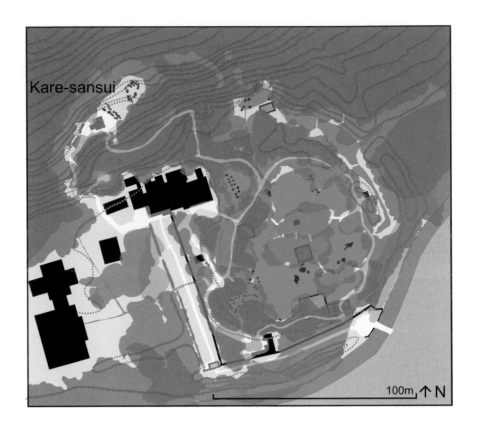

Kare-sansui

100m ↑ N

7.32 a, b, c Tenryu-ji is a Zen Buddhist temple with borrowed scenery, a dry waterfall and raked gravel beside a pond. In the thirteenth century it was an emperor's detached palace, with 'detached' meaning outside the city of Kyoto.

100m ↑ N

upward thrusting than the placid stones of Saiho-ji. The waterfall composition is 'only meant for contemplation; all is to be viewed from the abbot's quarters that face the garden scenery'.[40] Additionally, Tenryu-ji uses the principle of 'borrowed landscape' (*shakkei*) to draw in the wider landscape and has *kare-sansui* compositions of raked gravel and stone:

> *Not for one moment would we suspect these rocks of Tenryu-ji of being nature's handiwork. They were created as art, bold and rugged – designed perhaps, to excite the imagination and carry it far away from Japan's softly contoured mountains to the never-never land of vast Chinese landscapes, its painting, and its traditions.*[41]

7.33 Bamboos at Tenryu-ji.

Muromachi gardens, 1336–1573

Muromachi is a district of Kyoto which became popular with military leaders after the fall of the Kamakura government. In Kuck's opinion, the Muromachi shoguns produced a set of gardens which 'for sheer beauty and artistry have never been excelled in any period or in any country'. She was thinking particularly of the gardens of what are now called the Gold Pavilion (Kinkaku-ji) and the Silver Pavilion (Ginkaku-ji). In part, their excellence resulted from the increased influence of Zen Buddhism on garden design. Discipline appealed to the military mind. Warriors became scholars, almost forming a Japanese equivalent of the scholar officials who made gardens in Chinese towns. In Japan, gardens became places for contemplation and works of art, subject to the aesthetic disciplines of poetry and painting. They were places to be viewed from within buildings, from verandas and, significantly for the future, from aesthetically planned garden paths. This affected both temples and palaces. In palace gardens, boating ponds were replaced by ethereal woodland pools. In Zen temple gardens, real ponds were replaced by symbolic ponds of raked gravel.

Palace gardens

Kinkaku-ji's owner was the third Muromachi Shogun, Yoshimitsu (1358–1408). Before starting this garden, Yoshimitsu had set a design style for the new era at an estate known as the Flowery Palace on account of its cherry trees. It has gone but his retirement home, acquired in 1394, survives in the Kitayama district of Kyoto. At the time of its acquisition it was planned in the *shinden* style and known as the Kitayama Palace. Today it is often called the Gold Pavilion Temple: Kinkaku-ji. This implies opulence. But Yoshimitsu had a different conception. Thinking of the park in which Buddha first preached, at Isipatana (see p. 142), and untroubled by the lack of animals, he called it a deer park. Even today, the proper name is the Deer Garden Temple (Rokuon-ji).

7.34 Kinkaku-ji was Shogun Yoshimitsu's retirement palace before it became a Zen Buddhist temple garden. The Golden Pavilion houses Buddhist relics.

7.35 Kinkaku-ji is at the foot of the mountains outside Kyoto.

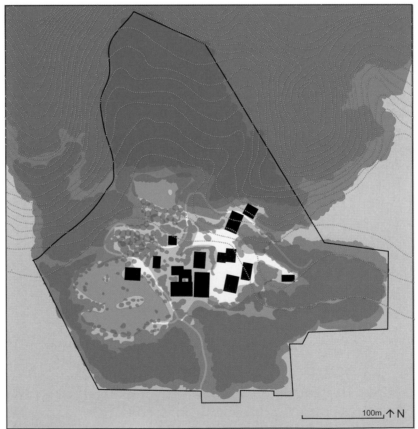

7.36 The Silver Pavilion and Pure Land pond at Ginkaku-ji. The garden began as a retirement palace for Shogun Yoshimasa and is now a Zen Buddhist temple.

7.37 Raked gravel at Ginkaku-ji.

7.38 The Togu-do at Ginkaku-ji is believed to be the place where the tea ceremony was first performed.

Kinkaku-ji was designed as a paradise garden in which to stroll and meditate, as the Buddha had done in the Jetavana. Yet the symbolism of the stone work is Daoist in origin. The shore of the lake is ornamented with rocks and a tortoise island divides it into two sections. The Gold Pavilion itself was inspired by the style of the Southern Song. It stands on the north side of the lake and was both a Buddhist relic-house and a place to receive guests. The pond was a place of contemplation and after Yoshimitsu's death the estate became a Zen Buddhist temple. Kuck knew the garden well and wrote a lyrical account of its beauty:

> *In spring, azaleas cast scarlet shadows into the water, while purple irises bloom in shallows along the shore. In summer, the water's surface is patterned with the green circles of native lily pads. In autumn, tall reeds rally their pointed spears around the islets, and on the distant shore maples blaze gorgeously. In winter's grey light, the white flames whirl lazily above the silvery surface of the water, piling up whiteness on every rock and tree.*[42]

The present Gold Pavilion, clad in gold leaf, is a replacement for a less-gaudy pavilion burned by a psychotic monk in 1950. Visitors enjoy a brilliance which garden historians find excessive, because Kinkaku-ji was not designed for jollification. The layout is a step in the transition from the gaudiness of the *shinden* style to the restraint of the Zen style. In gardens, transitional styles are often the best, as in the case of the Villa Lante, as Renaissance became Baroque, and Studley Royal, as Augustan became Serpentine.

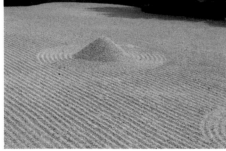

7.39 The Moon Washing Spring at Ginkaku-ji.

7.40 Raked gravel (at Kodai-ji) symbolizes 'mountains and water' (*sansui*).

Ginkaku-ji, the garden of the Silver Pavilion is the other key example of the Muromachi style and a further step away from the *shinden*-style. Formerly known as the Eastern Hill Villa (Higashiyama-dono), it was made by Yoshimitsu's grandson, the Shogun Yoshimasa Ashikaga (1435–90). As a man of taste, Yoshimasa can be compared to his Italian contemporary, Lorenzo de Medici (1449–92). Both men relished the company of artists and scholars: Lorenzo discussed Plato's philosophy in his garden; Yoshimasa gathered Zen Buddhists to conduct formal tea ceremonies in his garden. Yoshimasa was a Pure Land Buddhist with a taste for the aesthetic simplicity of Zen Buddhism. Flower arranging (*ikebana*) and Noh Theatre flourished during his shogunate. He wore Chinese clothes and made himself a vassal of China.[43] Gardens were the 'axis' of his aesthetic life.[44]

Temple gardens

Ginkaku-ji began as a residence and became a temple after its creator died. Yoshimasa is believed to have directed the overall design but to have employed specialists (e.g. in rockwork) and to have helped establish a new class of tradesmen with garden skills to do work formerly undertaken by Buddhist priests. Yoshimasa admired Saiho-ji. Ginkaku-ji has a stone garden and a contemplative pond as its central feature. A carefully planned walk leads around and across the pond. A cascade tumbles into the Moon Washing Spring. The moon was full at the moment of Buddha's birth and it became a symbol of his enlightenment. Yoshimasa composed a famous poem about the moonrise:

> *My little hut stands*
> *At the foot of the mountain*
> *'Waiting for the Moon'*
> *And my thoughts go to the light*
> *Of the moon sinking in the sky.*[45]

The Silver Pavilion, which is not clad in silver leaf, contains an image of the compassionate Buddha, Kannon. A small Amida Hall also survives, the Togu-do, which is believed to be the place where the first tea ceremony was performed. The name Togu-do has the literal meaning 'east seek hall' and the expanded meaning 'a person in the East who seeks the Pure Land in the West'.[46] The dry garden of white sand at Ginkaku-ji is thought to have been part of the original design but the flat-topped cone is believed to be a later addition.

The old Japanese term for what is now called a Zen garden (*zen niwa*) was a dry garden (*kare-sansui*). The term Zen garden is convenient but, as noted above, was not used before the 1930s. Zen gardens now attract worldwide interest for a number of reasons: they are beautiful; they often have no planting; they are unique to Japan; they are designed to be viewed like paintings. Above all, they are religious art, more akin to shrines than to Western gardens with patios, barbecues and hammocks. The two sources for the Zen garden, as reflected in the term 'zen niwa', are the Zen approach to landscape composition, derived from China, and the Japanese niwa (see p. 238). Japanese priests visited Hangzhou and brought back artwork from the monasteries. The Ch'an monasteries outside Hangzhou had cloister-like courtyards enclosed by roofed walkways. They may well have had stone and tree compositions, but perhaps not the raked gravel which features in Japan's Zen gardens.

The oldest known use of the term *kare-sansui* is in the *Sakuteiki*. As an essentially practical manual, the *Sakuteiki* has more information on how to make gardens than about design concepts. It simply states:

> *There is also a way to create gardens without ponds or streams. This is called the Dry Garden Style* (kare senzui [sansui]) *and should be created by setting stones along the base of a hill or with Meadows in the garden.*[47]

The translator comments: 'At the time the *Sakuteiki* was written (*c.*1060), the use of water was so prevalent that *kare-sansui* simply referred to an area within the larger garden where water was not used.' *Kare* meant 'withered', 'shrunken', or 'dead' in connection with plants, and came to mean 'dry' in connection with gardens. *Sansui* is from the Chinese *shan shui*, ('mountain-water') and is translated as 'landscape' in connection with painting or 'nature' in connection with gardens. *Kare-sansui* can be read as 'dry mountains and dry water'. The idea derives from religious concepts underlying the artistic representation of mountains and water. As discussed in regard to Chinese gardens (see p. 187) these ideas were partly Daoist and partly Buddhist. Shinto, in Japan, had long viewed certain rocks (*iwakura*) as being sacred because they are inhabited by gods (*kami*). Zen gardens are sacred in the sense of being set aside for reverence. They are a product of Shinto beliefs overlain by Daoist and Zen Buddhist beliefs.

The most famous example of a dry Zen garden, and the most famous garden in Asia, is Ryoan-ji.[48] It was begun in 1488, two years before Yoshimasa's death, on the site of an older temple. Meditation took place in halls with low illumination to avoid the distraction caused by bright light. The dry garden is about the size of a tennis court and is enclosed on one side by a roofed corridor and on the other three sides by walls and by a small moss garden. The raked gravel has 15 stones arranged in five groups: 1 of five stones, 2 of three stones and 2 of two stones. Unlike the stones in Chinese gardens, their shapes are not themselves remarkable. The interest comes from the arrangement. It takes time to absorb. The garden is said to be at its best when a damp mist enhances the textures – and to become more fascinating with repeated viewing. It can be seen as a landscape, a riverscape, a seascape or a microcosm of the creation. Complexity boosts its fascination. Kuck summarized the character of Ryoan-ji as follows: 'A sermon in stone, a whole philosophy bound up between the covers of

7.41 a, b Ryoan-ji is a Zen Buddhist Temple with the most famous *kare-sansui* garden. It is usually photographed, as here, with a wide angle lens which exaggerates the apparent size of the space.

7.42 Ryoan-ji is the most famous garden in Asia, partly because it is religious art.

7.43 Imperfection, as a symbol of transience, is part of the *wabi-sabi* aesthetic. Europeans would surely have dressed the stone, felled the trees and built a path (gate at Saiho-ji).

7.44 a, b, c Kodai-ji was begun in 1601 by the wife of the great *daimyo*, Toyotomi Hideyoshi.

an earthen wall – undoubtedly this garden is one of the world's great masterpieces of religiously inspired art.'[49]

It should be noted, however, that Zen Buddhism lacks some of the key characteristics of a religion, including belief in a creator God and belief in the efficacy of prayer. Furthermore, the Ryoan-ji garden is unlike other works of 'religious art' in not being either didactic or iconographic. It is best conceived of as aid to contemplation, like the Chinese tray gardens (see p. 190) it resembles – which were also popular in Muromachi Japan.

Azuchi-Momoyama gardens, 1568–1600

The Azuchi-Momoyama period takes its name from two castles: Azuchi was Nobunaga's castle-palace, 50 km north-east of Kyoto, and Momoyama, meaning Peach Hill, which was the site of a castle in Kyoto. It was reconstructed from illustrations in 1964 and is now called Fushimi Castle. The military commander Toyotomi Hideyoshi (1536–98) used a system of castles to pacify Japan after a century of warfare. Castles and cannon, the first European military ideas to take root in Japan, enforced the stability of the Edo Period. Toyotomi Hideyoshi had a portable tea room, covered with gold leaf and lined with gossamer. He also liked gardens and it was in his lifetime that the tea ceremony became a significant factor in garden design.

Drinking fermented black tea (from *Camellia sinensis*) was popular in Ancient China and the practice was introduced to Japan in the ninth century by the Buddhist monk Eichu. In the twelfth century, the drinking of unfermented green tea became a religious practice in Zen Buddhist monasteries. This habit also came from China. Tea heightened monks' awareness and kept them alert during long periods of meditation. The solemnity and spirituality of a tea ceremony place it closer to a Christian mass than an English tea party and the ceremony is conducted in an especially tranquil setting. Samurai warriors took up the practice and an elaborate tea ceremony ritual developed in conjunction with what is called the *wabi-sabi* aesthetic.

Precise definitions of aesthetic concepts are difficult. Originally, *wabi* referred to the solitary joy of natural living and *sabi* meant 'lean' or 'withered'. In time, *wabi* came to mean simplicity and *sabi* to mean the patina which comes with age. Brought together by the Buddhist ideal of monastic retreat, the *wabi-sabi* aesthetic found beauty in simple construction, imperfections, natural environments and the tea ceremony. *Wabi* and *sabi* are sometimes used interchangeably. The tea pavilion became a miniature world: a clean, compact, simple and orderly place in which wealth is spiritual, not material. Conduct of the tea ceremony grew into a sophisticated art requiring years of study. The tea garden which evolved from the *wabi-sabi* aesthetic was, in essence, a path to the tea pavilion. Called a *roji*, meaning 'dewy ground', it was designed as a

7.45 a, b, Stone lanterns were originally placed outside temples (Byodo-in) but, with the making of tea gardens, came to be a characteristic feature of Japanese gardens (Kyoto Gosho).

psychological prologue for the perfection of the tea ceremony. This required a just balance between movement and rest, action and contemplation, tension and calm. The influence of contrasting ideals on design became pervasive.

The Monoyama period is associated with divergent trends: luxury and simplicity. The return of peace allowed luxurious gardens to be made and the *wabi-sabi* aesthetic resulted in simplicity becoming the design aim. The hermit ideal flourished with Buddhism and became an influence on both poetry and design. The famous Buddhist poet, Kamo no Chomei, retired to the hills and published an account of his simple life in *A Ten Foot Square Hut* (1212):

> *Thus as old age draws on my hut has grown smaller and smaller. It is a cottage of quite a peculiar kind, for it is only ten feet square and less than seven feet high ... As to my surroundings, on the south there is a little basin that I have made of piled-up rocks to receive the water that runs down from a bamboo spout above it, and as the forest trees reach close up to the eaves it is easy enough to get fuel ... But though the valley is much overgrown it is open toward the west, so that I can contemplate the scenery and meditate on the enlightenment that comes from the paradise in that quarter. In the spring I behold the clusters of wisteria shining like the purple clouds on which Amida Buddha comes to welcome his elect.*[50]

Kyoto was ravaged by war in 1467. The poets fled and as they travelled through country areas, they gained an appreciation of natural scenery and recited poems in tea houses to earn food. Nature poetry thus became associated with tea houses and people began to make polite versions of the hermit's hut. They became known as tea gardens and their characteristic features were stone lanterns, stone water basins and stepping stones. Lanterns were needed because tea ceremonies were often held at night and a convenient model was found in the votive lanterns outside Buddhist temples. There are old examples of temple lanterns at Joruri-ji and Byodo-in. Stone water basins

7.46 a, b A tea pavilion at Shosei-en in Kyoto (built in 1643 and restored in 1865).

allowed guests to purify themselves by washing. Stepping stones made it possible to keep one's feet clean and walk through a naturalistic area without damaging plants. The juxtaposition of stone lanterns (*ishidoro*) with washing basins (*tsukubai*) became a characteristic garden feature. Moss was encouraged and evergreens were planted. Showy flowers were judged incompatible with the seriousness of the tea ceremony.

Tea gardens were maintained with great care but were modest structures and few early examples survive. Sen no Rikyu (1522–91), the person most closely associated with development of the tea ceremony, also set standards for the design of tea rooms and tea gardens. He was an aesthetic adviser to Toyotomi Hideyoshi and his three grandsons set up schools for the ceremony, each with a pavilion and a garden. The nexus of ideas around the tea ceremony has been called 'the element that perfected the beauty of Japanese-style garden spaces'.[51] Tea gardens encapsulated the beauty of simplicity and the simplicity of beauty. The associated architectural style is known as *sukiya-zukuri* ('tea house style of building').

Samboin, now part of the Daigo-ji temple complex, has a garden in which Toyotomi Hideyoshi took a personal interest. The garden has a collection of valued garden stones and is regarded as a transitional stage in the development of Edo stroll gardens. Kentei, a famous designer whose name means 'excellent gardener' was involved with the project for twenty years. Treib comments that the design is 'never at rest; the composition feels complete, but this is a restless landscape'.[52] A visitor seeing the garden from the verandah of a *shoin* residence is drawn in to explore new views.

7.47 View of Edo Castle (from a seventeenth-century panelled screen).

Edo gardens, 1603–1867

The Edo period is named after the town which became the real seat of power in 1603. Its name was changed to Tokyo when it became Japan's capital in 1868 and a resolution between the divergent attractions of luxury and simplicity was achieved through the stroll garden. Opulent in scale but aesthetically austere, stroll gardens are tea gardens on a palatial scale. The austerity was of *wabi-sabi* origin. The luxury became possible through the reunification of Japan under a powerful shogun. His name, Tokugawa, is sometimes applied to the Edo period itself and the semi-feudal system he established. Many of the senior *daimyo* were his relatives, so that the family gained control of the imperial court and the country's religious institutions. New palaces were built, a new legal code was enacted, everything was regulated – and foreigners were progressively excluded. Though more interested in Western science than China, Japan also turned in upon itself. Political stability led to economic prosperity, urban expansion and garden construction.

7.48 The moat and walls of Edo Castle – now Tokyo Imperial Palace.

Stroll gardens have lakes, islands and long paths leading to buildings and points of interest. Muromachi gardens also had paths, unlike older Japanese gardens, but the paths in Edo gardens are planned like routes through an art gallery and lead to spaces composed from every point of view. The scenes could be drawn from famous places in Japan or China, particularly if they had been described by well-known poets. As in the eclectic gardens of Victorian England, a planned garden walk became a substitute for long-distance travel. The best-known practitioner of the stroll garden style was Kobori Enshu (1579–1647), who also excelled in painting, poetry and flower arrangement. Enshu had studied Zen and the tea ceremony, under Sen no Rikyu, and helped train his friends and relatives in garden making. This resulted in his name being associated with more gardens than there are records of his having designed. Rikyu also popularized the idea of borrowed scenery and it is possible that he knew of the description of this technique in the *Yuan Ye* (see p. 224).[53] When one *daimyo* created a view in accordance with this idea, Enshu congratulated him as follows: 'This is really a

7.49 A Buddhist lantern at Katsura.

lordly garden: real mountains and water are summoned to present the garden form.'[54] It had outward views. Earlier Japanese gardens, like medieval European gardens, had been enclosed by high walls.

While stroll gardens were being made outside the castles of feudal lords, tea gardens continued to be made within towns. Some were run as commercial establishments and others were the private gardens of merchant families. A manual of 1670 stated that a tea garden

> should look like the hermitage of a recluse found in the shadows of an old forest in the countryside. A thicket should be planted, a narrow path must be laid out, a gate of planted bamboo or a garden wicket is built. In appearance it should be simple and calm.[55]

Taxation, onerous during the Edo period, was computed on the width of a property frontage. This resulted in narrow widths and long gardens, well suited to the layout of winding paths leading to tea pavilions or dwellings for other members of the family. The spaces between were called *tsubo* gardens with '*tsubo*' meaning both a ceramic pot and a small area, equal to two *tatami* mats. Applied to gardens, *tsubo* means 'enclosed' so that courtyards came to be called *tsubo niwa*.

Palace gardens

Prince Toshihito, an emperor's brother, acquired a property below the hills, west of Kyoto, *c.*1615. He built a rustic cottage on the site and over the next forty years he and his son, Prince Toshitada, made what is now the Katsura Imperial Villa – one of the most admired landscape and architecture compositions in the world. Its character results from *wabi-sabi* simplicity deployed on the scale of a luxurious palace garden. The architectural style is described as *sukiya-zukuri* and draws upon *shinden-zukuri* and *shoin-zukuri* traditions. *Sukiya* describes the restraint of a garden building appropriate for the tea ceremony. Katsura was made in an era which, as Sylvia Crowe remarked, 'coincides with great epochs of garden-making in other parts of the world'.[56] In 1620, Shalimar Bagh was made in Kashmir, de Caus' design for the Hortus Palatinus was published in Germany and the *Mayflower* reached America. The Villa Lante was designed in 1566 and Vaux le Vicomte in 1658.

In essence, Katsura is a *roji* extending round a pond. The 'Katsura Tree' (*Cercidiphyllum japonicum*) was associated with the God of the Moon and the garden has a platform to view its rise. The 6.9 ha site is low-lying and near the Katsura River. Material was excavated to make a 0.8 ha lake and arranged to make banks, islands and hills. The garden has paths, stepping stones, bridges, tea houses, rocks, pebble beaches, stone lanterns and stone wash basins (*tsukubai*). A restrained aesthetic guided the detailing, the architecture and the integration of elegantly-proportioned interiors with well-composed outdoor space. The result makes designers catch their breath.

7.50 a–d Katsura has a famous palace garden. The design was guided by Zen ideas and can be viewed as a tea garden with a long *roji*.

Prince Toshihito probably led the Katsura design team himself but also employed professionals. The design was formerly attributed to the leading garden designer and tea master, Kobori Enshu. But it is now thought that Enshu influenced the project through his taste and his brothers but was not personally involved in supervising the work. Additions, made when a ruling emperor first visited Katsura in 1658, included an extension to the garden, an imperial gateway and an avenue lined with clipped hedges. The latter was a new idea in Japan, and may have been influenced by reports of European gardens.

Modernist architects, as discussed in the next chapter, took a great interest in Katsura. Seeking an abstract composition to support their own design theories, they failed to appreciate the importance of Buddhism to its design.

7.51 Katsura Imperial Villa garden is near the river, west of Kyoto.

7.52 a, b Walter Gropius considered the rock compositions near the Shokintei 'overcrowded'.

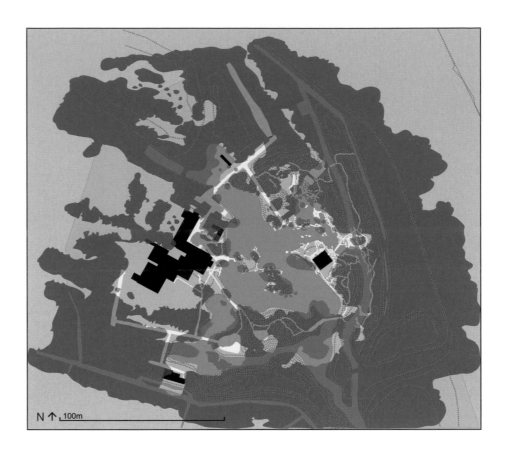

N ↑ 100m

In Kenzo Tange's view, the rustic cottage with which Toshihito began the project was 'more than likely a very ordinary thing, different in no material way from the many farmhouses of the surrounding area'.[57] Tange believed the brilliance of Katsura resulted from the 'true vitality of the Japanese race' (Jomon culture) married to 'the aristocratic Yayoi tradition'.[58] From a Chinese perspective, he might have called these aspects yin and yang. Following Professor Mori, Tange traces the aristocratic aspect of Katsura to Toshihito's love for *The Tale of Genji*. The Prince copied out passages from the *Tale*, including the following 'In the southeast rose a mountain, where all sorts of trees bearing spring flowers had been planted. The pond was excellent and delightful.' Mori takes this as the starting point for Katsura. Another passage in *The Tale of Genji* speaks of a moonlit night with the sounds of lutes and pine trees. Katsura has a Pine-Lute Pavilion, the Shokintei, and a Moon Viewing Platform which projects from the Old Shoin.

Katsura's garden is transitional. It exemplifies the refinement of Zen detailing on the scale of a stroll garden. The pond garden was used for boating parties, as in Heian times. The stroll path was used to conduct guests to tea pavilions in which Zen-

7.53 a, b Katsura. The area between the pond, the Shoin and the Moon Viewing Platform are blank, partly because of the lawn and partly because the façades are no longer open verandahs.

7.54 a–c The Sento Gosho in Kyoto has a carefully tended stroll path and a pebble beach.

inspired tea ceremonies were held. On the way, guests experienced a sequence of carefully composed scenes with literary and poetic allusions, as in Chinese gardens. Walter Gropius considered the rock compositions around the Shokintei 'overcrowded'. I disagree but Katsura has changed over the years. There was once a 'bridge with red-lacquered balustrade over the pond in front of the Shokintei'[59] and in my view there is a problem with the area in front of the Shoin, now managed as a European lawn. One possibility is that it was formerly a gravel niwa. This would accord with the *shinden-zukuri* garden style and would have contributed brilliance to the garden view from the Moon Viewing Platform.

A second Kyoto palace garden, for the Sento Gosho ('Retirement Palace'), was made for the Emperor Go Mizunoo (1596–1680) whose wife was a grand-daughter of Shogun Tokugawa. The Sento Gosho was begun in 1634 and the design was guided by Kobori Enshu's taste. The palace was burned and rebuilt several times but the garden survives. It is a 7.7 ha stroll garden with a large lake. The dry stone beach on the south shore of the lake is surfaced with pebbles of almost uniform size and is known as Odawara Isshoishi beach.

7.55 Shugakuin Imperial Villa is a stroll garden on the scale of a landscape park. It borrows scenery from around the Kyoto Valley.

A third Kyoto palace garden, for the Shugakuin Imperial Villa, was made by Emperor Go Mizunoo in 1655. He is said to have produced the design himself with a clay model and to have conceived it as a country retreat for himself and his court. It has a stroll path but the scale is closer to that of a landscape park than a domestic garden. Rice fields are included within the estate and there are planned views of borrowed scenery. It was a place to experience the countryside. Western visitors may compare Shugakuin with the landscape parks made in eighteenth-century Europe.

The fourth palace garden in Kyoto belongs to the imperial palace, the Gosho. It was begun in the Edo period but was often destroyed and took on its present character after 1855. It is of interest as a reconstruction but not as a historical relic. The gravel courtyard is in the *shinden-zukuri* style, though it would have had the main hall opening onto a lake and a stream winding through the gravel.

Aristocratic palace gardens were also made on what were then the outskirts of Edo (Tokyo). Koishikawa Korakuen Garden, 2.5 km north of the imperial palace, was started by *daimyo* Yorifusa Mito, in 1629, and completed by his more famous successor *daimyo* Mitsukuni Mito. Part of the garden survives as a public park. The name Korakuen, which means 'enjoying afterwards', was inspired by the Chinese proverb that 'a ruler should enjoy himself only when his people are contented'. Korakuen was made in the same period and for the same role as Katsura, to hold tea ceremonies for important guests. The main features are a lake and a long tea path with representations of famous views

7.56 a, b Koishikawa Korakuen in Tokyo has a tea path with representations of famous views.

7.57 a, b Rikugien Garden in Tokyo. The name means 'garden of the six forms of *waka* poetry'.

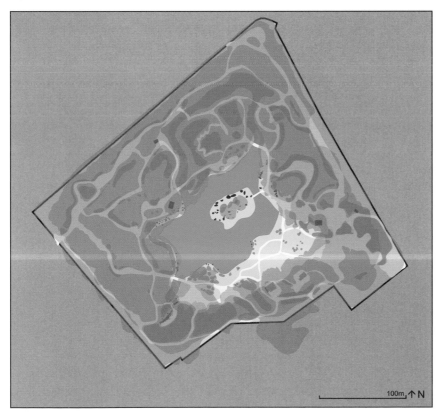

7.58 Konchi-in has a Zen garden with a rectangle of sand enclosed by a hall and a planted bank.

in China and Japan. One of the Chinese views was inspired by the mountains where a Pure Land sect, the White Lotus Society, had been founded in the thirteenth century.

Because of the owner's wealth, Korakuen has a sufficiency of boulders. Other Edo gardens created comparable visual effects by clipping shrubs into tight boulder-like shapes and some were built on marine inlets to make use of the water in Tokyo Bay. The Hama Rikyu (Beach Palace) is a surviving example. Rikugien was designed in 1702 with the aim of symbolizing famous scenes from a tenth-century anthology of poetry (*The Collection of Ancient and Modern Times*). The name Rikugien means 'garden of the six forms' of *waka* poetry. The garden also drew upon 88 scenes from famous poems.

Temple gardens

Japan's temples suffered during the wars of the sixteenth century but received fresh support after Shogun Tokugawa re-established order. A Zen monk, Ishin Suden, was appointed to control the monasteries and in 1611 a garden was made for the Konchi-in temple in Kyoto. It has a rectangle of sand enclosed on one side by a hall and on another side by a planted bank with a stone garden. One stone symbolizes a bridge, others symbolize a tortoise and the Islands of the Immortals (see p. 186). These Daoist symbols of longevity indicate the continuing influence of Chinese religious ideas on Japanese gardens. Kobori Enshu, also employed by the Tokugawa Shogunate, may have advised on the design.

Another Zen courtyard garden was made for the Daitoku-ji monastery in Kyoto. It is larger than the garden at Konchi-in, but is also rectangular and has a symbolic composition of raked gravel, rocks, plants and a dry cascade. 'Dry water' from the cascade flows onto an expanse of raked gravel.

Town gardens

Japan's military rulers became poorer during the eighteenth and nineteenth centuries, as merchants, industrialists and the professional classes became wealthier. The result was a decline in the making of large gardens and a growth in the making of small urban gardens. As in Victorian Britain, the new bourgeoisie tended to rely more on published manuals than on religious principles, artistic principles or professional expertise. Various arts, including garden design, were explained in Secret Books drawn from the sayings of former masters. *Creating Landscape Gardens*, by Enkin, was published in 1735 and a second part was added by Akizato Rito in 1828. The book was illustrated and has been republished many times – to the detriment of Japanese garden design. One can make a comparison with the works of William Halfpenny and J.C. Loudon, popular in eighteenth-century and nineteenth-century Britain. It was a time when 'the Japanese garden, like almost all other aspects of Japanese art, became stereotyped and degenerate'.[60] The 1828 section of Akizato Rito's book classified Japanese gardens as *shin*, *gyo*, and *so* (meaning 'elaborate', 'partly simplified' and 'greatly simplified'). For example, Katsura is *shin*, Daisen-in is *gyo* and Ryoan-ji is *so*. These terms are an unhelpful nineteenth-century historicism. Kuck puts the matter as follows:

> *The classification mentioned above, into shin, gyo, and so types, is one that still haunts writers on Japanese garden subjects, although the garden makers themselves never seem to have paid much attention to it. The three words were originally invented to designate*

GYO (INTERMEDIARY) STYLE OF HILL GARDEN (FROM AN ILLUSTRATION IN "TSUKIYAMA TEIZO-DEN")

I.—" Guardian Stone."
II.—" Cliff Stone."
III, IV.—" Cascade Stones."
V.—" Water Tray Stone."
VI.—Abbreviation of Hill " D," in Shin style.
VII.—" Bridge-Edge Stone."
VIII.—" Seat of Honour Stone."
IX.—" Perfect View Stone," or " Stone of Two Deities."
X.—" Worshipping Stone."
XI.—" Cave Stone."
XII.—" Moon Shadow Stone."
XIII.—Stone Lantern of " Snow-viewing " style.
XIV.—Stone Lantern of " Kasuga " style.
XV.—Water Basin as " Waiting Stone."

7.59 Akizato Rito's 'secret book' led to stereotyped designs for Japanese gardens.

*three styles of writing Chinese characters ... Dr Tatsumi sums and dismisses the whole
matter: '[their use] was only a fashion of the time, without any particular meaning'.*[61]

Josiah Conder, an Englishman, adapted the illustrations from several Secret Books for
his own 1893 book entitled *Landscape Gardening in Japan*.[62] It was the first systematic
treatment of Japanese gardens in a European language and helped the spread of over-
simplified ideas, akin to notions of *the* oriental mind and *the* oriental garden. Though
his treatment is sophisticated, the introduction and title of Ito Teiki's 1972 book, *The
Japanese Garden: An Approach to Nature*, reveal the continuing influence of Josiah
Conder and Akizato Rito on the interpretation of Japanese gardens. Ito asserts that:

> *There are only two attitudes toward nature. One confronts it or one accepts it ... In
> the Occidental garden, trees are ordered, paths are straightened, and a visible form
> is imposed ... In the Oriental garden it is nature and not the gardener which does the
> creating ... Man finally and firmly becomes a part of nature itself. There is no assumption
> that there is something better than nature.*[63]

Ito is equally misguided in his interpretation of Occidental and Oriental gardens: both
are concerned with the 'nature of Nature' – not with the raw materials of nature.

Meiji gardens, 1868–1912

The modernization of Japan had been in progress for half a century when Commodore
Perry steamed into Tokyo Bay with a squadron of warships. Perry delivered a letter
from the President of the United States to the Emperor of Japan. It required Japanese
ports to open for trade. An agreement was signed in 1854 and the Westernization of
Japan began in earnest. The Meiji restoration of 1868 returned nominal power to the
young Emperor Meiji. He moved to the capital and its name was changed to Tokyo. But
real power passed from a deeply conservative shogun to a group of reforming *daimyos*.
Japan began to industrialize rapidly, helped by the import of Western technology,
artifacts and architectural styles. A new style of building was introduced and appeared
to require a new style of garden design. The Japanese began to make flower beds,
lawns and gravel paths, decorating them with manufactured ornaments.

Villa gardens

The making of large gardens resumed as Japan's wealth grew. Since the new patrons
were businessmen and financiers, their homes can be described as villas. The new
rich lacked military or civil power but much of Japan's new industrial leadership was
drawn from the former *samurai* class, which had lost its old sources of income. Yataro
Iwasaki (1835–1885) is a good example. He was the great-grandson of a man who
had sold his *samurai* status to pay his debts. Iwasaki founded the Mitsubishi shipping

7.60 a, b Mitsubishi's founder made an Italianate villa, a Swiss chalet and a European garden for his guests – but a Japanese house and garden for his own family.

empire which grew into an industrial conglomerate (*zaibatsu*). As a wealthy man, he restored the Edo stroll garden at Rikugien and then purchased land for the Kiyosumi Garden near Tokyo Harbour. The latter was made into a stroll garden by digging a lake and using Mitsubishi ships to import rocks. A Tudor palace, designed by Josiah Conder, was built on the edge of the garden. Both estates were given to the City of Tokyo in the 1930s and are now open to the public.

The Iwasaki family's main residence, designed by Conder in 1896, survives in Kyu Iwasaki-tei Gardens. It has the oldest lawn in Tokyo and one of the few Swiss chalets in Japan, originally a billiard room. Conder was interested in Japanese design but helped introduce a Mixed Style to Japan. He taught at the Imperial College of Engineering and educated the first generation of Westernized Japanese architects. In architecture he used Gothic, Renaissance, Tudor and Islamic styles. His most influential design, for the Rokumeikan Pavilion had a garden which might have been lifted straight from J.C. Loudon's *Suburban Gardens*.

A gardenesque approach to planting design also flourished in Japan, though it is hard to say whether it arose spontaneously or came about through Western influence. In 1931 Kuck interviewed the leading Meiji garden designer, Jihei Ogawa (1860–1933), and he told her:

> In the old days only certain plants were allowed in the garden, and these only in certain places. But I decided there was no reason why any plant should not be used, even a foreign one, provided it was harmonious with its surroundings.[64]

Ogawa belonged to the seventh generation of a family of gardeners and Kuck reports that 'he never became interested in Western gardens'.[65] Yet the garden of the Heian Shrine, one of his major projects, makes extensive and un-Zen-like use of flowers.

7.61 a, b The Old Furukawa villa in Tokyo has a Victorian-style upper garden and house. The lower garden is Japanese.

Ogawa also designed the Murin-an garden in Kyoto with 'a blend of traditional technique and creative composition'.[66]

Temple gardens

Buddhism suffered as a result of the Meiji Restoration. Temples were demolished, texts burned and Buddha images destroyed. The persecution was short-lived but there were further difficulties in the twentieth century when, in a nationalistic spirit, Shinto became the state religion. After the Second World War, Shinto and Buddhism were placed on an equal footing. Article 20 of the 1946 Constitution stated that: 'Freedom of religion is guaranteed to all. No religious organization shall receive any privileges from the State, nor exercise any political authority.' Buddhism has flourished since the end of the Pacific War but the worldwide drift to secularism has affected Japan and at the time of writing temple gardens are not at the leading edge of Japanese garden design.

7.62 Matsumoto Castle was restored after the Meiji Restoration.

Part 4
North, West, South and East Asia

CHAPTER 8

Abstract Modernist gardens in Asia

8.1 International Abstract Modernism became the dominant design style for Asia's twentieth-century cities. But, as in Mumbai, the sun may be setting.

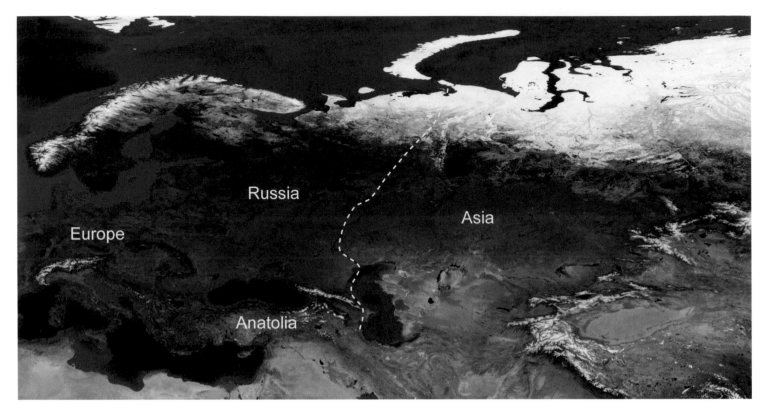

8.2 Herodotus called Anatolia 'Asia'. The dividing line between Europe and Asia is now taken to follow the Ural River and Mountains from the Barents Sea to the Caspian Sea, from whence it runs to the Red Sea. 'Russia' began as a small European state around Kiev and Moscow. The modern states of Russia and Turkey are part-European and part-Asian – both geographically and culturally.

This chapter offers an opinionated sketch of the period in which Modernism became the dominant design style across Asia. There are subsections on North, West, Central, South and East Asia. Examples of design projects are drawn from public landscape architecture, not private garden design, because most recent gardens are still in the ownership of the families which made them and because professional designers have found more employment on public projects, both municipal and corporate, than in private gardens. There is an obvious need for books on modern Asian gardens by local historians. But an interim overview may also have value. It is preceded by a brief discussion of an earlier period in which there was an international dimension to the belief systems of North Asia: that of nomadic herdsmen. The characteristic religion of this vast tract at that time was summarized by Eliade:

> *Morphologically, this religion is, in general, close to that of the Indo-Europeans: in both there is the same importance of the great God of the Sky or of the Atmosphere, the same absence of goddesses (so characteristic of the Indo-Mediterranean area), the same function attributed to the 'sons' or 'messengers' (Asvins, Dioscuri etc), the same exaltation of fire.*[1]

The design history of North Asia is touched upon in the next section to set the stage for the twentieth-century advance of Modernism into Asia.

North Asian Modernism

Modern Russia dominates North Asia and although it is the largest country on the Eurasian continent, it has not been mentioned in this book hitherto. The reason for the omission is that the cultural divide between the European and Asian parts of the Eurasian Continent runs from the Black Sea to the Ural Mountains, making the historic culture of Russia predominantly European.

The Principality of Muscovy (Moscow) was the medieval state which became Russia. In 1450, it was a small Christian state on the European side of the Urals, tracing its religion to Byzantium and calling its emperors 'Czars', the title deriving from the Roman 'Caesar'. By 1700, Russia had become an empire stretching from the Baltic to the Pacific. But its Christian culture was west-facing and its gardens had European roots. Peter the Great (1672–1725) worked and travelled in the West before returning home with a determination to modernize and Westernize Russia. His palace and gardens, the Peterhof, have an Eastern flamboyance but a German name to remind us that the design style is European. The array of gilded statuary in the garden is not so much a sign of Eastern opulence. It is an expression of the owner's taste and the limitless resources at his command. Similarly, the gardens made by Catherine the Great were European in style, if Asian in scale.

Russia's advance beyond the Urals took place in the sixteenth and seventeenth centuries, as did the European advance into the Americas. Fur hunting was the objective. At the time, Siberia was inhabited by nomads, including Nenets, Huns, and Uyghurs. They had been conquered by the Mongols in the thirteenth century and incorporated into a Siberian Khanate.

The belief systems of pre-Russian Siberia were analysed by Eliade in *Shamanism* and summarized in the above quotation (see p. 282). They are imperfectly known because they were unwritten, but, as Eliade explains, may have been close to the beliefs of the Proto-Indo-Europeans (PIEs) who are thought to have lived between the Black and Caspian Seas. Central Asians took the world to have physical and spiritual aspects. By going into a trance, shamans could cross the divide and exercise powers of divination and healing. Shamanism was widely influential. Eastward, the ideas spread into China (see p. 183), Japan (see p. 238) and the Americas. Westward, they spread with the Celts into Europe. Southward they spread with the Aryans into Iran and North India.

Shamanistic beliefs were suppressed by the Russian Empire, initially because they were not Christian and then because they were not Communist. 'Superstition' was seen as a threat to the newer faiths. The little information about shamanism available from travellers' tales, anthropology and linguistics has left the field wide open for speculation, to which I will contribute.

8.3 a, b The Peterhof Garden has an Eastern flamboyance but its design inspiration is Western.

8.4 Burkhan Cape on Lake Baikal is a sacred place for Shamans and Buddhists. The rocks are of white marble and have a small cave (the temperature was -30°C when the photograph was taken).

Central Asian nomads did not build temples or carve statues. Assuming them to have been at least as spiritual as other peoples, this gave a greater significance to the holiness of individuals. It seems likely that some holy men stopped travelling and took up residence as hermits in holy places with shelter. One can imagine an oasis or valley with sufficient water and trees for a few residents but not enough to support a tribe. Some men are naturally active and others prefer a life of seclusion and retreat. Holy men could collect knowledge from travellers, dispense wisdom and learn the medicinal uses of herbs. The early societies of India and China are known to have had holy men (*rishis* in India and *shengren* in China) who withdrew from settlements to live beside sacred rivers, near sacred mountains, in sacred woods and in sacred caves. They had a shamanistic tendency. *Sadhus* (Hindu ascetics) and Buddhist monks continue their ascetic habits. Buddhists organized the first property-owning communities of monks centuries before the advent of Christian monasticism in Egypt. As discussed in Chapters 4 and 5, Hindu *ashrams* and Buddhist monasteries were typically in forest and mountain settings, near but outside settlements.

At a later date, when Buddhist monasticism had become institutionalized and devotional, some holy men sought to return to the life of meditation chosen by the Buddha himself (see p. 139). They developed Ch'an Buddhism in China and Zen Buddhism in Japan. When the high priests of Western Modernism visited Japan in the early twentieth century, they were not slow in finding a kinship between the *wabi-sabi* aesthetic and International Modernist design (see p. 312). Perhaps they were making contact with a heritage of spirituality and restraint, flowing from shared ancestors in North and Central Asia. Before 1917, Holy Russia had been a religious society imbued with monasticism. Even after 1917, the river of asceticism ran deep in North Asia.

The spiritual aspect of Modernism, drawing on ancient roots, found ready acceptance in many parts of Asia. But the thoughtless transplant of North European architectural and landscape design styles to hot and arid climates was a social and environmental disaster. As the Japanese have sometimes shown, Modernism was a style which could and should have been adapted to local cultures, local materials and local traditions in the use and design of outdoor space.

8.5 A shaman from the Tuva region of South Siberia.

8.6 *Sadhus* are cultural descendants of Central Asia's ascetics.

Russian Modernism

Karl Marx despised the old faiths and damned religion as 'the sign of the oppressed creature, the heart of a heartless world, and the soul of soulless conditions. It is the opium of the people.'[2] Lenin considered religion an unfortunate consequence of feudalism and capitalism. But Communism's lack of a god has not stopped commentators from seeing it as a religion. Asia has several godless faiths and Ninian Smart, a great expert on Eastern religions, made the following observation on Marx's vision of 'a glorious future when a new form of life on earth will have been created':

> This corresponded to the Second Coming and to the Millennium of which many Christians have dreamed and for which they have lived in hope. And the joys of the hereafter would come through the sufferings of a chosen people – the proletariat whose present miseries might well be capped by the bloodshed and adversity of the revolutionary struggle.[3]

Russia's modernization was underway by the late nineteenth century but the country remained backward, with the authorities looking to the past and the revolutionaries looking to the future. Defeat by the Japanese in 1905 encouraged the revolutionaries and administered a shock to the authorities. Between 1890 and 1930, Russia

8.7 Lenin hoped to lead his people to the promised land of a modern Russia. His gesture is that of a religious leader.

8.8 *Dachas* were the only places with private gardens during the Communist era.

became a leading country in the advance of modern art, notable for Suprematism, Constructivism and Futurism. What might have been achieved is indicated by the interest taken in Wassily Kandinsky (1866–1944) by Jellicoe and others. Kandinsky taught at the Bauhaus. The October Revolution checked the trend to abstraction and Stalin exiled the artists. Socialist realism became the official art of Communism, with Russian garden and landscape design trailing in the wake of Russian politics. Bolshevist ideology had no place for private gardens, seen as capitalist baubles, but found a way to accommodate the *dacha*. A *dacha* is a house in the country. The word was originally applied to country retreats for the aristocracy, but the idea of a peasant cottage in the country is much older. Communism allowed only squatters' rights but a 1955 law established gardeners' partnerships as a legal entity, providing the land was used for agriculture. This made *dachas* a locale for folk art but not a field in which the art of garden design could advance – until the collapse of Communism and the return of private ownership in the 1990s. The *dacha* represents 'space, repose, "Russianess"',[4] a place to settle and grow one's own food.

Socialist realism influenced town planning and the design of public open space throughout the empire. Stalin turned from a dynamic new art to a drab version of the late-baroque. Constructivist ideas were condemned as 'decadent'. The Baroque style was used in Russia to glorify Communism, as it had been used in Rome to glorify the church, in Paris to glorify the king and in Washington, DC, to glorify democracy. Part of Moscow's Ostankino Park was used in 1935 to lay out the All-Union Agricultural Exhibition (VSKhV). Oltarzhevsky produced a Master Plan and Stalin had him arrested because the plan was insufficiently grandiose. No one could say this of the park's

8.9 The original designer of VDNH was arrested because his plan was insufficiently grandiose. His successor did not repeat the error.

8.10 The Gardenesque treatment of Gorky Park exemplifies the style of the once-hated now-admired capitalists.

1950s redesign as the VDNH. The Exhibition of National Economy Achievements is as fine an example of Stalinist landscape architecture as one could wish for.

With state power exalted and individual wealth despised, Russia had no place for private gardens. In their place, central government and industrial organizations built Culture Parks beside Palaces of Culture. The first culture park, made in 1928, is now an amusement park with a Gardenesque assembly of hills, trees, shrubs, flowers and amusements. The conceptual problem in designing a 'Culture Park' is the selection of whose culture to represent. Aesthetically, the Gardenesque was a fair choice. Politically, it was inept. Gardenesque was the style used by the capitalists Marx despised. Perhaps it was a Soviet-era joke, like the one about an official offering Khrushchev proof that the Garden of Eden had been in Russia: 'Adam and Eve had no clothes, they had no roof over their heads and had only apples to eat. Yet they thought they lived in Paradise. What else could they have been but Russians?'[5]

West Asian Modernism

By 1800, Islam had become a major religion in West, Central and South Asia. European ideas and arms then caused a setback: British rule allowed a Hindu revival in India; the First World War destroyed the Ottoman Empire; Islam was suppressed in the Russian Empire. But the discovery of oil gave some West Asian countries great wealth and a world role they had not enjoyed for centuries. With it came a design problem: should

8.11 The Atlantis Hotel in Dubai was described as follows in the *Sunday Times*:

Peter Jackson fantasy meets arabesque meets Hilton high-rise, all painted a slightly queasy frozen-prawn pink ... the beach is fine, though don't expect much from the scenery. It faces back to Palm Island, which may look great on a map, but is surprisingly ugly close up, with its densely packed, colourless villas and miles of strangely arid, unwelcoming beachfront. Nature does islands rather better than man.*

Note: *Bleach, S. *Sunday Times*, 27 July 2008.

the character of the new cities, public spaces and gardens be Traditional Islamic, Modern Islamic, International Modern or something new? The dimensions of the question are at once religious, cultural, technical, political, ecological and aesthetic. This was so in all the Asian countries but nowhere more than in the Fertile Crescent and Arabia. The region was keenly aware of its centrality in world history, of its relative weakness in 1900 and of the opportunities arising from the 'walls of money' which struck after 1973. Initially, there was a tendency for people from outside the region, like me, to prefer traditional styles, albeit with plumbing and air-conditioning, and for the residents of West Asia to prefer International Modernism.

Architectural critics resisted the temptation to hold their fire. Peter Davey, then editor of the *Architectural Review*, wrote in 1983:

> *With very few exceptions, export architecture is junk. In the last two decades, Western architects have covered the newly rich oil nations with a taffy tide of crude commercial kitsch. Local forms are endlessly trivialized, bastardized and wedded to the worst aspects of Western speculative 'architecture'.*[6]

Paul Finch, who succeeded him in 2004, was less restrained and made the following comment on a 2007 conference in Dubai which reviewed the place of sustainable design in making new urban environments: 'Diagrams are built rather than developed. Appropriateness is dismissed as the aesthete's niggle. Context is financial rather than physical ... dumb architecture dominates the scene. One feels entitled to criticise Dubai as "Las Vegas without the gambling"' and as a place in need of 'proper policies about infrastructure, water, energy and balanced communities'.[7] Catherine Slessor, also in the *Architectural Review*, wrote: 'Rooted in Northern European experience,

8.12 a, b New Gourna in 2004.

Modernism provided a rational, universal model that could be applied anywhere, with the addition of the odd brise-soleil'[8] but 'In the same way that rich patrons would once collect exotic specimens of plants, animals, wine, art and cars, so it is now with architecture'.[9] In 2007, the *Lonely Planet* recognized the victory of style over substance:

> *Peninsula architecture has become diverted from the traditional principle of functionality ... Increasingly architects are expected to refer, in an almost talismanical way, to the visual vocabulary of Arab art: hence the pointed windows, false balconies, wooden screens and tent motifs of modern buildings across the Peninsula. Perhaps this is because many traditional buildings, with their economy of style and design, achieve something that modern buildings often do not – they blend in harmoniously with their environment.*[10]

One might expect this line of criticism from the modern movement in architecture but not from a tourist guidebook. Tourism would be a less appealing activity if cities turned their backs on local character.

Egypt

The most thoughtful approach to the problem of context-sensitive design in an Islamic country came from Hassan Fathy (1899–1989). Egypt was not wealthy in his lifetime but its architectural tradition extended over 5,000 years and included buildings in European styles. In 1926, Fathy graduated in architecture from a school of engineering. Teaching in the Faculty of Fine Arts in Cairo in the 1930s he came in contact with International Modernism and watched the growing enthusiasm for concrete buildings.

8.13 Seen from Ibn Tulun Mosque, Cairo resembles Paris or London. But it has a different climate, a different culture and different traditions in the use of open space.

8.14 a, b Al-Azhar Park, designed by Dr Maher Moheb Stino, is a postmodern Islamic pastiche.

In full acceptance of the principle that form should follow function, Fathy judged them inappropriate: the materials had to be imported; they were culturally alien; the interiors became too hot; sunlight glared through the windows. 'On the one hand, Fathy respected and admired European traditions and on the other he resented them as part of a colonial legacy that had threatened Egypt's identity.'[11] He had a deep sensitivity to cultural traditions, materials and design with climate.

Reading Fathy in Cairo, as I did in a Modernist government office block in 1975, brought home the extent of his wisdom.[12] Mostly we just suffered with the flies. Sometimes we closed the blinds and tried to coax the air conditioning into action. Sometimes, when the sun was not blazing through un-curtained windows, we would open them and fan the breeze. The elevators did not work and we were usually sticky-hot on arrival, after walking to work along unshaded streets with diesel air – a day in Cairo was said to cause as much lung damage as 40 cigarettes.

Between 1946 and 1953, Fathy worked with Egypt's Department of Antiquities on the village of New Gourna, on the west bank of the Nile at Luxor. The project failed, because the planned residents preferred to live as tour guides and tomb robbers in Old Gourna, but the excellence of New Gourna's design was widely appreciated outside Egypt. Within Egypt, the mud brick used for its construction was seen as a symbol of backwardness. Fathy admired mud for its economy, for its thermal capacity and for the ease with which traditional design motifs could be re-interpreted. Fathy's mosque and a few other buildings survive but most of New Gourna was demolished. Old Gourna was itself vacated in 2007.

8.15 a, b Sultan Ahmet Square in Istanbul, looking towards Hagia Sophia. The garden was designed by the Chief Engineer for Lyons (André Auric) before the First World War.

As enthusiasm for Modernism wanes, hotel gardens and parks in Egypt are being designed in a hybrid Islamo-Modern style which one could well describe as pastiche. Al Azhar Park, in Cairo was designed by an Egyptian landscape architect (Dr Maher Moheb Stino) who is also a member of the American Society of Landscape Architects (ASLA). It may be a postmodern caricature of the Islamic garden tradition, but the use of water and palm trees is climatically appropriate.

Turkey

When I first visited Istanbul, in 1968, it felt like an Asian city. After three months travel in Turkey I had expected the great metropolis to be the most European part of the country. But it felt more Asian than Ankara, the capital, and the cities along Turkey's Mediterranean and Black Sea coasts. Even Van seemed more Western. But in 2005, when I went back, Istanbul felt European. There were many tourists, some in beachwear, but the big change was the Europeanization of Turkish culture. Most of the dust, most of the animals and most of the smells had gone. I found few of the old wooden buildings I remembered and there was no need to recall my Turkish. English was spoken, cappuccino was sold, vehicles were modern and the street management looked Central European, possibly the work of ex-*Gastarbeiten* (guest workers in Germany). It was an easier city to visit, but less Asian and less interesting.

Designing a Gardenesque park in front of what was once the greatest church in Christendom (Hagia Sophia) raises cultural and chronological issues. The church was built in 558 and the park is in the style of Europe's nineteenth-century public parks.

8.16 a, b Istanbul's waterfront is now dominated by a road and some flabby 'green space' – but it has capabilities.

Both are Christian. Yet Istanbul is now a Turkish city and the park does not have the slightest aesthetic or functional kinship with an Islamic garden. Since it is beautiful and refreshing, perhaps this does not matter. An International Modern style might have suited Kemal Ataturk's ideology, if not his personal taste. Functionally, one could make a case for a park where sitting on the grass and roasting kebabs were allowed. These activities, the most traditional and most popular Turkish uses of outdoor open space, can be seen by the Sea of Marmara in Istanbul and the Haus der Kulturen der Welt in Berlin. The landscape treatment of Istanbul's waterfront is also Western. It illustrates Ian McHarg's brilliant criticism of highway engineers: 'There are other aspirants who vie to deface shrines and desecrate sacred cows, but surely it is the highway commissioner and engineer who most passionately embrace insensitivity and philistinism as a way of life and profession.'[13]

In Byzantine and Ottoman times, the Istanbul waterfront was extensively developed with private villas and gardens (see p. 101). They were swept away to make a highway but, fortunately, the engineers left a stretch of dull parkland between the road and the Sea of Marmara which could still be used to build sound barriers, mounds, earth-sheltered buildings, restaurants, yacht harbours and bathing beaches. Istanbul could recover the place it had 1,000 years ago: Europe's greatest water city and even, perhaps, Europe's greatest city. But the view from the air is alarming. It looks as though Le Corbusier's *plan voisin* has been adopted by the city authorities. Tower blocks gape at each other across broad roads and expanses of dry 'green space' which are, of course, less suited to Istanbul than to the country of Le Corbusier's birth (Switzerland) or his adopted homeland (France).

Israel

Israel drew its modern wealth from industry and agriculture, not oil. Ancient monuments with Jewish connections were meticulously conserved but the same cannot be said for Islamic and Christian archaeological sites. Not having visited Israel, I will quote William Dalrymple's impressions on a journey from the Mediterranean to China:

> Israeli busses are the fastest, most comfortable and efficient in Asia. They are the only ones in which you can write a diary and read the results afterwards. But the view from their windows is invariably depressing: you read much about how the Israelis have made the desert flower, but little about the cost. The dual carriageway from Jerusalem winds past not a land of milk and honey, but a scape of scarred hillsides, rubbish dumps, telegraph wires, pylons, concrete, dirt and dust. The towns are charmless and ugly; there is barbed wire everywhere ... I thought: No. You've taken the oldest country in the world, one of the great centres of civilization, a kind of paradise – and you've turned it into suburbia. New Acre confirmed my prejudices. It has the decaying, unloved look of a provincial Californian town of the late fifties – all parking lots and spurious palm trees.[14]

One day, perhaps, the energy which has gone into defence and nation-building will be available for conservation and renewal of a historic landscape.

Saudi Arabia

An ancient land of nomads, Saudi Arabia began the path to modern statehood in the eighteenth century. After a prolonged struggle with the Ottoman Turks, the Saudi state was recognized as an independent kingdom in 1927. Oil was discovered in 1938 and

8.17 Hassan Beq Mosque, in Jaffa, was built by the Ottoman Turks in 1916. The Arab-Israeli War began nearby, in 1948, and the minaret became a sniper post. The mosque was saved from demolition, by Menachim Begin, but the surrounding Arab town has been replaced by high rise buildings, European-style parkland and a parking lot.

8.18 The Jeddah Corniche was designed by a British firm (RMJM) in 1977. The main features are a collection of modern sculptures and what is said to be the world's largest fountain. They are no substitute for good landscape planning and good landscape design.

8.19 A car sculpture on the Jeddah Corniche makes one wonder what future awaits the city when the oil runs out or loses its value.

modernization began with the help of an expatriate workforce. Two factors distinguish the Saudi urbanization from that of other West Asian countries. First, more money was available. Second, Saudi Arabia was the home of Islam. In consequence, more attention was given to conservation and some effort went into the creation of an Islamic environment. Old cities have, however, been drastically changed and one is left with the overall impression that much more could have been done. The author of *The Traditional Architecture of Saudi Arabia* is depressed by what has happened:

> In recent years, as cities have been modernized, many of the old buildings that constitute the extant evidence of the indigenous Arabian architectural tradition have disappeared. Whatever can still be done in the way of conservation, it is clear that the architectural traditions involved are dead.[15]

A similar point could be made about landscape and garden traditions which were, in any case, never as strong at the architectural tradition. There was a tendency for western consultants to create the types of public open space made in the West.

The name Jeddah derives either from the Arabic word for 'seashore' or 'grandmother', the latter because the tomb of Eve (Adam's wife) is said to have been here. Jeddah is an ancient port which was walled for protection against the Portuguese after being taken by the Ottoman Turks. The walls were demolished and used as landfill. The city grew from 1.5 sq km in 1940 to over 500 sq km in 1990. The following comment on the old town (Al-Balad) was published in 1995:

> There are a few unsympathetic intrusions by office blocks but these have at least
> followed the narrow, winding street patterns inside the vanished walls. Today Al-Balad
> is almost a ghost town. The inhabitants simply closed the shutters and locked the doors
> of their old houses when they left during the 1980s. It is eerily quiet for an Eastern city,
> with only a handful of small, Indian-run shops, a few poor immigrant families, and tribes
> of skinny alley cats. It is also one of the cleanest cities, since the earthen streets were
> paved with polished granite a few years ago. For the majority of Saudis, new means good
> ... That so much of Al-Balad remains is due mainly to a former city mayor, Mohammed
> Farsi, who introduced the foreign concept of listing buildings of historic interest. He
> fought to conserve old Jeddah when he realised it was the only substantial remaining
> example of Red Sea architecture in Saudi Arabia.[16]

As Jeddah began to spread along the coast, a road and promenade were built. It is called the Jeddah Corniche. The word 'corniche' comes from the French *route à corniche* ('road on a ledge'), often used for waterside roads. This led to its use for the Nile Corniche, in Cairo, and the Beirut Corniche, beside the Mediterranean, and, more recently, for coastal promenades and beaches in the Gulf States. The Jeddah Corniche was designed by British consultants in the 1970s. It catches the breeze but suffers from too much glare, too many cars and too few trees. The outdoor sculpture collection on the Southern Corniche, also planned by Mohammed Farsi, does something to provide visual interest. The King Fahd Fountain projects a column of sea water over 300 m into the air when the Saudi king is in Jeddah. In summer, the Corniche is enjoyed from within air-conditioned vehicles. At the time of writing, the Corniche is being redesigned.

United Arab Emirates

The United Arab Emirates (UAE) comprise seven states in the Arabian Peninsula. Rich in oil and gas, they have seen rapid economic growth since the union was formed in 1971. Dubai and Abu Dhabi are the largest Emirates in terms of population and land area.

Dubai had a population of 20,000 in 1945. A construction boom began in the 1960s and by 2005 Dubai, with a population of 1.4 m, was one of the fastest-growing cities in

8.20 The King Fahd Fountain in Jeddah.

8.21 An artificial beach is a popular feature of the Abu Dhabi West Corniche.

the world. The pre-1945 city should of course have been conserved in its entirety but there was no reason to make the new city resemble the old city. Unfortunately, clean sheets often bring out the worst in planners and designers. With nothing to relate to, except each other, highway engineering and show-off architecture flourish. Dubai became a hotch-potch of International Modernist, postmodern and junk architecture. Some of the quality is good but the 'just balance' between unity and diversity weighs towards diversity. The aim is to have 'the tallest', 'the largest', 'the first' and the 'most famous' in each category. This may help the quest to become a tourist destination, like Las Vegas, but from a design standpoint, what the city needed was an enlightened landscape structure plan with inventive approaches to climatic design, hydrological design, ecological design, the use of colour and the use of materials.

A book on the *Architectural Heritage of the Gulf* gives the following summary of conditions before and after the 1990 spike in the oil price:

> The lanes were usually sandy underfoot, or at the most covered with a layer of clay. This too meant that they were cooler than the asphalt roads of today. Since their width generally did not exceed three metres, they could be roofed over with beams and a palm-front covering, especially in the more heavily used lanes of the souq ... In the days before cars there was also no advantage in the present widespread, open plan of today's garden suburbs. In the past, city dwellers had to be within easy walking distance of the souq, the sea front or the mosque. Street maps of the cities of the Gulf today show very clearly the closely-built areas of the old towns, their street plan all jumbled, in sharp contrast to the grid plan of the newer districts.[17]

Oil prices rose again after 2003 and the development frenzy reached fantasy levels:

> Adrian Smith, the designer of the Burj Dubai tower, admits that he was inspired by the towers of the Emerald City in the film version of The Wizard of Oz ... which ... chronicles the voyage of Dorothy, a young girl from Kansas played by Judy Garland in the movie, to the Emerald City, residence of the Wizard of Oz. Accompanied by a Lion, a Scarecrow and a Tin Woodsman, Dorothy first sees gleaming green towers at the edge of the forest: 'There's Emerald City', she says. 'Oh, we're almost there at last! It's beautiful, isn't it?'[18]

The 2008 oil price collapse left some commentators wondering whether the Lion, the Scarecrow or the Tin Man would be the best pointer to the future.

Abu Dhabi is larger than Dubai and, with greater oil wealth, its population has grown fast. A conservative policy was chosen, socially and architecturally, which allowed time for lessons to be learned from the experiences of other Gulf States. The Abu Dhabi West Corniche is a case in point. The project was not treated, like the Jeddah Corniche, as an engineering project to be ornamented with sculpture. The infrastructure engineers (Parsons) appointed an experienced landscape architecture firm (LANDinc) to undertake the design of a 50 ha, and 5 km, stretch of waterfront. A wave form structure was used to integrate the town with the coast and it was planned with both

cultural and recreational facilities. Tented structures provide shade. The Corniche is popular and even in the humid heat of mid-summer is used for cycling, jogging and other activities. In winter weekends the park and the artificial beaches are crowded.

Kuwait

After the discovery of oil in 1938, Kuwait grew rich. In 1950, Monoprio, Spenceley and Macfarlene were commissioned to prepare a master plan for the expected urban growth. They were a British firm and the Kuwait plan was based on British new town master plans. This included a network of greenways – which are yellow-brownways without expensive irrigation. The annual rainfall is 100 mm and 75 per cent of Kuwait's water is distilled or imported. This makes Kuwait's greenways 'unecological' and a great deal more expensive than British greenways. An alternative would be to use the water for gardens and apply a US-style xeriscaping policy to the transport infrastructure. Xeriscaping is a way of establishing plants without irrigation.

Iraq

Iraq gained independence from Turkey in 1923 and from Britain in 1932. It then became a monarchy and, in 1958, a socialist republic. A programme of modernization followed but, compared to Saudi Arabia, Iraq had less money, less faith and worse government. Cities and parks were badly designed and a particularly regrettable aspect of Saddam Hussein's regime (1979–2003) was the unnecessary attempt to glorify Iraq by reconstructions of ancient monuments. The country which invented cities, writing and

8.23 A re-creation of the Ishtar Gate in Iraq was an excellent idea – but it should not have been done on an archaeological site (photograph 1967). Saddam Hussein 'restored' a considerable part of Babylon.

8.24 a, b Baghdad: the Martyr's Memorial and the Monument to the Unknown Soldier.

the wheel had no need to boast. Re-workings of old sites obscure and distort history. A better plan would have been to assemble a team of experts and make full re-creations of archaeological sites on different land. The regime had more success with the design of geometrically elegant war memorials.

Iran

Iran began to modernize in the late nineteenth century and the process gathered pace under the autocratic rule of Mohammad Reza Shah Pahlavi (reign 1941–7). There was a hiatus during the Iran–Iraq War (1980–88) and when modernization resumed, with increased oil revenues, it was done in a more Islamic framework. Religious monuments were cared for but old cities were not cherished. The *Architectural Review* devoted a special issue to Isfahan in 1976 and called for its conservation:

> *For Iran is in danger of forsaking its own culture by allowing Western influences to infiltrate and gradually destroy its traditional values ... To continue along this road will turn Iran, as it has other parts of the Middle East, into a cheap America and Iranians into ersatz Americans.*[19]

The Islamic Revolution of 1979 was politically and culturally anti-American – but did nothing to stop the Westernization of Iran's cities. Except for religious buildings, the old structures and spaces have been progressively replaced with anywhere-architecture in anywhere-landscapes. The Maidan in Isfahan, once used for markets, tents, parades and polo, now resembles a poorly maintained football pitch with a Baroque fountain. Similar fates have befallen many parks and gardens in Iran, though some spaces have received a more culturally appropriate treatment.

8.25 Isfahan used to be a city of mud brick, It is being rebuilt in concrete, glass and steel.

8.26 A modern park in Tehran manages to be modern without being excessively Western.

8.27 A Europe-esque avenue, driven through the ancient city of Yazd and centred on a traffic island in front of the Amir Chaqmaq Takiyya Mosque.

8.28 a, b The Maidan in Isfahan has been converted from a great multipurpose space into a lawn with a baroque fountain. (See also Figure 3.12.)

8.29 A gratuitously Western public park in Kerman.

8.30 The garden of a library in Kerman is enclosed and planted in a style which is both climatically and culturally appropriate.

Central Asian Modernism

Uzbekistan

The Russian Empire pushed into Central Asia at the rate of 140 km^2/day during the nineteenth century.[20] In Uzbekistan, the Russians were provoked by the emirs' habit of kidnapping Russian girls for their harems. They captured Tashkent in 1867 and Khiva in 1873. The palace and garden of a Russian-influenced emir survive outside Bukhara. Sitorai Makhi Khosa is a cross between a Russian *dacha* and an Islamic garden. Though the town has reached its gates, the setting is more rural than the fortress (Ark) in Bukhara and one can still sense the relationship between a fortified encampment and a country retreat of the kind enjoyed by Central Asian princes since ancient times. But Timur Tamerlane's garden, in Shahr-e Sabz has become a Soviet baroque park.

The Bolsheviks took control of Uzbekistan in 1920 and a programme of Sovietization was begun. There were campaigns against Islam, polygamy, the Hajj and Arabic. Nomads were settled. Agriculture was collectivized. Ancient cities were modernized. Dust roads were replaced with bitumen, mud architecture with concrete shacks. The town of Khiva was a lucky exception. It was recognized as an ancient monument, of urbanism, and largely preserved. Municipal authorities throughout Asia must wish the same policy had been applied to their walled cities, with Modernism held at their city gates. Mosques and madrasahs were also conserved in other Uzbek towns. But instead of being used for atheist propaganda, like churches in Soviet Russia, they were made into craft workshops, cafés and tourist emporia, re-introducing capitalism to the soul of the state.

8.31 A Soviet avenue runs across the site of Timur's palace garden in Shahr-e Sabz .

8.32 A madrasah used as a tourist restaurant in Bukhara.

8.33 a, b This is not Austria: it is the City Square in Taohkont.

Kazakhstan

Kazakhstan lies between Russia and Uzbekistan, on the dividing line between Europe and Asia – the Ural River. It is the ninth-largest country in the world and may be the region where the horse was domesticated. A northern Silk Route crossed Kazakhstan and it was overrun by the Mongols. In the nineteenth century, the country became subject to Russification and then, after 1917, to Sovietification. Agriculture was

8.34 The Presidential Palace in Astana could be a spoof by Borat or a bauble won from a lucky throw in Las Vegas.

collectivized and towns rebuilt. Independence was declared in 1991 and, because of the country's oil wealth, Western firms became involved in redevelopment projects. The character of the cities then began to change – from Russian provincial towns to American provincial towns. Borat made the country famous with his 2006 movie, *Cultural Learnings of America for Make Benefit Glorious Nation of Kazakhstan*, but did not find time to mock the standard of landscape and garden design in 'My glorious homeland of deflowering gardens'.

South Asian Modernism

India

On the evidence of the *Ramayana*, India had, as it will surely have again, the most wonderful gardens. But at the start of the twentieth century, it was difficult to know which direction should be taken. Constance Villiers-Stuart, the first Westerner to write about Indian gardens, used the title *Gardens of the Great Mughals*. She knew that gardens had been made in pre-Islamic India but, like us, could find little information concerning their character. American authors have been less than generous in seeing her book as an exercise in yoking garden design to the imperialist ox. Westcoat recognizes her sympathy for, and knowledge of, Indian culture but states that: 'She ardently believed that the spiritual meaning and beauty of gardens could foster loyalty among Indian subjects.'[21] As evidence for this misinterpretation, he quotes part of Villiers-Stuart's comment on the plan for New Delhi, formulated while she was in India: 'It has to convey the idea of a peaceful domination and a dignified rule of the life of India by the British Raj.' This remark was a quotation, by Villiers-Stuart, from a town planning report. She took exception to the attitude it displayed, writing that 'Ideas of "peaceful domination" or "dignified rule" are but a poor exchange for Indian religious feeling.' Her next paragraph begins as follows:

8.35 a, b, c Edwin Lutyens designed New Delhi in a Mughal-British style instead of the Ashokan style that Constance Villiers-Stuart recommended.

The material advantages of our good government – peace, laws justly administered, education, sanitation, hospitals, even the fairyland of European science – leave the mass of India cold ... Here lies the great opportunity for New Delhi, for the motive that can really move and lead India must be a religious one. The truth is cut deep in the edicts of Asoka.[22]

The remark that 'material advantages ... leave ... India cold' and the final sentence, which is not quoted by Westcoat, clarify Villiers-Stuart's own position: she considered Indian-ness more appropriate than British-ness for India's new capital. She was the wife of a British army officer and her remarks about 'good government' can be read as a wish for India to enjoy the benefits of European science and government, as it has done. Personally, I support Villiers-Stuart's position. Edwin Lutyens read her book on his voyage to India[23] but his idea of 'Indian-ness' was to borrow ideas from India's Mughal conquerors, not from the Buddhist faith and 'edicts of Asoka'. Carlton believes the British aspired to a second Mughal empire and displayed 'That crude racism (which has always been part of the British mindset in dealing with other peoples).'[24] He should compare the work of the Archaeological Survey of India (ASI) with the work of other Western powers, including that of America in Iraq.

Working with Gertrude Jekyll, Edwin Lutyens helped design some of the best gardens ever made in England. At the time, he was a delicate youth and she was a strong woman at the height of her powers. The later gardens which Lutyens designed, without Jekyll at the helm, because she had lost her eyesight, are of lower quality. He was a great architect but needed her help and judgement in the design of outdoor space. The overall plan of New Delhi is like Lutyens later gardens: rather formal, rather French and rather vacant. The Mughal Garden he designed for the Viceroy's House (now the President's Palace, *Rashtrapati Bhavan*) is Indian in the sense that Mughal Gardens are Indian – but in inspiration it is Islamic, owing nothing to the Buddhist style of Villiers-Stuart's imagination. Though well crafted like all Lutyens' work, it is not even planted like a Mughal garden. Villiers-Stuart knew what was required; Lutyens did not. It should have been an orchard garden, so that India's leaders could stroll in the shade, enjoying fresh scents and ripe fruits as they took wise decisions.

For the first half-century after independence, India was a poor country. There was little money for new gardens or for training garden designers and landscape architects. But tourism was a significant source of foreign currency and more money was spent on the garden treatment of archaeological sites than on public parks. Once again, Villiers-Stuart's excellent advice went unheeded. Indian horticulture advanced from where British horticulture left off in 1947: resolutely opposed to International Modernism. Indian temples, some of the greatest works of art in Asia, were treated like bandstands in British parks. One wonders if the staff concerned were trained in the parks departments of provincial English towns, or hoped for new jobs with the old imperialists. Either way, they'll regret it.

8.36 a, b The landscape setting of the Khajuraho Temples may have been date palms but is now (left) UK-style parkland.

The Khajuraho Temples are a case in point. Their setting now has lawns, rose beds and temples treated as bandstands. Only the crazy golf is missing. The original character of their setting (950–1050) is unknown but it is unlikely to have resembled Skegness. The name Khajuraho, derived from the Hindi word *khajur* (date palm) gives a hint, as does the survival of muddy pools around the visitor centre. Parts of the town could be re-planned so that it becomes possible to view the temples in an oasis setting with pools and date palms. Reflections in the water would be beautiful. There could also be habitat-creation work around the periphery of Khajuraho village, still leaving part of the site as the popular green park it has become.

Nepal

Nepal is a Himalayan kingdom bordering Tibet to the north and Bihar to the south. As discussed in Chapter 5, it was influenced by the Bon culture of Tibet and the Hindu culture of India. Though retaining its independence, Nepal came under British influence during the Rana Dynasty (1846–1953). It now has a British-influenced Royal Botanic Garden, outside Kathmandu, eight National Parks (an American idea) and a number of other wildlife reserves and conservation areas. They are useful 'scientific' introductions, like airports, mobile phones and the practice of garden restoration. In 2006, the former Kathmandu palace garden of Field Marshall Kaiser Shumsher Jung Bahadur Rana (1892–1964) was restored and opened to the public as the Garden of Dreams. The Field Marshall, having spent time in England and being an admirer of Austria's Kaiser Franz Joseph, made an eclectic Anglo-Austrian garden. It is right that

8.37 a, b The Garden of Dreams in Kathmandu is Anglo-Austrian in style and has been well restored.

8.38 a, b, c Kenzo Tange's Corbusian Master Plan for Lumbini is equally at odds with Buddhist traditions and with the local environment.

it should have been carefully restored, despite its largely un-Nepalese character. The garden has pavilions, balustrades, flagstone paths and a sunken flower garden with a pond.

East Asian Modernism

Chinese Modernism

Paul Kennedy wrote that in 1500 Europe was relatively weak and Chinese society was technologically precocious and 'the envy of foreign visitors'.[25] The scales had swung by 1900, with the West throwing its weight around and China little changed from 1500. By 2000, the scales were swinging again. Kennedy highlights political diversity as the factor behind the rise of the West but from an Asian perspective the decisive factor was a Chinese invention: gunpowder. It was cannon built with scientific expertise that powered the Mughal conquest of India in 1526, the Russian advance into Asia detailed above, the acquisition of Hong Kong from China in 1843 and, in 1905, Japan's sinking of the Russian fleet in the Tsushima Straits. And it was a belief in science and technology, not in democracy, which became the driving force in Asia's modernization. Religion therefore had to be split from education and government: China's last Son of Heaven was deposed in 1911, Russia's royal family was shot in Yekaterinburg in 1918.

By 1800, Western galleons were a common sight in East Asia. Europeans used their own architectural styles in some ports, but most urban houses and gardens were unaffected and there was little demand for European manufactures. The British worried that too much gold was flowing to India and China in exchange for cotton, silk and other Eastern products. This situation changed during the nineteenth century. Western products were found to have their uses, especially in battle, and Western design styles became fashionable. The fabulous success of reason in making machines and in managing the natural world led to a parallel deployment of reason in art, architecture and gardens. As rationalism advanced, religion retreated, not so much metaphysically as in its capacity to regulate natural phenomena, drive government policy and inspire the arts. Religious beliefs vary between countries but the abstract truths of science are everywhere the same. Therefore, if art and design are to be guided by analytical thought, instead of beliefs, they too will be everywhere the same – which will be a pity.

China had a bad experience with Europe in the nineteenth century and when the People's Republic of China was established in 1949 it looked to Russia for advice on modernization. There was discussion about a Beijing Master Plan and Chen Zhanxiang (1916–2001), who had been an assistant to Sir Patrick Abercrombie in London, recommended keeping the old city and building a new administrative district outside the walls. Sadly, the government took advice from Soviet experts and demolished the walls to make a ring road. Professor Liang Si-cheng said that 'demolishing the

8.39 Watched by guards, people stand around Tiananmen Square with nothing to do and nowhere to sit.

wall is like peeling off my skin!'[26] From 1949–76, Chinese cities were modelled on Soviet cities. China then adopted a policy of 'socialism with Chinese characteristics' (regarded by foreigners as 'capitalism with Chinese characteristics'). Architecturally, except for some tacked-on ornaments, the new style of urbanism was 'capitalism *without* Chinese characteristics'. This was because so many students from Hong Kong and Mainland China studied in the US. American planning replaced Soviet planning. Europe, the region with the greatest expertise in making good cities, was ignored on account of the bad reputation it had earned in the nineteenth century and relative lack of economic prowess in the twentieth century.

8.40 Shanghai's new skyline is an exotic landscape composition.

8.41 a, b Tai Ping Qiao Park, by SOM, has unsentimental dragon curves. Lujiazui Park, Pudong, is 'Western with Chinese features' but the mown grass is not available for public use.

Touring some Chinese cities in 2007, I felt empathy with the problems faced by China's landscape architecture profession. It was small and there was no Chinese tradition for the design of urban squares, town parks or public gardens. Travel to Europe, where examples of bad and good urbanism could have been studied, was difficult. Nor was the literature of urban landscape architecture readily accessible. The two open space types in which China had ancient expertise – scenic parks and private gardens – were despised by the authorities on account of their association with imperial elites. A further problem is that landscape architecture was regarded merely as a design profession. In practice, good landscape design is entirely dependent on good landscape planning.

8.42 a–d Abstract Modernism in Shanghai.

Construction and planting can be very good, as they generally are in China, without the places being remotely successful. Three types of modern park were evident in China: (1) Western-inspired parks in Chinese dress; (2) Western-inspired parks in Western dress; and (3) hybrids.

Tiananmen Square is a case in point. Chairman Mao's government decided that the capital of the world's most populous country should have the world's largest public square. No open space type is less suited to the alternating dust, heat and cold of Beijing's climate and, though of occasional use for pro-government parades and anti-government demonstrations, it is an otherwise function-less space – albeit with sacred status in the People's Republic. The people stand around with nothing to do but wonder at its extent. Moscow's Red Square once had a role as a market place. Perhaps the Modernist town planners responsible for the design of Tiananmen Square concluded that because it had so little function it did not need a form. In 2007, I found no public seating in the square but it did have a flotilla of police vans to stop people sitting on the few small patches of grass. Commands barked at me from loudspeakers could either have been 'Get off the grass' or 'Go to jail'. Tiananmen Square is a totalitarian memorial to Soviet master-planning.

The redevelopment of Shanghai is a happier tale. The Bund was recognized as a landscape resource and re-designed as a public garden and riverside promenade with cafés and outdoor seating. An equivalent space was designed on the Pudong bank of the Huangpu River. Within Shanghai, the Xintiandi district was re-developed along traditional lines, remembering the lanes of old China. SOM were commissioned to design the nearby Tai Ping Qiao Park, which fires on many cylinders: it makes use of land above an underground car park; its sinuous lakeside steps are unsentimentally Chinese; its fountains, for which there is no precedent in China's historic cities and gardens, are well handled and cool the air; it has many places to sit and sufficient flowers to create a garden atmosphere; the open space and its surrounding buildings are in scale and enhance each other.

Japan: Meiji modernization

The Meiji Restoration (see p. 276) launched a period of intensive modernization. 'Meiji', meaning 'Enlightened Rule' is a posthumous name used to describe the character of the emperor's reign from 1868–1912. The enlightenment he brought was political and technical. Japanese experts were sent to discover how things were done elsewhere and foreign experts were invited to Japan. Germany was admired both for its political arrangements and its technical education. Britain and America were admired for their engineers and designers. The 3,000 experts invited to Japan were known as hired foreigners (*o-yatoi gaikokujin*). Josiah Conder, as discussed in Chapter 7, was one of the foreign experts. He left England in 1877, at the age of 25, to become professor of architecture at Japan's Imperial College of Engineering and a consultant to the

8.43 a, b The visual role of the courtyard at the Byodo-in Museum is traditional but the design is modern.

8.44 Mirei Shigemori's own garden.

Ministry of Public Works. Conder lived in Japan until his death in 1920 and is buried in the Gokoku-ji Temple Cemetery. He had trained in London with an architect who worked on the Great Exhibition. This gave Conder eclectic tastes. His buildings were influenced by Tudor, Gothic, Islamic and Indian styles. He became known as the 'father of Japanese architecture', though 'father of Japanese eclecticism' would be more apposite. Conder wrote the first English book with detailed information about the gardens of Japan (see p. 277) – and detailed design interested him more than design theory. When he designed a European building, he supplied a European garden.

Japan: Showa modernization

By the 1920s, America had become a Great Power and, because it was also a Pacific Power, a significant influence on Japan. Showa, meaning 'Bright Peace', is a posthumous name for the reign of Emperor Hirohito (1926–89). He was associated with the rise of military nationalism in the 1930s and with its overthrow in 1945. On 1st January 1946, he stunned the nation by announcing that he was no longer a god. Japan became a democracy and a second phase of modernization was launched, with America now the dominant influence.

Mirei Shigemori (1896–1975) became the best-known Japanese garden designer of the period. The author of a 26-volume study of Japanese gardens, he wished to both modernize and sustain the tradition. He admired European culture but had no more wish to see imitations of Western gardens than stale imitations of old Japanese gardens being made in Japan. His solution was to take the nature-inspired tradition forward with the introduction of modern materials and with an awareness of modern art. His biographer sees him as a 'rebel in the garden'.[27] In terms of geometry and

8.45 a, b The Silver Moonlight Garden at the 2008 Chelsea Flower Show, by Haruko Seki and Makato Saito, is both Japanese and contemporary.

materials, this is correct. But he used traditional design features and his use of cement and concrete can be seen as a regrettable departure from the *wabi-sabi* aesthetic.

Leonard Koren, looking across a wide range of design categories, compares Japanese Modernism with the *wabi-sabi* aesthetic (see p. 264). He sees Modernism as 'the dominant aesthetic sensibility of mid- to late-20th century international industrialized society'[28] and *wabi-sabi* as 'the most conspicuous and characteristic feature of what we think of as traditional Japanese beauty'.[29] Koren's list of differences between the two aesthetics is longer than his list of similarities, but the similarities are striking: 'Both eschew any decoration that is not integral to structure; both are abstract, nonrepresentational ideals of beauty; both have readily identifiable surface characteristics.' His summary of the differences is that: 'Modernism is seamless, polished and smooth. *Wabi-sabi* is earthy, imperfect, and variegated.'[30] When applied to architecture, another difference was the use of steel, concrete and glass by practitioners of International Modernism.

Koren's analysis helps explain why Japan proved such fertile ground for the Modernist aesthetic. The similarities made it seem as though Modernism had existed in Japan centuries before it appeared in the West. The differences, centring on *wabi-sabi*, could scarcely be accommodated within Modernist buildings but found a ready application in outdoor space. In Europe, the application of Modernist ideas to outdoor space was rarely successful: unsuitable materials were used to make dysfunctional spaces which merely framed buildings in the way pre-modern painters had framed paintings. In Japan, Modernists created courtyards framed by buildings, instead of buildings framed by open space, and they used natural materials instead of white paint and grey concrete.

As the first East Asian country to industrialize, Japan was also the first to make contact with International Modernism. Rarely has a design seed fallen on more fertile soil. As discussed above, Zen Buddhism had long fostered an abstract approach to art and design. Buildings, exemplified by the Katsura Palace, were austere and disciplined. Zen gardens abstracted the 'essence' of mountains, water and natural principles. Modernist designers from the West found highly developed precedents for the style they were stumbling towards. Abstraction became a fundamental characteristic of Modernism.

Japanese designers approached the issues raised by International Modernism with great seriousness. They wanted to modernize and they wanted to retain Japan-ness. Bruno Taut, a Modernist architect from Germany, visited Japan in 1933 and at once identified the Ise Shrine and Katsura Imperial Villa as masterworks. At Katsura, he believed: 'The presence of the garden dominates the interior so much that all the surfaces of the walls appear designed to reflect it, and the reflection is especially vivid in the opaque gold and silver of the sliding partitions.'[31] The Ise Shrine was seen as an

8.46 Hiroshima Peace Park. The Peace Museum has a proportional system which drawn on both Modernism and traditional Japanese proportions. A baroque fountain can be glimpsed beneath the pilottis.

8.47 Hiroshima Peace Park. The Peace Dome ruin is at the other end of the baroque avenue.

Eastern equivalent of the Acropolis and Katsura as a precursor of Modernist principles, pre-dating International Modernism by three centuries. In 1960, Walter Gropius and Kenzo Tange wrote about Katsura with equal enthusiasm.[32] Japanese architects, having regarded their country's traditional buildings as 'mostly wooden shacks'[33], were intrigued by the flattering attention of Western Modernists. Tange wrote that 'Buildings in the *shinden-zukuri* style were not merely open but were completely integrated with the gardens surrounding them. They were prime examples of the interpenetration of building and setting – a quality typical of Japanese architecture in general.'[34]

Unfortunately, the appreciation of Katsura as an architecture-and-landscape composition was not reflected in Tange's design projects. He admired Le Corbusier but was also a proud patriot who, during the war, thought it would be better for Japan to die than surrender. His pre-1946 work had Mondrianesque façades with sweeping Japanese roofs. After the war, he took off the sweeping roofs, but continued with the Mondrianesque façades and adopted a tragically European approach to site planning. Tange's first major project was the Peace Museum and Memorial Park in Hiroshima. The museum building is a Modernist structure with a Japanese proportional system. The landscape has a central axis running from a European-style fountain to the 'A-Bomb Dome' – a bomb-damaged fragment of the former Industrial Promotion Hall. The design therefore symbolizes the Western ideas which led to Japan's downfall: scientific rationalism and baroque imperialism. The avenue runs from a symbol of triumph (the fountain) to a symbol of disaster (the dome). It is a journey from hubris to nemesis. One can see it as symbolizing the failure of war or one can read it, as Tange presumably

8.48 The Bell of Peace Garden in Hiroshima (1964) has a more Buddhist and more Japanese character, without being a traditionalist pastiche.

8.49 a, b, c Wadakura Fountain Park uses postmodern geometry in a European-type square without European urban planning.

did, as symbolizing the triumph of peace. It has been suggested that a Buddhist design would have been more appropriate, perhaps resembling the lotus pond round the Bell of Peace. But the Peace Park remains an accurate symbol of Japan's post-war decision to spurn militarism and take a new pride in applied rationalism.

It was the Corbusian aspect of Tange's approach which came to dominate Japanese urbanism. There were some architectural wonders but, in the main, dull roads were lined with dull buildings to make dull cities. The Wadakura Fountain Park in Tokyo is an early instance of an urban square in Tokyo – early in the sense that Japan, like China, had no tradition of public squares. Wadakura was built to celebrate the wedding of the Crown Prince in 1961 and reconstructed in 1995. The paving design uses a postmodern geometry and the fountains are impressive, but the 'park' has none of Katsura's virtues. Paving and water have not been integrated with the other compositional elements of landscape design: vegetation, landform and buildings. Furthermore, the Wadakura Fountain Park is an abstract composition, lacking religious, cultural, philosophical, narrative or poetic meaning. It is a 'park' only in name. Across the highway (Uchibori-dori) is the Kokyo Gaien, shown on English maps as the Imperial Palace 'Plaza' or 'Outer Garden'. This is a lawn planted with pine trees and signs forbidding walking, bonfires and camping. As in Europe, the 'don't signs' erected by authorities reveal a good understanding of what people would like to use the space for.

The Roponggi Hills development in Tokyo shows a more sophisticated approach to the development of urban space, made possible because it had a wealthy private developer (Minoru Mori). It has a roofed plaza, with outdoor video screen, and a

8.51 a, b The Roku-roku Plaza at Roponggi Hills is both visually dramatic and a sensible climatic response: the water and mist provide cooling; the glazed roof provides shelter from downpours.

8.52 a, b Benesse House Hotel on the island of Naoshima is a climatically appropriate composition of landform with water, vegetation, paving and structures.

somewhat traditional Japanese garden. The combination of modern glitz with a sentimental theme resulted from the involvement of the Jerde Partnership, a US firm specializing in retail architecture. Gardens and amphitheatres characterize Jon Jerde's approach, if not Japan's traditional urbanism.

Tadao Ando has become Japan's best-known architect and landscape architect. He was not trained in either discipline but was inspired by Le Corbusier's sculptural prowess, if not his dreary planning. This led on to an enthusiasm for Frank Lloyd Wright and an admiration for the way Wright merged a sculptural approach to architecture with a love of nature, as at Falling Water, Bear Run, Pennsylvania. Ando's buildings are minimalist contextual sculptures. They use primary geometrical forms, integrated with the natural landscape and, increasingly, with environmental concerns. Benesse House Hotel, on the island of Naoshima, creates enclosed outdoor space as an integrated composition of landform, buildings, water, vegetation and paving. This is a promising start for the re-working of Japan's urban landscapes – and a fair example for the rest of Asia.

Afterword

There is a possibility that science will answer all the great questions which face mankind: why we are here, how the universe began, how life began, how we should live and how we should design our gardens. But for the present, science has little to say on these topics. There is, for example, no scientific proof that murdering people is wrong or that murdering farm animals or garden pests is right. We can argue that killing animals is not murder, but that distinction involves beliefs, philosophy and the world of ideas. As old scientific books illustrate, scientists are no less prone to error than priests. Any modern doctor who tried the remedies in my great-great grandfather's medical books would end up behind bars.

A.1 Looking to the future from the Suzhou Museum (by I. M. Pei).

Afterword

A.2 A Gulf skyline shows science-based modern architecture and landscape design at their unsustainable worst. The failures of Modernist planning in Asia are unnatural disasters. As after dam failures, there should be far-reaching investigations of the technical, professional, supervisory, political and metaphysical circumstances which may have contributed to such glaring design failures.

Over-reliance on Modernism, as we saw in Chapter 8, has damaged Asian gardens and the cities they should inspire and glorify. Modernism has made them too similar, too Western and too unsustainable. The abstract art of the twentieth century derived from an analytical process not unlike that used by scientists. Instead of trying to represent beliefs about the natural world, as their predecessors had done, designers turned to the analysis of shape, line, colour, mass, pattern and proportion. Art became abstract, as did the design of buildings, cities and gardens. Aesthetic taste therefore became internationalized, as outlined in the preceding chapter, because its analytical basis was as international as its intellectual foundations. If science is everywhere the same – then science-based design should be everywhere the same. Or shouldn't it? For architecture, Oleg Grabar put the question as follows, in a book on Islamic architecture:

> *Thus we return to what I see as the fundamental question of our time: how can one preserve, in dignity, and with success, separate identities, when technology, ecology, economics and the media all tend to homogenize their impact and their control? Should one even try?*[1]

The related question 'Do we want gardens and urban landscapes to be everywhere the same?' can be answered with relative ease: 'No'. I have never met or heard of a person who wants places to be everywhere the same. Tourism, said to be the world's largest business, depends on difference. We take pride in our localities and admire those of others. As travellers, we expect Portugal to be Portuguese, China to be Chinese and America to be American. But nationalistic branding is a difficult issue for designers: should modern Chinese gardens use red lacquer and Taihu stone, or would this be overly sentimental? And should North Asian gardens have trolls?

The geographic dimensions of context-sensitivity are simpler. Different plants flourish in humid and arid climates; cold gardens need to collect heat and hot gardens need to disperse heat. Context-sensitive design can also be inspired by politics, religion, ethnicity, geology, hydrology, sociology, ecology and many other -ologies. Intensive irrigation *can* make gardens in South Australia *resemble* those in the humid tropics, but this approach would be irresponsibly unsustainable. The availability of water must always be a leading consideration in garden design.

The rich countries of West Asia convert oil-wealth into water-wealth by desalinization and by draining aquifers, which are relatively unsustainable practices. Hot arid regions have also built cities which depend on air-conditioned buildings and cars for the comfort of their citizens. This too is relatively unsustainable. It would be wiser to plan cities which recycle their wastes, catch God's breath, and give their citizens glare-free courtyards and cool shady walks along which they can enjoy the scent of flowers while picking lush fruits. But why do this? I can provide no scientific proof that 'better' places would result – but I *believe* it to be so. This takes us to another question: has Abstract Modernism passed its sell-by date in matters of urban design? My answer is 'Yes'. In a book entitled *City as Landscape: A Post-Postmodern View of Planning and Design*, I argued that:

- *Modernist planning* was rationalist, utopian and misguided.
- *Postmodern planning* was merely anti-planning and idiosyncratic.
- *Post-postmodern planning* should be founded on reason + belief.

City as Landscape cited some evidence for the hoped-for change coming about:

> *There are signs of post-Postmodern life, in urban design, architecture and elsewhere. They are strongest in those who place their hands on their hearts and are willing to assert 'I believe'. Faith always was the strongest competitor for reason: faith in a God; faith in a tradition; faith in an institution; faith in a person. The built environment professions are witnessing the gradual dawn of a post-Postmodernism that seeks to temper reason with faith. Designers and planners are taking to the rostrum and the pulpit.*

Since this was written, in 1996, the most significant move towards a new role for belief in the planning and design process has, unexpectedly, come from scientists. At the time of writing, there is a broad consensus that global warming is a global problem in need of a global solution and that life on earth should be made more sustainable. The relative contributions of carbon emissions and climatic change to global warming are unknown, as are the beneficial effects of the proposed changes to our urban and transport systems. But in the absence of certainty, scientists still believe it necessary

A.3 a, b Should modern Chinese gardens look like this? ('Through the Moongate' at the 2007 Chelsea Show). And should gardens in North Eurasia have trolls to make them look Northern?

to act. Some of the impacts of a global warming agenda on the design of gardens and urban landscape architecture are listed below. If adopted, they might heal the rift between garden design, landscape design and urban design:

- Most roofs should be vegetated, as roof gardens, roof parks, wildlife habitats and facilities for water detention and/or evapo-transpiration.
- The walls of buildings should be either vegetated or used for energy generation, unless there is a good reason for them to be lifeless.
- Municipal composting should follow in the wake of garden composting.
- Cities should stop discharging waste water into rivers: it should be recycled in buildings, gardens, parks and other areas of urban green space.
- City walks and cycleways should become more like garden walks and woodland greenways. In terms of route selection, if not total expenditure, they should take priority over vehicular routes in city planning procedures.
- Citizens should have private and communal green space.
- More urban green space should be used for urban agriculture, so that cities become more like the productive pleasure gardens of Ancient Asia.

A.4 a–e Asian cities would benefit from making better use of roofspace and courtyards: a roof in Singapore Botanic Gardens, the roof of Kyoto Station, a courtyard in Suzhou (by I. M. Pei), a roof garden in Singapore and a seaside lookout in Saudi Arabia.

These things will be done if and when their implementation is *believed* to be right. When analytical science ruled the urban environment, each of the scientifically-based professions assembled 'proofs' of what should be done. In the planning of road and water systems, for example, statistics of rising demands were collected and project- ed, 'proving' the need for extra capacity. Patrick Geddes was a keen gardener, the greatest planning theorist of the twentieth century and a man who spent many years working in India. He was also the first European to call himself a landscape architect and stated the problem as follows:

> *Each of the various specialists remains too closely concentrated upon his single*
> *specialism, too little awake to those of others. Each sees clearly and seizes firmly one*
> *petal of the six-lobed flower of life and tears it apart from the whole.*[2]

Among the petals which have been seized by over-zealous planners and designers are hills, valleys, rivers, lakes, footpaths, roads, housing, commerce, industry, parks and gardens. One by one, they have been ripped off and 'planned' in cruel, ugly, abstract and soulless isolation. Considerations relating to the landscape which sustains life on earth have been neglected. Urbanization works best when buildings are related to landform and land uses are designed in relation to each other. Planners and designers cause aesthetic and ecological chaos when they fail to practise Environmental Impact Assessment (EIA) and Environmental Impact Design (EID). Architects, like other consultants, focus on the professional discipline in which they were trained – or on the instructions of often-selfish land users who commission their services. Yet a good relationship with architecture and planning is a critical factor in the design of good gardens, both public and private. When cities are planned by blinkered specialists, the design of good gardens and the planning of good landscapes become impossible. Garden design can again be the crucible for urban design, as it was in Rome, Isfahan, Paris, London, Washington, DC, and Dadu-Beijing. This is because the composition of buildings, landform, water, vegetation and planting is conceptually simpler at the garden scale than the city scale. The fringes of Asia are recovering their economic dynamism and should now recover their prowess in the arts of garden and landscape design. They can turn away from the vacancy of Abstract Modernism. They can murmur:

> *Mmmm ... life can be more beautiful, more interesting, healthier and more sustainable.*
> *Our heritage is rich and diverse. Europe and Asia are one mighty continent. It is the*
> *mainspring of world culture. It is the ancestral home of the world's great gardens. New*
> *dawns can grow from the roots of ancient dawns. 'The farther back you look, the farther*
> *forward you are likely to see.'*[3]

A.5 Token green space is welcome – but inadequate.

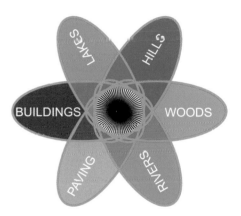

A.6 The six-lobed flower of life.* To design good gardens, and cities, the compositional elements of the outdoor landscape should be composed.

Note: *Turner, T. *Landscape Planning and Environmental Impact Design*, 1999, p. 357.

Notes

Preface, pp. vii–xii

1   There is, or rather was, a small exception to this generalization in the Desert Garden in the Sacred Precinct in Mexico's capital. Tenochititlan was founded in 1325. Maria Elena Bernal-Garcia connects the garden to shamanistic ideas and explains its character in a way which supports my hypothesis. She writes: '[It] represented, in miniature, the vast desert lands through which the Mexicans migrated southward from Azlan, their city of origin.' See Maria Elena Bernal-Garcia, 'The dance of time, the procession of space at Mexico-Tenochititlan's desert garden', in M. Conan, *Sacred Gardens and Landscapes: Ritual and Agency* (Washington, DC: Dumbarton Oaks, 2002), p. 70.

2   Hunt, J.D., *The Italian Garden: Art, Design and Culture* (Cambridge: Cambridge University Press, 1996), p. 4.

3   Ninian Smart's book on *The Religious Experience of Mankind* (London: Fontana, 1969) was published a year later, in 1969. A friend gave me a copy which has been near my desk since then.

4   Kemp, B.J., *Ancient Egypt: Anatomy of a Civilization* (London: Routledge, 1991).

1   Beliefs and gardens, pp. 3–36

1   Locke, J., *Observations Upon the Growth and Culture of Vines and Olives: The Production of Silk: The Preservation of Fruits* (London: W. Sandby, 1766).

2   Locke, J., *Two Treatises of Government* (London: Awnsham Churchill, 1689), First Treatise, Chapter 19: 2.222.

3   This is the version in my head, and is probably Scots. I prefer it to Shakespeare's original: 'Golden lads and girls all must, As chimney-sweepers, come to dust', *Cymbeline*, Act iv, Scene 2.

4   Smart, N., *The Religious Experience of Mankind* (London: Fontana, 1969), p. 11.

5   The phrase 'daughters of Eve' is from Sykes, B., *The Seven Daughters of Eve* (London: Corgi, 2004).

6   Fortson, B.W., *Indo-European Language and Culture* (Oxford: Blackwell, 2004), p. 22.

7   James, E.O., *The Worship of the Sky-God* (London: Athlone Press, 1963), p. 20.

8   Redford, D.B., *Egypt, Canaan, and Israel in Ancient Times* (Princeton, NJ: Princeton University Press, 1992), p. 5.

9   *Encyclopaedia Britannica Online*, entry for 'garden', http://www.britannica.com/; accessed 4 January 2006.

10   The place of public goods in landscape architecture is the subject of Turner, T., *Landscape Planning and Environmental Impact Design* (London: Routledge, 1998).

11   Jellicoe, G.A. and Jellicoe, S., *The Landscape of Man* (London: Thames and Hudson, 1975).

12   Jaspers, K., *The Origin and Goal of History*, trans. M. Bullock (New Haven, CT: Yale University Press, 1953).

13   A 'god slot' is a regular time for religious programmes in a broadcasting schedule, like the BBC's *Thought for the Day*.

14   Doniger, W., 'Foreword', to the 2004 edition of Eliade, M., *Shamanism: Archaic Techniques of Ecstasy* (Princeton, NJ: Princeton University Press, 2004), p. xiv.

15   Frazer, Sir James, *The Golden Bough* (London: Macmillan & Co., 1890).

16   Eliade, M., *Patterns in Comparative Religions* (London: Sheed and Ward 1976), p. 109.

17   Ibid., p. 193.

18   Ibid., p. 216.

19   Ibid., p. 253.

20   Ibid., p. 278.

21   Ibid., p. 380.

22   Eliade, M., *Shamanism: Archaic Techniques of Ecstasy* (Princeton, NJ: Princeton University Press, 2004), p. 270.

23   Eliade, *Patterns in Comparative Religions*, p. 361.

24   Ibid., p. 354.

25   Ibid., p. 355.

26   Ibid., pp. 370–1.

27   Ibid., p. 369.

28   Ibid., p. 375.

29   Govinda, A., *The Way of the White Clouds* (London: Hutchinson, 1966), p. 198.

30   Jiro Takei and Keane, M.P., *Sakuteiki: Visions of the Japanese Garden* (Boston: Tuttle Publishing, 2001).

31   Ji, Cheng, *The Craft of Gardens*, trans. Alison Hardie (New Haven, CT: Yale University Press, 1988).

32   As, for example, by the Society for Ethnomusicology, founded in Philadelphia in 1980.

33   Baumgarten, A.G., *Aesthetica Trajecti cis Viadrum* (Frankfurt-on-the-Oder, 1750).

34   Coomaraswamy, A., *Introduction to the Art of Eastern Asia* (reprinted from *The Open Court*, March 1932) 1932, p. 18, emphasis added.

35   Turner, T., *Garden History, Philosophy and Design* (London: Spon Press, 2005), p. 14ff.

36   Russell, B., *History of Western Philosophy* (London: Allen & Unwin, 1946), p. 136.

2   Polytheist gardens, pp. 27–59

1   National Geographic Society, *Atlas of the Human Journey*, available at: https://www3.nationalgeographic.com/genographic/atlas.html.

2   Folz, R.C. *Religions of the Silk Road* (New York: St Martin's Press, 1999), p. 23.

3   Kramer, S.N., *History Begins at Sumer* (London: Thames & Hudson, 1958).

4   Halloran, J.A., *Sumerian Lexicon: A Dictionary Guide to the Ancient Sumerian Language* (Oxford: Logogram, Oxbow, 2007).

5   The Sumerian king list: translation; available at: http://www-etcsl.orient.ox.ac.uk/section2/tr211.htm 17; accessed December 2008.

6   Leick, G., *Mesopotamia: The Invention of the City* (London: Allen Lane, 2001), p. 2.

7   Bottero, J., *Religion in Ancient Mesopotamia* (Chicago: University of Chicago Press 2001), p. 78.

8   Layard, A.H., *A Popular Account of Discoveries at Nineveh* (London: John Murray, 1852), p. 317.

9   Crawford, H.E., *Sumer and the Sumerians* (Cambridge: Cambridge University Press, 2nd edn., 2004), p. 53.

10 Leick, *Mesopotamia*, p. 50.

11 Brusasco, P., 'Family archives and the social use of space in Old Babylonian houses at Ur', *Mesopotamia*, vol. XXXIV–XXXV (1999–2000), pp. 3–173.

12 Bottero, *Religion in Ancient Mesopotamia*, p. 58.

13 Gray, J., *Near Eastern Mythology* (Feltham: Hamlyn, 1969), p. 13.

14 King, L.W. (ed.), *The Seven Tablets of Creation, or the Babylonian and Assyrian Legends Concerning the Creation of the World and of Mankind*, Vol. 2 (London: Luzac and Co. Luzac's Semitic Text and Translation Series, 1902), Tablet 1.

15 Eliade, M., *A History of Religious Ideas*, Vol. 1 (Chicago: University of Chicago Press, 1978), pp. 75–6.

16 Bottero, *Religion in Ancient Mesopotamia*, p. 157.

17 Eliade, *A History of Religious Ideas*, pp. 61–2

18 *The Historical Library of Diodorus the Sicilian, in fifteen books. To which are added the fragments of Diodorus, and those published by H. Valesius, I. Rhodomannus, and F. Ursinus*, trans. G. Booth. Vol. J. (London: Davis, 1814), pp. 108–9.

19 National Geographic Society, *Atlas of the Human Journey*, available at: https://www3.nationalgeographic.com/genographic/atlas.html.

20 Redford, D.B., *Egypt, Canaan, and Israel in Ancient Times* (Princeton, NJ: Princeton University Press, 1992), p. 0.

21 Lacovara, P., *The New Kingdom Royal City* (London: Kegan Paul International, 1997), p. 80.

22 Van Lepp, J., *Is the Hieroglyphic Sign Niwt a Village with Cross-roads?* (Göttinger: Miszellen, 1997), no. 158, pp. 91–100.

23 Eliade, *A History of Religious Ideas*, p. 88.

24 Macaulay, G.C., *Herodotus* (London: Macmillan, 1890), available at: http://www.gutenberg.org/files/2131/2131-h/2131-h.htm, accessed 10 December 2008.

25 Lacovara, *The New Kingdom Royal City*, p. 58.

26 Ibid., p. 66.

27 Ibid., p. 33.

28 Ibid., p. 35.

29 Kemp, B.J., *Ancient Egypt: Anatomy of a Civilisation* (London: Routledge, 1989), p. 215.

30 Life of St Philibert, Abbot of Jumièges, quoted in Braunfels, W., *Monasteries of Western Europe: The Architecture of the Orders* (London: Thames and Hudson, 1972), Documentary Source II.

31 Cyrus' claim is disputed. See Waters, M., 'Cyrus and the Achaemenids', *Iran – Journal of the British Institute of Persian Studies* vol. xlii (2004), pp. 91–102.

32 *Encyclopaedia Iranica*, Online edition. Alphabetical entry on 'Charbagh' (ùahaúrbaúgú), available at: http://www.iranica.com/newsite/articles/v4f6/v4f6a048.html, accessed 16 June 2007.

33 *Encyclopaedia Iranica*, Online edition. Alphabetical entry on 'Zoroastrianism', available at: http://www.iranica.com/newsite/articles/ot_grp9/ot_zorhist_2005 1007.html, accessed 16 June 2007.

34 Stronach, D., 'The Royal Garden at Pasargadae. Evolution and Legacy', in *Archaeologia Iranica et Orientalis Miscellanea in Honorem Louis Vanden Berghe* (Ghent: Peeters Presse, 1989), pp. 475–502.

35 Pinder-Wilson, R., 'The Persian Garden: Bagh and Chahar Bagh', in E.B. Macdougall and R. Ettinghausen (eds) *The Islamic Garden* (Washington, DC: Dumbarton Oaks, 1976).

3   Islamic gardens, pp. 60–102

1   Ettinghausen, R. and Grabar, O., *The Art and Architecture of Islam 620–1250* (Harmondsworth: Penguin, 1987), p. 20.

2   Eliade, M., *A History of Religious Ideas*, vol. 1 (Chicago: University of Chicago Press, c.1978–c.1985), p. 75.

3   Quran, Sura ix.

4   Goode, P. *et al.*, *Oxford Companion to Gardens* (Oxford: Oxford University Press, 1986), p. 105.

5   Khansari, M. and Minouch, Y., *The Persian Garden: Echoes of Paradise* (Washington, DC: Mage Publishers, 1998).

6   Ruggles, D.F., *Gardens, Landscapes and Vision in the Palaces of Islamic Spain* (University Park, PA: Pennsylvania State University Press, 2000), p. 215.

7   Koch, E., 'The royal gardens of Farahbad and the fall of Shah Sultan Husayn revisited', in M. Conan (ed.), *Middle East Garden Traditions: Unity and Diversity* (Washington, DC: Dumbarton Oaks, 2007), pp. 139–59.

8   Procopius, *History of the Wars*, trans. H. B. Dewing (Cambridge, MA: Harvard University Press and Wm. Heinemann, 1914; reprint edn, 1953–54), Book I.

9   Ammianus Marcellinus, *Roman History* (London: Bohn, 1862), Book 14, Part IV.

10 'The poem of Imru-Ul-Quais', in F.E. Johnson (trans.), *The Hanged Poems* (with revisions by Sheikh Faiz-ullah-bhai) from *The Sacred Books and Early Literature of the East*, vol. V, *Ancient Arabia*, ed. C.F. Horne Parke (New York and London: Austin, and Lipscomb, 1917). *Citrullus colocynthis* is the Bitter Apple.

11 Casson, L., 'The Greek and Latin sources for the southwestern coast of Arabia', *Arabian Archaeology and Epigraphy*, vol. 6 (1995), pp. 214–22.

12 King, G.R.D., 'Creswell's appreciation of Arabian architecture', in *Muqarnas: An Annual on Islamic Art and Architecture*, vol. 8, *K. A. C. Creswell and His Legacy* (1991), pp. 94–102.

13 Ettinghausen and Grabar, *The Art and Architecture of Islam, 650-1250*, pp. 83–6.

14 Personal communication from Alistair Northedge, 2007.

15 Ruggles, *Gardens, Landscapes and Vision*, p. 87.

16 Ibid., p. 90.

17 Pinder-Wilson, R., 'The Persian garden: bagh and chahar bagh', in E.B. MacDougall, *The Islamic Garden* (Washington, DC: Dumbarton Oaks, 1976), p. 80.

18 Leisten, T., 'Between orthodoxy and exegesis: some aspects of attitudes in the Shari'a toward funerary architecture', in *Muqarnas*, vol. VII, *An Annual on Islamic Art and Architecture*, Oleg Grabar (ed.) (Leiden: E.J. Brill, 1990), pp. 12–22.

19 Dickie, J. (Yaqub Zaki), 'The Mughal garden: gateway to Paradise', in *Muqarnas*, vol. 3, (1985), pp. 128–37.

20 Quran, suras ix, 73, xiii, 23, xvi. 33, xviii. 30, xix. 62, xx. 78, xxxv. 30, xxxviii. 50, xl. 8, xli. 12.

21 Fitzgerald, C.P., *China: A Short Cultural History*, 4th edn (London: Cresset, 1986), p. 432.

22 Golombek, L., 'The gardens of Timur: new perspectives', in *Muqarnas*, vol. 12 (1995), pp. 137–47.

23 Chardin, Sir John, *Travels in Persia* (London: Argonaut Press, 1927), p. 77.

24 de Bruyn, Cornelis, *Travels into Muscovy, Persia and Part of the East Indies* (London: Bettesworth, 1737), vol. 1.

25 Ibid., p. 242.

26 O'Kane, B., 'From tents to pavilions: royal mobility and Persian palace design', in Proceedings of the Symposium on Pre-Modern Islamic Palaces', *Ars Orientalis*, vol. 23 (1993), pp. 245–64.

27 Tabbaa, Y., 'The "Salsabil" and "Shadirvan" in medieval Islamic courtyards', *Environmental Design: Journal of the Islamic Environmental Design Research Centre*, vol. 1 (1986), pp. 34–7.

28 Moynihan, E.B., 'The Lotus Garden Palace of Babur', in *Muqarnas*, vol. 5 (1988), pp. 135–52.

29 Thackston, W.M., *The Baburnama, Memoirs of Babur, Prince and Emperor* (Oxford: Oxford University Press, 1996), p. 403.

30 Ruggles, D.F., 'Humayun's tomb and garden: typologies and visual order', in A. Petruccioli (ed.) *Gardens in the Time of the Great Muslim Empires* (*Muqarnas Supplements*, vol. 7) (Leiden: E.J. Brill, 1997), pp. 173–86.

31 Koch, E., 'Mughal palace gardens from Babur to Shah Jahan (1526–1648)', *Muqarnas*, vol. 14 (1997), pp. 143–65.

32 Kipling, R., *Letters of Marque* (Allahabad: A. H. Wheeler & Co., 1891), p. 215.

33 Necipoglu, G., *Architecture, Ceremonial and Power: The Topkapi Palace in the*

Fifteenth and Sixteenth Centuries (Cambridge, MA: MIT Press, 1991), p. 13.

34 Atasoy, N., 'Ottoman garden pavilions and tents', *Muqarnas*, vol. 21 (1995). pp. 15–19.

35 Quran 15: 45–6, Abdul Majid Daryabadi translation, 1941.

36 Necipoglu, *Architecture, Ceremonial and Power*, p. 52.

37 Ibid., p. 91.

38 Ibid., p. 183.

39 Necipoglu, G., 'The suburban landscape of sixteenth-century Istanbul as a mirror of classical Ottoman garden culture', in A. Petruccioli (ed.) *Gardens in the Time of the Great Muslim Empires: Theory and Design* (Leiden: E.J. Brill, 1997), pp 32–71.

40 Villiers Stuart, C.M., *Gardens of the Great Mughals* (New Delhi: Cosmo Publications, 1983), p. 71.

4 Hindu gardens, pp. 105–37

1 *Rig Veda*, VII 96.1.

2 Schumacher, H., 'Nachwort zu Marie Luise Gotheins "Indische Garten"', in M.L. Gothein, *Indische Garten* (Berlin: Gebr. Mann Verlag, 2000), p. 8.

3 *Rig Veda*, II 20.7. See also Gothein, M. L., *Indian Gardens* (London: Gardenvisit.com, 2008).

4 Pramar, V.S. *A Social History of Indian Architecture* (New Delhi: Oxford University Press, 2005), p. 155.

5 *Rig Veda*, X 89.13.

6 Trautman, T.R. (ed.), *The Aryan Debate* (Oxford: Oxford University Press, 2005).

7 Anthony, D.W., 'The opening of the Eurasian steppe at 2000 BC', in V.H. Mair (ed.), *The Bronze Age and Early Iron Age Peoples of Eastern Central Asia* (Washington, DC: The Institute for the Study of Man), vol. 1 (1998), pp. 94–13 (*Journal of Indo-European Studies* Monograph 26).

8 Sarvepalli, R., *The Hindu View of Life* (London: George Allen and Unwin, 1926), p. 30.

9 *Rig Veda*, 10.101.5.

10 *Rig Veda*, 4.33.7.

11 *Rig Veda*, 2.13.7.

12 *Rig Veda*, X 97.3.

13 *Riv Veda*, X 97.15.

14 *Rig Veda*, RV I.8.7.

15 Goldman, R.P. (ed.), *The Ramayana of Valmiki: An Epic of Ancient India*, vol. 1, *Balakanda* (Princeton, NJ: Princeton University Press, 1984), p. 3.

16 Goldman, R.P. (ed.), *The Ramayana of Valmiki*, vol. 2, *Ayodhyakanda* (Princeton, NJ: Princeton University Press, 1986), Sarga 15, p. 113.

17 *Book V (Sundara Kanda)*, Canto VI.

18 Goldman, R.P. (ed.), *The Ramayana of Valmiki*, vol. 3, *Aranyakanda* (Princeton, NJ: Princeton University Press, 1991), Sarga 48.

19 Ibid., Sarga 46.

20 Pramar, *A Social History of Indian Architecture*, p. 42.

21 Shamasastry, R. (trans.), *Kautilya's Arthashastra*, Book II, 'The duties of government superintendents', Chapter 1, 'Formation of villages' (Mysore: Oriental Research Institute, 1915).

22 Ganguli, K.M. (trans.), *The Mahabharata of Krishna-Dwaipayana Vyasa* (Calcutta: Bharata Press, 1893–96), Book 1, Section LXXIV.

23 Ganguli, K.M. (trans.), *The Mahabharata of Krishna-Dwaipayana Vyasa*, Book 3, Section CLXLI.

24 Ganguli, K.M. (trans.), *The Mahabharata of Krishna-Dwaipayana Vyasa*, Book 2, Section III.

25 Ganguli, K.M. (trans.), *The Mahabharata of Krishna-Dwaipayana Vyasa*, Book 3, Section CCLIX.

26 Scully, V., *The Earth, the Temple and the Gods* (New Haven, CT: Yale University Press, 1962), p. 1.

27 Ganguli, *The Mahabharata of Krishna-Dwaipayana Vyasa*, Book 3, Section LXXXIX.

28 Ryder, A.W. (trans.), *The Little Clay Cart (Mrcchakatika)* (Attributed to King Shudraka) (Cambridge, MA: Harvard University Press, 1905), Act IV, p. 68.

29 Ibid., Act IV, pp. 72–3.

30 Shokoohy, M., *Muslim Architecture of South India: The Sultanate of Ma'bar and the Traditions of Maritime Settlers on the Malabar and Coromandel Coasts (Tamil Nadu, Kerala and Goa)* (London: RoutledgeCurzon, 2003), p. 31,

31 Spodek, H. and Meth Srinivasan. D. (eds), 'Urban form and meaning in South Asia: the shaping of cities from prehistoric to precolonial times', in *Studies in the History of Art*, vol. 31, Center for Advanced Study in the Visual Arts, Symposium Papers XV (Washington, DC: National Gallery of Art, 1993), p. 127.

32 Kalidasa, *Sakoontala or The Lost Ring, An Indian Drama*, trans. M. Monier-Williams (London: Routledge, 1898), Act 1.

33 Ibid.

34 Ibid.

35 *The Kama Sutra of Vatsayana* (trans. R. F. Burton), Part IV, Chapter 1 (Benares: Kama Shastra Society, 1883).

36 Ibid., Part I, Chapter IV.

37 Ibid., Part V, Chapter V.

38 *Hymns of the Atharva-Veda together with Extracts from the Ritual Books and the Commentaries* (trans. M. Bloomfield) (Oxford: Clarendon Press, 1897), pp. vii, iii, 12.

39 Ibid., pp. ix, 3.

40 Ibid., x, xii, 1.

41 Ganguli, K.M. (trans.), *The Mahabharata of Krishna-Dwaipayana Vyasa*, Book 2: Sabha Parva, Section 1.

42 Bhat, R. (trans.), *Varahamihira's Brhat Samhita* (Delhi: Motilal Banardsidass, 1981), p. 475.

43 Ibid., p. 537.

44 Ibid., p. 527.

45 Ibid., p. 409.

46 Ibid., p. 547.

47 Pramar, *A Social History of Indian Architecture*, p. 3.

48 Kramrisch, S. *The Hindu Temple* (Delhi: Motilal Banarsidass, 1976), pp. 3–5.

49 Russell, R.V., *The Tribes and Castes of the Central Provinces of India* (London: Macmillan, 1916), p. 54.

50 Villiers Stuart, C.M., *Gardens of the Great Mughals* (New Delhi: Cosmo Publications, 1983), p. 56.

5 Buddhist gardens, pp. 138–70

1 Coomaraswamy, A., 'The gods of Mahayana Buddhism', *The Burlington Magazine for Connoisseurs*, vol. 27, no. 148 (July, 1915), pp. 138–41.

2 Ibid.

3 Pramar, V.S., *A Social History of Indian Architecture* (New Delhi: Oxford University Press, 2005), p. 6.

4 Legge, J., *A Record of Buddhistic Kingdoms, Being an Account by the Chinese Monk Fâ-hien of his Travels in India and Ceylon (A.D. 399-414) in Search of the Buddhist Books of Discipline*. Translated and Annotated, with a Corean Recension of the Chinese Text (Oxford: Clarendon Press, 1886), Chapter XXII.

5 Dhammacakkapavattana Sutta Samyutta Nikaya LVI, 11, available at: http://www.tipitakachanting.org/Tipi-3.htm.

6 Pramar, *A Social History of Indian Architecture*, p. 145ff.

7 Tucci, G., *Stupa: Art, Architectonics and Symbolism* (New Delhi: Aditya Prakashan, 1988), p. xxv.

8 Ibid., p. 23.

9 Bhat, R. (trans.), *Varahamihira's Brhat Samhita* (Delhi: Motilal Banardsidass, 1981), p. 538.

10 Wu, N., *Chinese and Indian Architecture* (London: Prentice-Hall International, 1963), p. 17.

11 Leidy, D.P. and Thurman, R.A.F., *Mandala: The Architecture of Enlightenment* (New York: Asia Society Galleries, 1988), p. 17.

12 Kramrisch, S., *The Hindu Temple* (Delhi: Motilal Banarsidass, 1976), p. 6.

13 Pramar, *A Social History of Indian Architecture*, pp. 121–5.

14 Leidy and Thurman, *Mandala*, p. 19.

15 *The Jataka*, vol. I, trans. R. Chalmers, ed. E. B. Cowell (Cambridge: Cambridge University Press, 1895–1913), no. 75.
16 *The Jataka*, vol. II, trans. W.H.D. Rouse, ed. E. B. Cowell (Cambridge: Cambridge University Press, 1895–1913), no. 220.
17 Geiger, W., *The Mahavamsa or the Great Chronicle of Ceylon* (London: Pali Text Society, 1912), Chapter 15.
18 Ibid., Chapter 11.
19 Coomaraswamy, A.K., *History of Indian and Indonesian Art* (New York: Dover Publications, 1965), p. 15.
20 Re. Megasthanes, see Majumdar, R.C., *The Classical Accounts of India*, ed. K.L. Firma (Calcutta: Mukhopadhyay, 1960), p. 414ff.
21 Rowland, B., *The Art and Architecture of India, Buddhist, Hindu, Jain*, 3rd edn (Harmondsworth: Penguin Books, 1967), p. 39.
22 Davids, T.W.R and Oldenbert, H. (trans.), *Vinaya Texts* (Oxford: Clarendon Press, 1881–85), *Sixth Khandhaka*, Chapter 4.
23 Geiger, W. and Rickmers, C.M. (trans), *Culavamsa Being the More Recent Part of the Mamavamsa*, Part I (London: Pali Text Society, 1929), pp. 39, v, 1–3, 5.
24 De Silva, R., *Sigiriya and its Significance: A Mahayana-theravada Buddhist Monastery* (Colombo, Sri Lanka: Bibliotheque (Pvt) Ltd, 2002), p. 36.
25 Ibid., p. 64.
26 *The Jataka*, vol. I, trans. R. Chalmers, ed. E. B. Cowell (Cambridge: Cambridge University Press, 1895–1913), no. 92.
27 Folz, R.C., *Religions of the Silk Road* (New York: St Martin's Press, 1999), p. 8.
28 Ibid., p. 45.
29 Mitra, D., *Buddhist Monuments* (Calcutta: Sahitya Samsad, 1971), p. 15.
30 Rowland, *The Art and Architecture of India*, Chapter 24.
31 Jordaan, R.E., 'Why the Sailendras were not a Javanese dynasty', in *Indonesia and the Malay World*, vol. 34, no. 98 (March 2006), pp. 3–22.
32 Rowland, *The Art and Architecture of India*, p. 264.
33 Wu, N., *Chinese and Indian Architecture* (London; Prentice-Hall International, 1963).
34 Rowland, *The Art and Architecture of India*, p. 268.
35 Freeman, M. and Jacques, C., *Ancient Angkor* (Thailand: Narisa Chakrabongse, 1999), p. 48.
36 Rowland, *The Art and Architecture of India*, p. 239.
37 Evans, D., et al., 'A comprehensive archaeological map of the world's largest preindustrial settlement complex at Angkor, Cambodia', *Proceedings of the National Academy of Sciences* vol. 104, no. 36 (2007), pp. 14277–82.
38 Ibid.
39 Rowland, *The Art and Architecture of India*, p. 253.
40 Standen, M., *Buddha in the Landscape* (Bangkok: M. Standen Publishing, 1998).
41 Muller, F.M. (ed.), *Sukhavati-vyuha: Description of Sukhavati, the Land of Bliss* (Oxford: Clarendon Press: 1883), Section 15.
42 Takakusu, J. (trans.), *The Amitayur-Dhyana-Sutra* (Sacred Books of the East. vol. 49) (Oxford, 1894); available at: http://web.mit.edu/stclair/www/meditationsutra.html.
43 Basham, A.L., *The Wonder That Was India* (London: Sidgwick & Jackson, 1954), p. 256.

6 Daoist-Buddhist gardens in China, pp. 173–236

1 Elvin, M., *The Retreat of the Elephants: An Environmental History of China* (New Haven, CT: Yale University Press, 2004), p. 9.
2 Ibid., p. 24.
3 Gernet, J., *A History of Chinese Civilization*, trans. J.R. Foster and C. Hartman (Cambridge: Cambridge University Press, 1996), p. 28.
4 'A comparative study on landownership between China and England', Feng Deng Chongqing University, December 1996, available at: http://mpra.ub.uni-muenchen.de/2241/01/MPRA_paper_2241.pdf.
5 Sun Tzu, *The Art of War*, trans. L. Giles ([S.I.]: Luzac, 1910), vol. III, p. 3.
6 Knapp, R.G., *China's Walled Cities* (Oxford: Oxford University Press, 2000), p. 4.
7 Siren, O., *Gardens of China* (New York: Ronald Press Company, 1949), p. 4.
8 Ibid., p. 4.
9 *Analects of Confucius*, Chapter IV.
10 Steinhardt, N. (ed.), *Chinese Architecture* (New Haven, CT: Yale University Press, 2002), p. 6.
11 Ibid.
12 Eliade, M., *A History of Religious Ideas*, vol. 2 (Chicago: University of Chicago Press, 1982), p. 16.
13 Hu, Dongchu, *The Way of the Virtuous: The Influence of Art and Philosophy on Chinese Garden Design* (Beijing: New World Press, 1991), p. 11.
14 Graham, D., *Chinese Gardens* (New York: Dodd, Mead & Company, 1938), p. 180.
15 *Analects of Confucius*, Chapter XXIII.
16 Ibid., Chapter XXI.
17 Wang, J.C., *The Chinese Garden* (Hong Kong: Oxford University Press, 1998), p. 12.
18 Ibid., p. 13.
19 Graham, *Chinese Gardens*, p. 101. Maggie Keswick remembered that an educated Chinese gentleman visiting Europe in the 1920s commented in amazement on

A mown and bordered lawn which, while no doubt of interest to a cow, offers nothing to the intellect of a human being. For the British, long settled on peaceful, damp and temperate islands, rolling swards of cropped green grass are soothing and restful to the eye. Behind each suburban patch lies a dream of country parkland, the wealth of acres. But the Chinese are rice-growers, and pastureland can suggest only, however faintly across the centuries, nomadic cattle-raiders – barbarians beyond the benefits of civilization – riding south to plunder Chinese settlements.
(Keswick, M., 'Foreword', to Ji Cheng, *The Craft of Gardens: Yüan Ye*, New Haven, CT: Yale University Press, 1988, p. 21)

20 Graham, *Chinese Gardens*, p. 40.
21 Ibid., p. 87.
22 Handlin Smith, J.F., 'Liberating animals in Ming-Qing China: Buddhist inspiration and elite imagination', *The Journal of Asian Studies*, vol. 58, no. 1 (Feb., 1999), pp. 51–84.
23 Elvin, *The Retreat of the Elephants*, p. 11.
24 Ibid., p. 5.
25 Kohn, L., *Monastic Life in Medieval Daoism* (Honolulu: University of Hawai'i Press, 2003), p. 28.
26 Schafer, E., 'Ritual exposure in Ancient China', *Harvard Journal of Asiatic Studies*, vol. 14 (1951), pp. 130–84.
27 Kohn, *Monastic Life*, p. 29.
28 Ibid., p. 26.
29 Wong, E. (trans.), *Lieh-Tzu: A Daoist Guide to Practical Living* (Boston: Shambhala, 1995), p. 53.
30 Cheng, L., *Private Gardens* (Vienna: Springer-Verlag, 1999), p. 116.
31 Ibid., 'Foreword'.
32 Xu Shen, *Shuowen jiezi* (Explaining single-component graphs and analyzing compound characters), c.100 CE (quotations from http://www.iep.utm.edu/y/yinyang.htm).
33 Legge, J., *Sacred Books of the East*, vol. 39, *The Tâo Teh King (Tâo Te Ching) of Lâo Dze (Lao Tsu)* (Oxford: Clarendon Press, 1891), Chapter 43.
34 Munakata, K., *Sacred Mountains in Chinese Art* (Champaign, IL: University of Illinois Press, 1991), p. 35.
35 Siren, *Gardens of China*, p. 6.
36 Porter, B., *Road to Heaven: Encounters with Chinese Hermits* (London: Rider, 1994), p. 2.
37 Steinhardt, N. (ed.), *Chinese Architecture* (New Haven, CT: Yale University Press, 2002), p. 256.
38 Xu, Y., *The Chinese City in Space and Time* (Honolulu: University of Hawai'i Press, 2000), p. 201.
39 Stein, R.A., *The World in Miniature: Container Gardens and Dwellings in Far Eastern Religious Thought* (Stanford, CA: Stanford University Press, 1990),

Notes

p. 114.

40 Rambach, P. and Rambach, S., *Gardens of Longevity in China and Japan: The Art of the Stone Raisers* (New York: Rizzoli International, 1987), p. 22.

41 Schafer, I.H., *Tu Wan's Stone Catalogue of Cloudy Forest: A Commentary and Synopsis* (Berkeley, CA: University of California Press, 1961), p. 3.

42 Rambach, and Rambach, *Gardens of Longevity in China and Japan*, p. 92.

43 Ibid., p. 27.

44 Blake, W., *Auguries of Innocence* (written *c*.1800–01).

45 Coomaraswamy, A., *Introduction to the Art of Eastern Asia* ([S.l.]: Open Court Publishing Co, 1932), p. 18.

46 *China* (Amsterdam: Time-Life Books, 1984), p. 17.

47 Dingle, E.J., *Across China on Foot* (Bristol: J. W. Arrowsmith Ltd., 1911), Chapter 12.

48 Graham, *Chinese Gardens,* p. 97.

49 Zhu, J., *Chinese Spatial Strategies: Imperial Beijing, 1420–1911* (London: RoutledgeCurzon, 2004), p. 32.

50 Kiyohiki Munakata, *Sacred Mountains in Chinese Art* (Chicago: University of Illinois Press, 1991), p. 4.

51 Steinhardt, N. (ed.), *Chinese Architecture* (New Haven, CT: Yale University Press, 2002) p. 26.

52 Fitzgerald, C.P., *China: A Short Cultural History* (London: Century Hutchinson, 1986), p. 45.

53 Cheng, L., *Imperial Gardens* (Vienna: Springer-Verlag, 1998), p. 122.

54 Schafer, E., 'Hunting parks and animal enclosures in ancient China', *Journal of the Economic and Social History of the Orient*, vol. XI (1968), pp. 318–43.

55 Clements, J., *First Emperor of China* (Stroud: Sutton, 2006), p. 132.

56 Yang, H., *The Classical Gardens of China* (New York: Van Nostrand Reinhold, 1982), p. 85.

57 Ibid., pp. 83–6.

58 Ibid., p. 89.

59 Ibid., p. 99.

60 Ibid., p. 105.

61 Ibid., p. 105.

62 Ibid., p. 107ff.

63 It should be noted that although Keswick, M., *The Chinese Garden* (London: Frances Lincoln, 2003) p. 43, and Steinhardt, p. 50, attribute the first instance of making 'three islands in one lake' to Emperor Wu of Han, Cheng in *Imperial Gardens*, p. 124, attributes the idea to Qin Shi Huang.

64 Weinstein, W., *Buddhism under the T'ang* (Cambridge: Cambridge University Press, 1987), p. 3.

65 Johnston, R.S., *Scholar Gardens of China* (Cambridge: Cambridge University Press, 1991), pp. 9–13.

66 Schafer, *Tu Wan's Stone Catalogue*, p. 4.

67 Shaw, M., 'Buddhist and Daoist influences on Chinese landscape painting', *Journal of the History of Ideas*, vol. 49, no. 2 (Apr.–Jun., 1988), pp. 183–206.

68 Ibid.

69 Siren, *Gardens of China*, p. 71.

70 Keswick, M., 'Foreword', to *Ji Cheng, The Craft of Gardens – Yüan Ye* (New Haven, CT: Yale University Press, 1988), p. 15.

71 Kenner, W.J.F., *Memories of Loyang – Yang Hsuan-chih and the Lost Capital (393–534)* (Oxford: Clarendon Press, 1981).

72 Ibid., p. 232.

73 Ibid., pp. 148–9.

74 Ibid., p. 173.

75 Ibid., p. 173.

76 Ibid., p. 148.

77 Ibid., p. 174.

78 Ibid., p. 221.

79 Ibid., p. 189.

80 Ch'en Shou-Yi, cited in Henry Inn, *Chinese Houses and Gardens*, ed. Shao Chang Lee (Honolulu: Fong Inn's Limited, 1940), p. 8.

81 Giles, H.A., *Religions of Ancient China* (London: Constable and Company, 1906), p. 63.

82 Tregear. M., *Chinese Art* (London: Thames and Hudson, 1980), p. 70.

83 Hu, K., *Scholars' Rocks in Ancient China: The Suyuan Stone Catalogue* (Trumbull, CT: Orchid Press, 2002), p. 1.

84 Washington Chinese Poetry Society, *A Bilingual Site of Classical Chinese Poetry*, trans. E.C. Chang, available at: http://www.classicalchinesepoetry.com/wangwei5l-4a.htm.

85 Columbia University, *Asian Topics*, trans. P. Rouzer, available at: http://www.columbia.edu/itc/eacp/asiasite/topics/WangWei/Fields/Text.htm.

86 Sullivan, M., *Symbols of Eternity: The Art of Landscape Painting in China* (Oxford: Clarendon Press, 1979), p. 28.

87 Ibid., p. 45.

88 Fitzgerald, C.P., *China: A Short Cultural History* (London: Century Hutchinson, 1986), p. 440.

89 Cheng, L., *Private Gardens* (Vienna: Springer-Verlag, 1999), p. 131.

90 Keswick, 'Foreword', p. 15.

91 Yang, X., *Metamorphosis of the Private Sphere: Gardens and Objects in Tang-Song Poetry* (Cambridge, MA: Harvard University Press, 2003), p. 38.

92 Benn, C., *China's Golden Age: Everyday Life in the Tang Dynasty* (Oxford: Oxford University Press, 2002), p. 92.

93 Xiong, V.C., *Sui-Tang Chang'an: A Study in the Urban History of Medieval China* (Ann Arbor, MI: Center for Chinese Studies, The University of Michigan, 2000), p. 81.

94 Benn, *China's Golden Age*, p. 68.

95 Ibid., p. 31.

96 Sullivan, *Symbols of Eternity*, p. 139.

97 Siren, O., *Gardens of China* (New York: Ronald Press Company, 1949), p. 87.

98 Yang Xiaoshan, 'Li Gefei's "Luoyang mingyuan ji" ('A Record of the Celebrated Gardens of Luoyang'): text and context,' *Monumenta Serica*, vol. 52 (2004), pp. 221–55.

99 Marco Polo, Yule, H. (trans), *Book of Ser Marco Polo* (London: Murray, 1921), Vol.2, Ch.11.

100 Ibid.

101 Ibid.

102 The foot-binding custom was opposed by the Manchus and was not followed by Manchu women. It was banned by the Republic of China in 1911.

103 Hu, Dongchu, *The Way of the Virtuous: The Influence of Art and Philosophy on Chinese Garden Design* (Beijing: New World Press, 1991), p. 37.

104 Yule, *Book of Ser Marco Polo*, Vol.2, Ch.11.

105 Ibid.

106 Coleridge, S.T., 'Kubla Khan', in *Christabel* (London: William Bulmer, 1816).

107 Johnston, R.S., *Scholar Gardens of China* (Cambridge: Cambridge University Press, 1991), p. 106.

108 Ibid., p. 106.

109 Clunas, C., *Fruitful Sites: Garden Culture in Ming Dynasty China* (London: Reaktion Books, 1996), p. 74.

110 Zhu, J., *Chinese Spatial Strategies: Imperial Beijing, 1420–1911* (London: RoutledgeCurzon, 2004), p. 5.

111 Clunas, *Fruitful Sites*, p. 71.

112 Clunas, C., *Elegant Debts: The Social Art of Wen Zhengming, 1470–1559* (London: Reaktion, 2004), p. 7.

113 Clunas, *Fruitful Sites*, p. 129.

114 Ji Cheng, *The Craft of Gardens*, trans. A. Hardie (New Haven, CT: Yale University Press, 1988), p. 122.

115 Ibid., p. 39.

116 Ibid., p. 53.

117 Cheng, *Private Gardens*, p. 133.

118 Finnane, A., *Speaking of Yangzhou: A Chinese City, 1550–1850* (Harvard East Asia Monographs, number 236) (Cambridge, MA: Harvard University Asia Center, 2004), p. 65.

119 Wang, J.C., *The Chinese Garden* (Hong Kong: Oxford University Press, 1998), p. 22.

120 Cranmer-Byng, J.L. (ed.), *An Embassy to China. Being the Journal Kept by Lord Macartney during his Embassy to the Emperor Ch'ienlung, 1793–1794* (London:

Longmans, 1962), p. 126 .
121 Ibid., p. 125.
122 Ibid., p. 132.
123 Ibid., p. 132.
124 Foret, P., *Mapping Chengde: The Qing Landscape Enterprise* (Honolulu: University of Hawai'i Press, 2000), p. 23.
125 Young-tsu Wong, *A Paradise Lost: The Imperial Garden Yuanming Yuan* (Honolulu: University of Hawai'i Press, 2001), p. 119.
126 Ibid., p. 119.
127 Johnston, *Scholar Gardens of China*, p. 98.
128 Ibid., p. 145.
129 Ibid., p. 146.
130 Ibid., p. 124.
131 Graham, *Chinese Gardens*, p. 92.
132 Cheng, *Private Gardens*, p. 130.
133 Xuoqin, C. *The Story of the Stone: A Chinese Novel*, in 5 volumes, trans. D. Hawkes (Harmondsworth: Penguin, 1973).
134 Cheng, *Private Gardens*, p. 324.
135 Ibid., p. 330.
136 Ibid., p. 335.
137 Private communication.

7 Shinto-Buddhist gardens in Japan, pp. 237–78

1 Shinoda, M., *The Founding of the Kamakura Shogunate, 1100–1185* (New York: Columbia University Press, 1960), p. 228.
2 Hayakawa, M., *The Garden Art of Japan*, trans. R.L. Gage (New York: Weatherill, 1981), p. 27.
3 *Encyclopedia of Shinto*, article on 'Shinto and Ancient Chinese Thought', available at: http://eos.kokugakuin.ac.jp/modules/xwords/entry.php?entryID=825.
4 Hayakawa, *The Garden Art of Japan*, pp. 16, 27.
5 Kuck, L.E., *The World of the Japanese Garden: From Chinese Origins to Modern Landscape Art* (New York and Tokyo: Walker, Weatherhill, 1968), p. 71.
6 Ibid., p. 77.
7 Paine, R.T. and Soper, A., *The Art and Architecture of Japan* (New Haven, CT: Yale University Press, 1981), p. 329.
8 http://www.city.kyoto.jp/koho/eng/historical/1200.html.
9 Paine and Soper, *The Art and Architecture of Japan*, p. 341.
10 Ibid., p. 341.
11 'The Collected Works of Shinran' (translated, with introductions, glossaries, and reading aids, by Dennis Hirota (Head Translator), Hisao Inagaki, Michio Tokunaga, and Ryushin Uryuzu) in *Hymn of the Two Gateways of Entrance and Emergence* (2), available at: http://www.shinranworks.com/shorterworks/gateways2.htm.
12 Ibid.
13 Watson, B. (trans.), *The Lotus Sutra* (New York: Columbia University Press, 1993), Chapter 11, 'The emergence of the treasure tower', available at: http://lotus.nichirenshu.org/lotus/sutra/english/watson/lsw_chap11.htm, accessed 16 June 2008.
14 Ibid.
15 'The Collected Works of Shinran' (translated, with introductions, glossaries, and reading aids, by Dennis Hirota (Head Translator), Hisao Inagaki, Michio Tokunaga, and Ryushin Uryuzu) *Major Expositions KGSS II*: 35–61, available at: http://www.shinranworks.com/majorexpositions/kgssII-35_61.htm.
16 Watson, B., *The Lotus Sutra*, Chapter 21, 'The mystic powers of the Tathagata' (New York: Columbia University Press, 1993), available at: http://lotus.nichirenshu.org/lotus/sutra/english/watson/lsw_chap21.htm, accessed 16 June 2008.
17 'The Collected Works of Shinran' (translated, with introductions, glossaries, and reading aids, by Dennis Hirota (Head Translator), Hisao Inagaki, Michio Tokunaga, and Ryushin Uryuzu), *Gutoku's Notes*, available at: http://www.shinranworks.com/shorterworks/gutoku2.htm.

18 Kuitert, W., *Themes in the History of Japanese Garden Art* (Honolulu: University of Hawai'i Press, 2002), p. 20.
19 Treib, M. and Henman, R., *A Guide to the Gardens of Kyoto* (Tokyo: Shufunotomo Company, 1983), p. 190.
20 Kuitert, *Themes*, p. 22.
21 *The Tale of Genji*, Chapter 40, available at: http://ota.ahds.ac.uk/.
22 Seidensticker, E.G. (trans.), *Murasaki Shikibu: The Tale of Genji* (London: Martin Secker & Warburg, 1992) p. 404.
23 Ibid., p. 919.
24 Varley, H.P., *Japanese Culture,* 3rd edn (Honolulu: University of Hawai'i Press, 1984), p. 53.
25 Kuitert, *Themes*, p. 11.
26 Ellwood, R.S., 'The Spring Prayer ("Toshigoi") ceremony of the Heian court', *Asian Folklore Studies*, vol. 30, no. 1 (1971), pp. 1–30.
27 Takei, J. and Keane, M.P., *Sakuteiki: The Vision of the Japanese Garden* (Boston: Tuttle Publishing, 2001), p. 41.
28 Inaji, T., *The Garden as Architecture: Form and Spirit in the Gardens of Japan, China, and Korea* (Tokyo: Kodansha International, 1998), p. 16.
29 Harada, J., *The Gardens of Japan* (London: The Studio, 1928), p. 7.
30 Paine and Soper, *The Art and Architecture of Japan*, p. 343.
31 Kuitert, *Themes*, p. 66 ff.
32 *Treasury of the Eye of the True Dharma*, Book 11, 'Principles of Zazen', available at: http://hcbss.stanford.edu/research/projects/sztp/translations/shobogenzo/translations/zazengi/pdf/Zazengi%20translation.pdf , 5 December 2008.
33 Varley, *Japanese Culture*, p. 122.
34 Kuitert, *Themes*, p. 129ff.
35 Kuck, *The World of the Japanese Garden*, p. 107.
36 Ibid., p. 105.
37 Ibid., p. 112.
38 Ibid., p. 123.
39 Kuitert, *Themes*, p. 78.
40 Ibid., p. 80
41 Kuck, *The World of the Japanese Garden*, p. 121.
42 Ibid., p. 129.
43 Keene, D., *Yoshimasa and the Silver Pavilion: The Creation of the Soul of Japan* (New York: Columbia University Press: 2003), p. 77.
44 Ibid., p. 131
45 Ibid., p. 95.
46 Ibid., p. 92.
47 Takei and Keane, *Sakuteiki*, p. 161.
48 The Taj Mahal is more widely known but people think of it more as a building than a garden.
49 Kuck, *The World of the Japanese Garden*, p. 167.
50 Sadler, A.L., *A Ten Foot Square Hut and Tales of the Heike* (Sydney: Angus and Robertson, 1928).
51 Hayakawa, *The Garden Art of Japan*, p. 135.
52 Treib and Herman, *A Guide to the Gardens of Kyoto*, p. 186.
53 Hayakawa, *The Garden Art of Japan*, p. 140.
54 Kuitert, *Themes*, p. 242 in 1988 edn.
55 Hayakawa, *The Garden Art of Japan*, p. 149.
56 Crowe, S. *et al.*, *The Gardens of Mughul India: A History and Guide* (London: Thames & Hudson, 1972), p. 54.
57 Tange, K. and Isimoto, Y., *Katsura: Tradition and Creation in Japanese Architecture* (New Haven, CT: Yale University Press, 1972), p. 41.
58 Ibid., pp. 44–5.
59 Isozaki, A., *Japan-ness in Architecture* (Cambridge, MA: MIT Press, 2006), p. 262.
60 Hayakawa, *The Garden Art of Japan*, p. 142.
61 Kuck, *The World of the Japanese Garden*, pp. 240–1.
62 Conder, J., *Landscape Gardening in Japan … With Numerous Illustrations* (Yokohama: Kelly & Walsh, 1893).
63 Ito, T., *The Japanese Garden: An Approach to Nature* (New Haven, CT: Yale University Press, 1972), p. 138.

Notes

64   Kuck, *The World of the Japanese Garden*, p. 252.
65   Ibid., p. 252.
66   Hayakawa, *The Garden Art of Japan*, p. 143.

8   Abstract Modernist gardens in Asia, pp. 281–316

1   Eliade, M., *Shamanism* (Princeton, NJ: Princeton University Press, 1992), p. 10.
2   Marx, K., 'Introduction', to *A Contribution to the Critique of Hegel's Philosophy of Right.* (written in 1843 but not published in Marx's lifetime) in *Early Writings* trans. and ed. T.B. Bottomore (London: Watts, 1963).
3   Smart, N., *The Religious Experience of Mankind* (London: Fontana, 1969), p. 652.
4   Humphry, C., 'Creating a culture of disillusionment', in D. Miller (ed.), *Worlds Apart* (London: Routledge, 1995), p. 58.
5   Winick, C., *USSR Humor* (Mount Vernon, NY: Peter Pauper Press, 1964), p. 17.
6   *Architectural Review*, March 2005 p. 55, Peter Davey (quoted from Jan. 1983).
7   *Architectural Review*, January 2007.
8   *Architectural Review*, August 2006, comment by Catherine Slessor.
9   *Architectural Review*, March 2007, Catherine Slessor, 'Fantasy Island', p. 30.
10   Walker, J. (ed.), *Oman, UAE and Arabian Peninsula* (London: Lonely Planet, 2007), p. 55.
11   Steele, J., *An Architecture for People: The Complete Works of Hassan Fathy* (London: Thames and Hudson, 1997), p. 6.
12   I spent six months working for the United Nations Development Programme and wrote a report on 'Environment' as part of the UNDP *Master Plan for the Suez Canal Zone.*
13   McHarg, I., *Design with Nature* (New York: Doubleday Natural History Press, 1971), p. 31.
14   Dalrymple, W., *In Xanadu, a Quest* (London: Flamingo, 1990), pp. 18–19.
15   King, G., *The Traditional Architecture of Saudi Arabia* (London: I.B. Taurus Publishers, 1998), p. 1.
16   Llewellyn-Jones, R., 'The coral city of old Jeddah – Saudi Arabia', *Architectural Review*, September, 1995.
17   Kay, S. and Sandi, D., *Architectural Heritage of the Gulf* (London: Motivate Publishing, 1991).
18   Jodidio, P., *Architecture of the Emirates* (Köln: Taschen, 2007), p. 10.

19   Iran Issue, *Architectural Review*, vol. CLIX, no. 951, May 1976, p. 255.
20   McLeod, M. and Mayhew, B., *Uzbekistan* (Hong Kong: Odyssey, 2004), p. 20.
21   Westcoat, J.L., 'Mughal gardens: the re-emergence of comparative possibilities and the wavering of practical concern', in Conan, M., *Perspectives on Garden Theories* (Washington DC: Dumbarton Oaks, 1999), p. 134.
22   Villiers-Stuart, C.M., *Gardens of the Great Mughals* (London: A&C Black, 1913), p. 275.
23   Carlton, C. and Carlton, C, *The Significance of Gardening in British India* (Studies in British History, 2005), p. 91.
24   Ibid., p. 85.
25   Kennedy, P., *The Rise and Fall of the Great Powers* (London: Fontana, 1988), p. 5.
26   Xue, Charlie Q. L., *Building a Revolution: Chinese Architecture Since 1980* (Hong Kong: Hong Kong University Press, 2006), p. 52.
27   Tschumi, C., *Mirei Shigemori – Rebel in the Garden – Modern Landscape Architecture* (Berlin: Birkhäuser, 2007).
28   Koren, L., *Wabi-Sabi for Artists, Designers, Poets and Philosophers* (Berkeley, CA: Stone Bridge Press, 1994), p. 25.
29   Ibid., p. 21.
30   Ibid., p. 26.
31   Taut, B., 'Reflections on Katsura' in Ponciroli, V. (ed.), *Katsura Imperial Villa* (Milan: Electa Architecture, 2004), p. 335.
32   Gropius, W., *Katsura: Tradition and Creation in Japanese Architecture* (New Haven: Yale University Press, 1960).
33   Isozaki, *Japan-ness in Architecture*, p. 293.
34   Tange and Ishimoto, *Katsura: Tradition and Creation in Japanese Architecture*, p.21.

Afterword, pp. 317–21

1   Grabar, O., 'The mission and its people', in *Architecture for Islamic Societies Today* (New York: Academy Editions, 1994), p. 11.
2   Tyrwitt, J., *Patrick Geddes in India* (London: Lund Humphries, 1947), p. 26.
3   The latter quotation is attributed to Winston Churchill, but with a lack of documentary evidence.

Illustration credits

The author and publisher wish to thank these individuals and organizations for permission to reproduce material. We are particularly grateful to NASA for making the satellite imagery available. Other photographs and drawings are by the author. Every effort has been made to contact and acknowledge copyright holders, but if any errors or omissions have been made we will be happy to correct them at a later printing and on the companion website: http://www.gardenvisit.com/asian_gardens_companion

Illustration credits

Index